PREFACE

THE PREFACE TO the first volume of *Practice and Theory of Psychoanalysis,* first published in 1948, could be applied to the present volume as well.

This second volume contains one paper, *The Unfulfilled Wishes According To Freud,* which actually should have been included in the first volume. A footnote explains why this could not be done.

I may perhaps call the reader's attention to the fact that, in these volumes, I endeavored to show the principles of psychoanalysis with the help of carefully selected clinical material which served me as a firm basis for my theoretical constructs.

Herman Nunberg

New York, November 7, 1964

Practice and Theory
of
Psychoanalysis

Volume II

By

HERMAN NUNBERG

INTERNATIONAL UNIVERSITIES PRESS, INC.

New York   New York

PRINTED IN THE UNITED STATES OF AMERICA

CONTENTS

PRACTICE AND THEORY OF PSYCHOANALYSIS

THE UNFULFILLED WISHES ACCORDING TO
FREUD'S TEACHINGS

Translated by PAUL FRIEDMAN, M.D.

THE POINT OF departure of psychoanalytic investigation is the unconscious. Its main characteristic is the wish. This was shown for the first time by Freud in his study of dreams.

As we know, Freud distinguished between the manifest and the latent dream. According to him, every dream represents a fulfillment of an unfulfilled wish. Besides, the dream is also a pictorial representation of a particular situation. In the manifest dream, imaginary events are created which do not exist in reality, and some details of these compositions appear with a lifelike vividness,[1] in hallucinatory form, as it were. However, when we analyze pictures of this kind—i.e., when we try to search out the latent content which is hidden behind them—we gain the conviction that each and every one of these pictures is composed of less complex elements that correspond to real experiences or to fantasies, and that, in the last analysis, they are also an amorphous mixture of manifold experiences. Any experience, in its turn, is a sum of perceptions and impressions which alter the psychic condition. It leaves traces, namely, the memories of these perceptions and impressions. As psychoanalysis has taught us, these memories may become activated under certain circumstances—i.e., after a

This paper was meant as an introduction to a series of lectures on psychoanalysis. It was presented in 1912, at the Second Congress of Polish Psychiatrists, Neurologists, and Psychologists in Cracow and published, subsequently, in *Neurologia Polska* (Nunberg, 1913).

I had completely forgotten that this paper existed until after the death of Dr. Ludwig Jekels, when it was turned over to me by his widow. I am grateful to Dr. Paul Friedman who volunteered to translate it into English.

[1] These pictures pertain not only to sight, but also to all other senses. Preponderantly, however, they are visual.

certain, even a long lapse of time, they may reappear with the same, unchanged intensity of the original experience.[2] Silberer (1909), in his experiments on hypnagogic hallucinations, has shown that in normal persons, during a state of sleepiness or of fatigue, a given idea may take on the form of a hallucination. An idea may, in some situations, assume characteristics of lifelike vividness. This process, which involves the stimulation and evocation of repressed memory images in their primary—and thus no further reducible—form, we call regression. A question arises as to the nature of the factors that force the psychic apparatus in the direction of regression. The most important of these is the wish. This process involves a tendency toward removal of momentary unpleasure through satisfaction by means of real or delusional experience, and through the resulting evocation of pleasure. This tendency aims at obtaining experiences which will provide pleasure. In this respect, we agree with Lipps (1907), who sees, in every fantasy, a wish, an attempt at a real experience *(Wirklichkeitsstreben)*. Similarly, we agree with Pikler (1908), who maintains that every fantasy comprises a tendency toward realization, and that each new experience involves an attempt to re-create something experienced in the past, i.e., that every experience models itself upon something which was already experienced before *(Beharrungsprinzip)*. These "tendencies" defined by Lipps and Pikler encompass, in a wider sense, our "fulfilled wishes" in the form of hallucinations modeled on the prototype of some previously experienced, actual perceptions and impressions. In this sense, we can also characterize wishes accurately as attempts to re-experience certain situations. This formulation is in agreement with the definition given above, a definition which we can now render more adequate by stating that the tendency we speak of aims at evoking previously experienced, primary impressions and, therefore, those impressions which are the least complex for a given person.

Although Silberer does not state explicitly that hypnagogic hallucinations are the expression of a wish, it is possible to show this, even on the basis of his own examples.

---

[2] In psychoanalytic treatment, it happens not infrequently that the patient produces a vision in the beginning, which, only in the later course of the analysis, can be traced back to a situation of his distant past.

In summary, we arrive at the conviction that regression transforms thoughts into images and that it reactivates the earliest experiences, breaking down the more complex psychological products into simpler components.

After this brief introduction of the concepts of regression and wish, we can take up a discussion of the vicissitudes of the latter.[3]

When a specific wish is fulfilled as soon as it arises, i.e., immediately after it has altered the momentary psychic state, there is nothing to be said about it, since it has ceased to exist.

Unfulfilled wishes are much more important. They can be divided into two groups: (1) *suppressed* wishes, i.e., wishes which arise in us every day, and which we must abandon for rational, logical reasons; (2) *repressed* wishes, i.e., wishes that remain with us, which it is difficult for us to master, and of whose existence we are largely unaware, but which are always ready to seek an outlet by whatever means. Of these two types of wishes the first are the less important, since they acquire importance only when they find a resonance in the second.

Speaking about repressed wishes, we must again digress slightly in order to give a brief explanation of the concept of *repression*.

We have seen that a wish is aroused as a result of an excitation producing unpleasure (in the broadest sense of the term). As a reaction to this, there arises a tendency to substitute pleasure for unpleasure, by means of fantasy. The child in the earliest periods of life, persons of low intellectual or moral level, and also primitive people satisfy all their wishes directly. In other words, they attempt to gratify almost every wish *without denying themselves, even for a moment,* the opportunity of attaining pleasure. In the course of individual as well as of cultural development, however, wishes develop, the satisfaction of which would be running counter to the personality or to the entire sociocultural order. To gratify them would not cause more pleasure but, on the contrary, unpleasure. *It is precisely this reversal of affects in relation to certain wishes which constitutes the essence of repression.* Wishes of this kind are unpleasurable. However, one of the characteristics of the organism is the avoidance of unpleasure. This may be achieved through

---

[3] I must emphasize that I shall by no means exhaust the topic. I would like merely to outline a few thoughts.

repression, which is one of the infantile defenses against un-pleasure. Such wishes do not find an outlet; they cannot be ful-filled. *Therefore, they become repressed.*

Repression begins at an early age. We can observe its prototype in children, who, in certain stages of development, manifest shame or disgust for some of the functions that had previously provided pleasure. But the repressed wishes had been a source of pleasure before the affect connected with them became reversed. We know, moreover, that wishes have a tendency to re-emerge. It is not sur-prising, therefore, that after being eliminated from consciousness, they continually seek pathways for expression, aiming to re-evoke the pleasure which had previously been experienced through their realization.[4] There is a variety of such pathways. We shall review the most important ones in broad outline.

Repressed wishes are wishes which have become interrupted in their course, i.e., which have not resulted in the satisfaction of a need. External as well as internal factors can interfere with the fulfillment of wishes. In the first case, the relevant factor is a lack of external conditions required to satisfy the need. In the second, it is a negative affect produced by repressive forces. Nevertheless, the organism aims at the attainment of pleasure at any price and by the shortest route. *From the very nature of the wish, it follows that this shortest route is provided by regressive re-evocation of images pertaining to experiences once known in reality.* To ex-press this more clearly: the wish finds hallucinatory fulfillment if it cannot find immediate satisfaction. *Thus, every wish must be fulfilled either in reality or in fantasy.* Since the repressed wish has a negative affect, however, it undergoes various transformations before it can become conscious, so that finally it is distorted beyond recognition and its real meaning can be uncovered only with the aid of analysis.

Unsatisfied wishes often find fulfillment in unchanged form in the dream fantasies of children; in children's games, however, they are masked to some extent. Games correspond to fantasies which

---

[4] I wish to call attention to the ambivalent character (Bleuler, 1912) of a repressed wish.

represent the fulfillment of wishes that had to yield to repression.[5] Fantasying is characteristic of childhood. But this kind of thinking is not encountered among children alone. For instance, there are many folktales in which the boldest wishes are fulfilled directly, by fantastic means, without the use of overly complicated symbolism. Moreover, the most recent studies (Abraham, Rank, Maeder, Jung) have shown that legends, myths, and religious systems of primitive peoples employ the same type of thinking. In the contemporary European adult we find the identical type of thinking in dreams, in the productions of psychic illness, artistic creations, etc.

The key to the discovery of the unconscious psychic function was the fantasy product *par excellence*—the dream fantasy. Here the unfulfilled wish is elaborated in a characteristic fashion. From the characteristics of the wish, it is possible to conclude theoretically that every wish is indestructible, that it always strives toward fulfillment, and that it dates back to the earliest years of childhood. Moreover, our experience confirms that *every wish in the dream must date back to the earliest years of childhood.* Freud correctly maintains that *the dream fantasy is a part of psychic life which we have already outgrown* (in waking life).

The discovery of the unconscious wish led to another very important discovery, namely, that *all psychoneurotic symptoms are expressions of unconscious wishes which have been repressed and which go back to the earliest years of childhood.* These symptoms represent conflict among various wishes,[6] and they are symbolic of these wishes.

Wishes may find fulfillment in *illusions* as well as in fantasies. Here the mechanism of *displacement* may perhaps be most easily discerned. In brief, since unconscious wishes cannot become con-

---

[5] To give a drastic example: one of my patients recalls that between the ages of six and nine he used to amuse himself by sitting at the window, taking the cords of the venetian blinds in one hand, and brandishing a whip with the other. In this instance, the game served to mask sadistic fantasies which had arisen for the first time in the fifth year of his life and which, of course, had to be repressed. However, these repressed fantasies—or, ultimately, desires—found an outlet in play. At a later age, they gave rise to psychoneurotic symptoms.

[6] I shall not develop this thesis further, because it would lead us too far afield, namely, to a discussion of the theory of neurosis.

scious as such, they seek a suitable object to which they can attach themselves in order to gain access to consciousness. We call this mechanism *displacement.*[7]

In addition to those described above, there are many other means by which unfulfilled wishes may manifest themselves. First among them are hallucinations and delusions. I have mentioned hallucinations in connection with dream fantasies. Even when they appear in waking life, they do not differ in any respect from dream hallucinations. Just like the sleep state, the life of hallucinating persons is isolated, self-contained, independent of the external world. They have lost almost all contact with the outside world, and live as though in a dream. The shift of the point of gravity in their psychic life is not due merely to the fact that reality circumstances have made it impossible for their wishes to be fulfilled. The disturbance in their relationship to the world stems from deeper causes: many of their wishes are so extreme, so strong, that their fulfillment under ordinary conditions becomes impossible. The reason for this should be sought in the fact that their desires are continuously being strengthened from the somatic side, i.e., by the drives. (More about this later.) Moreover, in the case of hallucinating patients, regression must go very far back, so that for them the oldest experiences become actual, changed in form but enlivened by sensory imagery.

The wishes fulfilled in the hallucinations of psychotics or in artistic visions are subject to the same laws as those fulfilled in dreams. They originate in childhood, and their function is the attainment of pleasure.

The situation is more complicated in the case of delusions. For example, in the case of delusions of persecution, which have thus far been studied most thoroughly, *the desires become separated from the self, are attributed to a given object, and then return, externalized, in the form of delusions of persecution.* The patient experiences his own opposition to these desires as opposition coming from the outside.

Thus, one of my patients had a strongly developed homosexual component of the sexual drive. In his work, he established a close relationship with his supervisor, a very gifted person. The patient

[7] Each of us can find sufficient examples in his own life.

admired him, was ready to do anything for him, *simply loved him*. However, after a period of time, it seemed to him that the supervisor wanted to enter into homosexual relations with him. In support of this, he cited a whole series of delusional proofs. *Then he developed a conviction that this man wanted to destroy him, that they were struggling with each other,* that the man was an evil spirit, a devil.[8] Finally he systematized his delusion so that the supervisor became the "King of the Negroes" and the patient himself "White King," the "Jewish King." These camps are at war with each other as "good" and "evil."

Thus, the previously unsatisfied homosexual desire goes through various transformations and reappears in the form of a delusion of persecution. This, however, is not the end. The wish becomes *systematized and generalized.* In the end the patient views the entire world from the standpoint of his repressed wish. Projection is not a characteristic of illness alone. We also find this mechanism in normal life; we use it every day without realizing it. Projection is very frequent in the thinking of children, of poets, and of primitive peoples who even project life onto lifeless objects and nature, attributing sensations and thoughts to them (animism).[9]

Even though the wish, before it can be projected, must find an appropriate object to which the desire can be attached, i.e., although *the substitution must take place first,* the two mechanisms should not be confused. We experience the projected wish as something foreign coming to us from the outside, often as imposed upon us, or even hostile. By contrast, we experience the substitute wishes, though changed in form, as subjectively felt, etc.

The following example illustrates the apparently strange paths that a repressed wish sometimes takes. A female patient in catatonic delirium told me:

"I killed my father, he is in heaven, he is God. I am the earth, I am the earth. The dear Lord [*der liebe Gott*—the patient was

---

[8] I cannot agree with Bleuler's (1912) statement that the fulfillment of all desires would have to lead to delusions of an expansive nature (autistic thinking).

[9] I am not discussing delusions of grandeur in this context, although they are evident in the above example.

Swiss] creates people out of earth masses [*Erdmassen*]." From her forehead, she removed a crust which actually looked like earth, and said: "You see, out of this."

She *identified* her father with God, and herself with the earth. She re-created the biblical creation of the world. If we designate this fantasy as a wish, it immediately becomes intelligible. We also find the above mechanism in everyday life, as well as in dream fantasies.

Without adding further examples, we can now state that, both in dreams and in mental illness, we find the same roots as in infantile thinking and in the thought processes of the primitive. We may confidently repeat Freud's statement that the dream fantasy demonstrates the primitive mode of operation of the psychic process. In this primitive mode of thinking, there was only one aim: the fulfillment of wishes. For primitive peoples, children, poets, and for the mentally ill alike, it is a matter of indifference whether certain wishes find fulfillment in reality or only in fantasy. They live in a different world. Our old wishes and those of all earlier generations thus continue to live in us for all time; they follow us at every step, just like our own shadow. And like the latter, they are intangible, but real nonetheless. Bleuler is correct in maintaining that life appears to us, not as it really is, but as we should like to see it.[10]

What is the usual content of a wish? As we have seen, wishes aim at a repetition of earlier experiences. Satisfaction of a need constituted such an experience. But we know from analytic experience that infantile sexual wishes and those childhood functions which had a sexual component are the most susceptible to repression in the course of development. No other needs, no other drives are subjected to such repression or undergo such transformation, between the cradle and the age of sexual maturity, as the sexual drive. It is not surprising, therefore, that the sexual wishes press toward

---

[10] That we evaluate the entire world from the standpoint of our own "I," has been convincingly proved by Freud's fundamental and brilliant discovery of transference. Many human motivations can be evaluated only by taking account of this factor. Further evidence of this is provided by the experimental work of Pfenninger (1911) and Aptekmann (1911). They show that *the individual characteristics of the experimenter* must be taken into account before the results of psychological experiments can be evaluated objectively.

re-emergence with particular force. When these wishes are re-inforced further by somatic factors—i.e., through some specific sexual striving which is either overestimated or more strongly developed, or which is out of harmony with other strivings—we have all the prerequisites for the expansion of vehement wishes. Thus, if one such striving is constitutionally stronger or becomes reinforced, its function is intensified from the very start. As a result, it leaves more memory traces of experienced need gratifications and, later on, presses more strongly for repetition. For all these reasons, *there is in us a strong, unconscious tendency toward re-creation of the first sexual impressions as a means of obtaining pleasure in its earliest form.* If these wishes become fulfilled, they disappear, since they have reached their aim, i.e., perversion.[11] If they continue to be repressed, however, they will find expression via regression. *The infantile way of sexual gratification is also found (permanently) in the form of undifferentiated wishes,* in the psychic productions mentioned above. To state this more clearly: *every repressed wish is traceable to unsatisfied, primitive, sexual needs.*

On the basis of the foregoing considerations, we have become convinced of the significant insight into the human psyche which is gained through the genetic conception of psychological proc-esses. From the psychoanalytic point of view, the unconscious psychic function belongs to the category of primitive functions, both in terms of the sequence of individual development and in terms of quality.

We have learned that the wish function is one of the main characteristics of the unconscious. Viewed from the dynamic stand-point, the unconscious has a *constant tendency* toward the attain-ment of pleasure, a tendency which manifests itself through the satisfaction of needs aroused by irritation or, in other words, by unpleasure. Freud states that this tendency is governed by the *pleasure principle (Lustprinzip).* The child and the primitive are not able to wait a long time for the attainment of pleasure. If real gratification does not follow, they obtain their pleasure by the shortest route, i.e., through hallucinations and fantasies in which

[11] The child's first sexual pleasure is a deviation—viewed from the standpoint of the adult, of course.

the wishes find their fulfillment. At a certain stage in the development of the individual and of mankind, fantasy was to some extent a substitute for thinking. This type of thinking is described *by Freud* (1911a) *as thinking in accordance with the pleasure principle, by Jung* (1911) *as fantasy thinking, and by Bleuler* (1912) *as autistic thinking.*[12]

To repeat: at some stage of development, the satisfaction of certain needs occurred in hallucinatory form. It is possible to explain this fact in various ways. I shall limit myself to a few words. Some unfulfilled wishes find fulfillment in fantasy. These wishes have arisen as a result of obstacles in the satisfaction of instinctual needs. Thus the wish is a psychic production stemming directly from the instinctual drives.

It happens sometimes that we wake up from a dream, even though the wish was satisfied in it. Thus one might dream that one is thirsty, that one drinks water; but, nevertheless, one continues to experience thirst and finally wakes up. In this phenomenon we have evidence that, despite the fulfillment of wishes in hallucinatory form, their satisfaction may not take place. This happens when the irritation has not been removed.[13] Moreover, there is a basis for the assumption that, in the development of mankind (and of the individual), there were occasions when wishes were fulfilled in hallucinatory form, but such fulfillment did not result in pleasure. The wish was then forced to seek other ways of gratification, i.e., it had to seek real experiences providing real pleasure. Thus, the psychic apparatus had to exert itself in the direction of changing the external life conditions so as to assure itself of pleasure. In this way there developed a psychic function which, to use Freud's words, is "oriented toward reality" (reality principle). A new mode of thinking developed, termed "realistic" by Bleuler (1912) and "directed" by Jung (1911). Realistic thinking is a higher function required in the process of development. That this is the case is confirmed by illnesses (hysteria, schizophrenia) in which the

[12] There are some differences among these authors, which I shall not take up here.
[13] This permits us to explain why some patients suffer in spite of the wish fulfillment in fantasies and hallucinations.

relationship to the real world is the first function to become disturbed. The transition from the one to the other mode of psychic functioning has had great significance for the development both of the individual and of mankind. And so we have learned to foresee, to think, to act in a coordinated way—in short, purposefully to modify conditions in the external world in accordance with our needs.

However, the organism did not completely and immediately abandon all possibilities of obtaining pleasure by direct means. Consequently, a particular form of thinking, governed by the pleasure principle, has survived. This is the production of fantasies, which I have mentioned here repeatedly. The impossibility of completely supplanting the one mode by the other—or, as Freud puts it, one principle by the other—results from the nature of sexuality. More specifically, sexual impulses aim, during a longer period, at the attainment of pleasure in primitive form, because in the beginning their satisfaction was not dependent on objects, i.e., on the external world. Indeed, we know that they possessed an autoerotic character, i.e., that they could be satisfied on the own body. *The sexual wishes should therefore be regarded as the prototype of wishes that can be satisfied in the form of hallucinations, i.e., which can be satisfied through regression.* For the same reason, we find, in patients, such a close connection between excessive fantasy and sexual disturbances. *Hallucinations and fantasies are strikingly autoerotic.*

It would appear that realistic thinking finally becomes completely independent of fantasy thinking; for the latter aims at the direct attainment of pleasure, the former at a purposeful modification of external conditions by removing obstacles to the attainment of pleasure. Thus, realistic thinking is likewise subject to the pleasure principle; but momentary satisfaction is renounced in favor of a longer-range plan designed to secure definite pleasure.[14] The formulation of the two above-mentioned principles of psychic functioning is of great practical import.

[14] E.g., a young man in love aims to establish a secure livelihood so that he can get married.

SUMMARY

We arrived at the conclusion that each person's unfulfilled wishes are stored in the depth of his psyche, the unconscious. These wishes stimulate the psychic apparatus into activity, sometimes in the direction of normal development and creation of social values, sometimes in a pathological and asocial direction. In both cases the wish has sought an outlet and has found it. Moreover, if we represent the wish as a straight line with a direction in space, then we find unpleasure at the beginning of this line and pleasure at its end. Thus, depending on whether we view the psychic function from the standpoint of causes or from the standpoint of aims, either unpleasure or pleasure may be regarded as the creative agent both in culture and in mental illness.

When we consider the cause of a temporary unpleasure, however, we become convinced that it originates from unsatisfied drives; the wish is their first direct psychic manifestation. Perhaps I should have taken this as the starting point of my lecture. This would have been justified if we knew more about the drives than is the case so far.[15]

---

[15] When originally given, this lecture concluded with the following statement: "I have cited from the literature only those writings which are presumably the least well known. I believe that it would have been superfluous to cite the works of Freud, which are becoming better known here."

PROBLEMS OF BISEXUALITY AS
REFLECTED IN CIRCUMCISION

SUBMISSION TO CIRCUMCISION

FREUD (1937a) SAYS THAT the deepest roots of the castration complex reach "bedrock" where psychology rests on biological foundations. Homosexuality which constantly crosses the path of heterosexuality, complicating and yet in its struggle enriching the life of man, may be distinguished as one of its biological foundations.

Among the most significant of the numerous manifestations of the castration complex are doubts of one's own sex or of another's, and fears of being of the opposite sex. Dissatisfaction with the sex bestowed by nature is widespread among primitive as well as among highly civilized peoples. It has found expression in the various forms of circumcision, practiced by savages and ancient Egyptians, still adhered to, for religious reasons, by Jews and Mohammedans, and performed in Anglo-Saxon countries today, allegedly for hygienic reasons.

As early as 1912 Freud (1912-1913) recognized the inner relationship between circumcision and castration, and Theodor Reik, in his excellent study of the puberty rites of primitives, proved that circumcision represents symbolic castration, its underlying motive being prevention of incest (Reik, 1915-1916). By means of these rites the boy is declared a man, introduced into the community of men, and granted sexual license with nonincestuous objects.

Why injury to the penis should make a man more masculine is not quite clear. The explanation that the initiation ties up homosexual libido and also facilitates identification with the father, is undoubtedly valid. It is equally true that the initiation releases heterosexual libido caused by the boy's separation from his mother

---

Reprinted from the book by the same title. London: Hogarth Press, 1949, pp. 1-83.

and his longing for her. Both these changes in the distribution of the libido foster the masculinity of the initiated boy.

Géza Róheim (1942) stresses the fact that circumcision and separation from the mother occur simultaneously, and according to my experience, the loss of the mother and the loss of the foreskin are closely associated in the boy's mind, as if femininity and foreskin were the same. Since, moreover, the glans is freed by circumcision, the boy's penis becomes similar to his father's. This similarity, encouraging the identification of the boy with his father and supporting his sense of equality with his father, strengthens his masculinity. The masculinity is further reinforced by the sexual freedom through circumcision.

And yet, it is also possible that the injury to the penis intimidates the boy and impairs his development to full virility. The injury leads to intimidation by and submission to the father, to the inhibition of erection and to the suppression of certain heterosexual, incestuous desires; briefly, to a weakening of the masculinity of the initiated boy. In other words, the circumcision stimulates the feminine as well as the masculine strivings of the boy.

Circumcision is, no doubt, a trauma, releasing a tendency in the ego to repeat it in one way or another and to form reactions to it. Through the work of Reik, Róheim, and others, we have to some extent become familiar with the sociological aspects of these reactions. Our knowledge of individual reactions, however, is scant, perhaps because we are still not entirely aware of the paramount importance of the castration complex. I do not intend to enter into a discussion of this complex as a whole, but I should like to illustrate some of its manifestations.[1]

---

[1] The concept of "castration complex" has been stretched; therefore I should like to delimit its scope in Freud's (1923b) own words:

"It seems to me, however, that the significance of the castration complex can only be rightly appreciated when its origin in the phase of *primacy of the phallus* is also taken into account.

"It has quite correctly been pointed out that the child acquires the idea of a narcissistic wound or deprivation of a part of its body by the experience of the loss of the nipple after suckling and of the daily production of its fæces, even already by its separation from the womb of the mother by birth. Nevertheless, the castration complex should be a term reserved for the occasion, when the idea of such deprivations becomes associated with the loss of the male organ."— Freud: "The Infantile Genital Organization of the Libido. A Supplement to the Theory of Sexuality" (p. 247).

It is not easy to find a patient who was circumcised at an age allowing psychoanalytic study of the reactions to the operation. Jewish boys are circumcised eight days after birth. Although Jews bear their stigma of sanctity and inferiority as if they realized the meaning of the circumcision, it is impossible for them to remember the actual event. Circumcision after puberty is too complicated for psychoanalytic study as it is superimposed upon a number of other shocks. The best cases are provided by circumcisions performed between the years of four and six. Yet, some very interesting material was also obtained from a patient whose son was circumcised while the father was in analysis; in his identification with the son, he gave infantile material.

First I should like to present a dream which a patient had two days before the end of his analysis. I quote: "I am playing tennis with a professional . . . I am losing. . . . He serves in a peculiar way. . . . I jump to get the ball. . . . I am all set to hit it, but I miss the ball and the professional wins the game. I say, it was a clever game but it was not a fair serve. I say, well, if that is the rule, that is all right. But I feel a little mad and funny."

The background of this dream was related to the prospective termination of the patient's analysis which had been set for the following day. This hour was the one before his last hour of analysis. He thought that his analysis was not quite complete and felt that I was fooling him; "it was not a fair play." Therefore he was angry at me.

The patient had frequently played tennis with his father, who used to defeat him. As he had, reluctantly and resentfully, accepted the rules of the game with his father, so he had grudgingly accepted the termination of his analysis. His analysis was thus a game in which he was defeated.

This dream, however, has a deeper meaning. The patient was, in childhood, often fascinated by the shape and size of his father's penis, particularly by its glans. Like so many boys who have the opportunity to observe their father's penis with the retracted foreskin, and wish to have an identical penis, so our patient wished to have one with a free and visible "head," as he called the glans. He once asked his father when he himself would have such a penis. His father answered that this would be when he grew older. In order to accelerate the growth of his penis he repeatedly tried to pull back the foreskin from the glans, masturbating so frequently that his penis became irritated and the foreskin inflamed. The foreskin was finally removed when he was about five years old. After the circumcision, he was so proud of his new penis that he showed it to the little sister and other playmates with great satisfaction, expecting to be admired and treated like an adult man, like his father. When his hopes did not materialize, he became disappointed, unhappy, and withdrew from his mother, his little sister and other playmates. Only one member of his family treated him in what seemed to him a decent manner, his considerably older brother who was kind to him, taught him many things, talked to him as to an equal and even permitted him to urinate in an upright position—which was to him the most important privilege in the world, hitherto not granted by mother and nurse. One can imagine how much he admired this brother and how fervently he wished to be like him. The love ultimately took the form of an overwhelming yearning to touch his brother's penis, which, however, he never dared to do. This is expressed in the manifest dream by the words "I hit the ball." In the latent dream, this corresponds to "having father's penis," "being like father or brother" and "touching brother's penis." In the "system Unconscious (Ucs)" these ideas replace each other and mean: having sexual relations with father. On the basis of many facts, such as his behavior in analysis, his attraction to father's penis, and other recollections, we assume that he had felt attracted to his father even before the circumcision. Circumcision increased the homosexual drive, but as a result of its frustration, he shifted his sexual wishes to his brother. Here his fears and inner inhibitions again caused frustration and disappointment. The end of his analysis produced in him the attitude he had felt in childhood toward his circumcision, namely, that he was ready to accept the loss of his foreskin, if by this loss he would become equal to his father and be permitted to play with him sexually. In the dream he felt frustrated as he did in childhood after the circumcision. In the psychoanalytic situation, he felt a similar frustration in relation to his analyst.

As already indicated, he thought that his analysis was incomplete, and was therefore reluctant to end the treatment. One of his recollections throws light on this particular resistance. When, after his circumcision, the wound was healed and he inspected the penis, he discovered that he had really lost "a little bit"—his prepuce— and wondered what had happened to it. While he was puzzling over its fate, the idea came to him that the doctor who had performed the operation had taken the foreskin for himself, and that from then on he was married to this man. We may, therefore, conclude that the patient felt homosexually tied to his father (the doctor) by the circumcision. Does that not mean that he could not finish his analysis unless he regained his foreskin?[2] I may add, in anticipation of further material, that he hoped, through undoing the circumcision, to free himself from his homosexual ties and become heterosexual again. The validity of this statement is shown by another detail of the dream. The dreamer thought that the professional did not serve in a correct way, that he tricked him. In association to this part of the dream, he called my attention to a memory on which we had already worked in another connection, that before the circumcision his mother used to wrap a piece of cotton around a toothpick and with it clean the pocket of his foreskin; she also used to put an ointment on his penis, wash it, and so on. Beyond doubt, these manipulations represented a kind of seduction to the little boy and were a repeated source of sexual pleasure. It is, therefore, not surprising that he wished his mother to continue these gratifications. When, after the circumcision, he urged her again and again to clean and wash his penis, she refused. He argued with her, accused her of unfairness and of trickery (as in the dream) by having promised that he would feel no discomfort after the operation. These arguments ended, as a rule, with attacks of rage. The dream in which the professional refuses to serve in a way agreeable to the dreamer and which ends in anger, seems, in its deepest level, to repeat the arguments with the mother after the circumcision.

The circumcision deprived him, indeed, of both the prepuce and the pleasure derived from his mother's care of his sex organs. If he could regain his foreskin, he thought obviously, his mother

---

[2] It happens rather frequently that a patient cannot finish his analysis because he (or she) did not receive, in his treatment, what he felt entitled to get, namely, a penis.

would once more take care of it. That made the loss of the foreskin and the loss of mother's love identical in his mind. Thus the circumcision, on the one hand, tied the patient homosexually to his father, and on the other hand, increased his longing for heterosexual gratification by his mother.

The next dream shows how the patient attempted to overcome his fixation on the circumcision: "I went with Ann to the hospital. It seems as if the hospital had given us a child to take home with us. I was carrying him to the taxi. He started to say 'wet.' I did not know what to do and told him to do it in his pants. I put him down on the floor and the urine poured out. Ann touched it and said 'wet.' I said, 'Do you suppose urine is dry?' "

This is a very rich dream, telling almost the whole life history of the patient. I cannot, of course, analyze the whole dream here, but I wish to take up one point which leads into the center of our problem, the circumcision. The patient had this dream under unusual circumstances. His wife woke him during the night asking him to take her to the hospital because she felt the beginning of her labor pains. He probably dreamt this dream while she was trying to wake him. This was the last dream in the analysis, a few hours before the birth of his child.

His first association to this dream was the recollection that his childhood questions about where children come from evoked the answer that children are born in the hospital. In the dream, he anticipated the birth of his child.

But what did birth mean to him unconsciously? The hospital in the dream reminded him of the hospital where his circumcision had been performed. Hence the hospital was a place where children are born and where they are circumcised as well. What, however, is the inner connection between birth and circumcision? A fantasy, represented in the dream, answers the question. After his circumcision the patient developed the following birth theory: father or mother is urinating, "peeing" out a child which is a boy and a girl in one person—a hermaphrodite; when the sex of the child has been decided upon, it is cut in two parts, the boy retains the penis, the girl gets the prepuce. This old fantasy, which reappeared in the dream in the form of the urinating child, obviously acquired new life through the expectation of a baby. The urinating child in the dream, however, not only represented the patient's child, but also the patient himself, because the dream reflected a rebirth fantasy.[3]

If this interpretation is correct, another question presents itself: Is the child reborn a hermaphrodite, a male, or a female? In the dream the child urinates in a standing position. We remember the patient's great satisfaction when his brother permitted him to urinate in an upright position, because it represented the fulfill-ment of his wish to become a grown-up man like father. Moreover, in the fantasy which helped to construct this dream, he was, through birth as well as through circumcision, separated from the woman whom he identified with his foreskin. His foreskin was given to the girl and the freed glans penis, the sign of masculinity, he kept for himself. Through identification of this part of his body with the whole body, he felt reborn as a man who can do as he pleases.

When he asked his wife with an air of superiority, "Do you suppose urine is dry?" he referred to the early disputes with his mother about his urination technique. He wanted to urinate in an upright position like a man, but because he splashed the urine, soiling floor and toilet seat, his mother prohibited his standing and forced him to urinate in a sitting position. He was convinced that his bed-wetting of a later period was a reaction to this frustra-tion. The bed-wetting became a new source of conflict with mother. However, he eventually succeeded in controlling himself. When he began puberty masturbation, he had a similar conflict within himself. Like so many boys, he was particularly afraid of the orgasm and learned to masturbate without ejaculation. He called this technique "dry masturbation." It seems as if he were saying to his mother, in this dream, that one cannot masturbate without orgasm, urinate without getting wet, and cohabit without having children; now circumcised and reborn as a man after his analysis, he would not only satisfy himself sexually as he liked, but he would also not inhibit and intimidate his children as his mother had done with him.

[3] Where a birth fantasy emerges in an analysis, there can always be found its counterpart, a *rebirth* fantasy, and *vice versa*. The child is always object as well as subject of the fantasy.

To put it briefly, this dream meant that one becomes a man by circumcision, which is equal to being reborn. It is obvious that this idea expressed the patient's reactions to the end of his analysis and to the expected birth of his child.

Not infrequently, patients feel the end of their analysis as a kind of rebirth. The various kinds of birth and rebirth fantasies are well known. Otto Rank (1924) first called our attention to them, but he overestimated their importance and did not discern their origin in the castration complex. Theodor Reik (1915-1916, pp. 116-118) has recognized rebirth fantasies in the ceremonies accompanying circumcision in puberty rites. And yet, the link between birth fantasy and injury inflicted precisely upon the reproductive organ seems to be missing. This gap may perhaps be filled by the following recollection of our patient. When he at last accepted the idea that the child is born out of the mother, he imagined that, in the hospital, the child is cut out of her in a way vaguely reminding him of the circumcision. In fact, by the circumcision the glans penis is freed; it emerges like an infant from the mother's womb; in other words, after the circumcision a new penis is born which looks like a phallus in erection with retracted foreskin. As in the system Unconscious or in primitive thinking a part is taken for totality, so here the whole body is identified with the new phallus: the child is born; the initiated, the circumcised boy, is reborn without a foreskin and is thus a man (Lewin, 1933).[4]

Since circumcision occurred at an age at which the patient was intensely interested in the problems of the difference between the sexes and the birth of man, we should not be surprised to find a number of fantasies related to these matters. Some of them have already been discussed. As we have seen, they are centered around the circumcision and, as we shall see later on, they are partly repetitions of, partly reactions to this event. As they express sexual ideas on the phallic level, we may call them phallic fantasies. So interwoven are they, that it is sometimes difficult to separate them. If we succeed in isolating one of these fantasies, we can see that it solves a certain problem. In the hermaphroditic fantasy the patient

---

[4] In his fascinating book, "*Thalassa, the Theory of Genitality*," Ferenczi (1924) arrives at similar conclusions, not, however, on the basis of individual analyses, but on the basis of "bioanalytic" speculations.

tried to solve two problems at once: the origin of man, and the difference between the sexes. According to this fantasy, the boy and girl constitute a unit before birth; at birth they are separated, the boy retains the penis, the girl obtains the foreskin; in other words, the unity between man and woman is destroyed by birth or castration.[5]

The fantasy that both sexes come into being by splitting a hermaphroditic creature into two parts, formed a basis for further fantasies and speculations of our patient. First of all, he thought that his sister, a year his senior, was a part of himself separated from him at birth, i.e., his twin sister. He also had the idea that the entire body is divided into two halves, "that it is dual," as he expressed himself. As evidence, he cited the fact that man has two arms, two eyes, two ears, and so on. He felt that these parts could never meet; as a matter of fact, he had a rather obsessional idea that they should always be kept apart.

The masturbatory origin of these ideas betrays itself; however, the prohibition of masturbation as expressed in the urge not to touch his body with his hands is coupled with the experience of circumcision. The prohibition itself seems to have been established even before the circumcision. When his mother caught him masturbating, she scolded him and warned him not to touch himself. He tried to obey, but without great success. So he imposed more severe precautions on himself. He not only avoided touching his penis with his right hand, but also tried to avoid touching the rest of his body with his *right hand*. When he succeeded temporarily in controlling his masturbation, i.e., when his right hand did not touch the left side of his body, he was convinced that his body was split into two separate parts, right and left. Without doubt the purpose of these obsessional ideas was protection from masturbation, yet, they seem also to be a form of repetition of the circumcision, in which one part of the body was separated from another part, the foreskin from the glans penis, the so-called twin sister from himself. Moreover, when his mother criticized him for his

[5] The corresponding fantasy of many female patients is that the mother has robbed them of the penis at birth. The boy, according to his fantasy, loses his femininity at birth; the girl, according to her fantasy, her masculinity. Therefore, she hates her mother. Significantly, for the same reason, the boy hates his mother and not his father, as might be expected.

behavior, when she called him a bad boy and presented his sister in contrast, as an example of a good girl, he thought that his sister was good because she did not masturbate and that she did not masturbate because she had no penis; so he wished to have no penis. If he had none, he imagined, he would please his mother and be like his sister whom everybody loved. This fantasy, carried out, implied full acceptance of the castration and definite renunciation of masturbation. But as he did not really like to lose his penis, to have his body split, to be separated from sister-mother, he gradually gave up this fantasy by forming other fantasies and obsessions. First, he tried to undo the division in his body, its separation into different parts, by attempts to reunify them in his mind. During latency, he used to spend nights and lonely hours worrying and speculating about the methods by which this unification might be accomplished; in other words, he tried to find a method by which he could join the left part of his body to the right, by which he could touch his penis without being caught by his mother. At last he found a solution in the idea that his worries would be over if he could "marry" his right arm to his left arm, his eyes as well as his ears to each other, his penis to his scrotum, and so on. However, this idea about the unification of his body did not offer complete satisfaction. He continued his speculations and conceived the idea that the best way to become a good boy was to marry a good girl, and such a girl was his sister. Since this sister was the girl whom he fancied separated from himself by circumcision, which in his fantasy coincided with birth, there is no doubt that, by marrying her, he hoped to regain this good part of himself. We remember that he identified this sister with his foreskin; thus marrying her meant at the same time retrieving his foreskin, or undoing the circumcision. It meant, also, uninhibited masturbation and sexual gratification with the help of mother, as we saw in connection with the first dream. After puberty he dropped the fantasy of marrying his sister, and substituted for it a sort of obsessional idea of having to marry a "good girl."

The marriage fantasy had still another root. We remember the first dream to which the patient associated a recollection of thoughts, which had occupied him after the circumcision—that the doctor who performed the operation kept the foreskin for himself and that the patient from then on was married to the doctor. We remember further that, in the transference situation, this fantasy represented a serious obstacle to finishing the analysis. The patient felt as if he were an inseparable part of his analyst, as if he were tied to him by invisible bonds.

The patient thus had two marriage fantasies, a homosexual and a heterosexual one. In his homosexual fantasy he was tied to the doctor-father, in his heterosexual fantasy to the sister-mother.

In fact, both fantasies were of a bisexual, hermaphroditic nature and expressed the idea that by marriage man and woman become united in one person, as was shown by his conception of the way in which "marriage" was carried out. Since he believed that the woman has a little penis hidden behind what seemed to him to be the female foreskin, analogous to the foreskin covering the glans penis, he imagined that in "marriage" the man's visible penis touches the woman's hidden one and is covered and *protected* by her "foreskin." The two genitalia, the male and the female, grow together, whereupon the husband's blood flows through his penis into his wife. As a result of this fusion a new human being is formed, a child, which at first is both male and female.

As to the details of the creation of the child, the patient again had two theories, both based, similarly, on the castration complex: first, the father puts his penis into the mother, where the child grows—"a pregnant woman is a woman with a swollen penis in her belly"—when the penis has grown big enough it becomes a baby which is cut out of the mother, whereupon the father dies.[6]

The second theory was as follows: the man is a man in front and a woman in back, the woman is a woman in front and a woman in back (the typical cloacal theory of childhood). The woman cannot have babies, the man can impregnate himself and have babies. Even at a fairly advanced stage of his analysis the patient still expressed the conviction that a hermaphrodite, a creature in whom he, like so many other patients, showed great interest, is the most enviable and the happiest being in the world, independent and omnipotent like God.

---

[6] This is again a confirmation of Freud's concept that in the unconscious, death is represented by castration. When our patient's wife was pregnant, he was afraid he would die at the child's birth.

Let us pause for a moment for a quick summary of his ideas about the origin of man: primarily, the human being was a hermaphrodite, man and woman in one person; at birth this bisexual creature is split into its component parts, man and woman, both craving reunion; by marriage they reachieve the prenatal state of their existence and become a hermaphrodite; from this creature a new being grows which is again split into two parts, and so on.

This is a striking fantasy; the more we listen to it, the more familiar it sounds. We recognize it as the core of the cosmogonic delusional systems of schizophrenia (Nunberg, 1948) as well as of the creation myth related by the Greek philosopher Plato.

In Plato's *Symposium* Aristophanes develops the following ideas: ". . . our original nature was by no means the same as it is now. In the first place, there were three kinds of human beings, not merely two sexes, male and female, as at present: there was a third kind as well, which had equal shares of the other two, and whose name survives, though the thing itself has vanished. For 'man-woman' [Hermaphrodite] was then a unity in form no less than in name, composed of both sexes and sharing equally in male and female; . . . then Zeus, putting all his wits together, spake at length and said: . . . I propose now to slice everyone of them in two . . . this done, the god was to heal them up. Then Apollo turned their faces about, and pulled their skin together from the edges over what is now called the belly, just like purses which you draw close with a string; the little opening he tied up in the middle of the belly, so making what we know as navel. . . . Now, when our first form had been cut in two, each half, in longing for its fellow, would come to it again; . . . Each of us, then, is but a tally of a man, since everyone shows like a flatfish the traces of having been sliced in two; and each is ever searching for the tally that will fit him. . . ."

There is an obvious similarity between the theory about the origin of mankind obtained through the analysis of our patient, and the creation myth as reported by Plato. Even the manner in which the wound is treated in the *Symposium* reminds us of circumcision. However, we know that the Greeks were not circumcised. How then is it possible that Plato, a Greek, used a circumcision fantasy, personified in a hermaphroditic figure split in two, as a basis for the origin of sexes?

According to Salomon Reinach (1928), the Hermaphrodites seem to have appeared in Greek art, at the latest in the fourth century B.C., when certain types of juvenile gods, such as Eros, Dionysos, and Apollon developed. The Attic sculptors endeavor to express a synthesis of male and female beauty in their figures of these gods. Under different names, they are, indeed, Hermaphrodites. . . . The cult of the god Aphroditus, represented as a bearded Aphrodite, had been brought from Cyprus to Athens in the fourth century B.C. In the fifth century B.C., however, there existed in Athens hermae of Aphroditus, or phallic statues with a female head. . . . Briefly, Reinach assumes that the bisexual god Hermaphroditus had been introduced in Greece from Asia Minor around the fifth century B.C. Since Plato lived from 427 to 346 B.C. it is likely that he was greatly influenced by the religions then flourishing in Asia Minor, and that he made them an integral part of his philosophic concepts relative to the origin of man.

It is not surprising that Freud's searching mind tried to penetrate to the sources of the Platonic mythological concepts about the creation of man. In discussions with H. Gomperz, Professor of Philosophy at the University of Vienna, he learned that they can be traced back to early Indian ideas (Upanishads), and from an article by K. Ziegler he drew the information that this creation myth is rooted in old Babylonian ideas (Freud, 1920).

Father J. Winthuis (1928), a Catholic missionary who lived for a long time among the primitives in Central Australia, goes a step further, being of the opinion that all primitives think and talk in *bisexual* terms, in bisexual connotations; that all customs, songs, legends, ceremonies, religious rites and myths are of bisexual nature. Their creation myths, he says, present the ancestor of the human being as a bisexual creature which was split in two, a man and a woman, whose goal is reunion, rebirth as a man-woman, as an androgyne. Winthuis asserts furthermore that not only the primitives express the belief that the human being was in the beginning androgynous, but that traces of this belief can also be found in the religions of nations with highly developed civilization, such as the Persians, Greeks and Hebrews. I do not consider myself competent to evaluate the validity of this theory, but I should like to refer to the ideas of Fr. Lenormant, a French archeologist, whom Winthuis quotes in support of his theory about the origin of certain religious concepts. I quote from Lenormant's book *Les Origines de l'Histoire* (1880, p. 51): "According to the version of the Vulgate, which in this point is in agreement with the Greek version of the Septant, we are accustomed to acknowledge that, according to the Bible, the first woman was formed out of a rib taken from the side of Adam. But it is very doubtful whether this interpretation is precise and correct. The Hebrew word 'cela' used here, means, in all other Biblical passages, wherever it is found, 'side' and not, indeed, 'rib.' Hence the philologically most probable translation of the text of the Genesis is the one we have adopted below.

"Yahveh Elohim caused a deep sleep to fall upon the man and he slept. He took out one of his sides and closed up the place with flesh thereof. And Yahveh Elohim formed the side which he had taken from the man into a woman and brought her unto the man. And the man said: 'This is now bone of my bones and flesh of my flesh, she shall be called "isschah" (woman) because she was taken from the "issch" (man).' That is the report of the Jehovist's document; in the Elohist document we have first: 'Elohim created the man in his semblance; male and female he created them' [Gen. i, 28]. The use of the plural pronoun seems, at first sight, to imply the notion of a couple of two distinct persons. But further on, this plural seems, on the contrary, to apply to the nature of a double being, male and female, constituting a single Adam; 'He created them male and female, and he blessed them and called their name Adam' [Gen. v, 2]. The text says 'Adam' and not 'HA Adam,' with an article, and the following paragraph proves that the word is used here as a personal name, and not as a generic designation. The Jewish tradition, Targumist as well as the Talmudic, and the scholarly philosophers, like Moses Maimonides, quite generally admit a similar interpretation in stating that Adam was created a man and a woman at the same time with two faces turned in opposite directions and that, in his sleep, the Creator separated from him Hava (Eve), his female half, to transform her into an individual person. Among the early Christian ecclesiastical writers, Eusebius of Cesarea adopted the same interpretation of the Biblical text and thought that the narrative of Plato on the primitive androgynes is in complete accord with that of the Holy Books."[7]

Thus, according to many scholars, Adam was an androgynous, bisexual creature, man and woman at the same time; the woman owes her existence to the fact that she was cut out from the man. Even in Greek mythology the Goddess Aphrodite (who was supposedly of Asiatic origin) came into existence by means of a similar, yet more clearly depicted event; Kronos fought with his father, Uranos, cut off his penis and threw it into the sea, whereupon Aphrodite sprang from the foam gathered around her father's membrum. Birth of the female from the male does not correspond to reality; the male is borne by the female. Hence the Greek myth, like the Biblical narration, represents a reversed version of the real event. Our patient had the idea that father puts his penis into mother where it grows and when it has become big enough it is cut out of her, a fantasy reflected in the myth in slightly changed form. Such mutation is a well-known defense mechanism. On the basis of voluminous comparative mythological material, Otto Rank (1912-1914) assumed that the creation myth as related in Genesis represents incest between Adam and Eve, who is the primal mother as well as the daughter. He believes that this myth further expresses the idea that woman was created by castration of man. These interpretations are still valid, but there is a discrepancy between the myth and our patient's fantasy, in relation to the difference between the sexes.

If we adopt our patient's idea that the prepuce represents the female part of the man, then his theory about the origin of the two sexes is identical with the myth as reported in the Bible. The words, "And the side which the Lord God had taken from man, made he a woman . . ." can thus be substituted by the sentence: God circumcised Adam and made a woman out of his prepuce. We see that in the fantasy of the individual as well as in the fantasy of a group, it is taken for granted that man is a bisexual, androgynous creature and that a distinct man and a distinct woman are formed by cutting

[7] Translated from the French text by the author of this study.

this creature in half. This theory is reminiscent of the well-known infantile "theory" about the origin of the two sexes, according to which only boys exist originally, and girls are made by castrating boys. However, it is significant that in none of the manifest texts—Biblical, Platonic, or the patient's—does the woman become a woman through castration: what they say is, that through circumcision the man loses his femininity, and that the part lost through circumcision is a woman. Now the man sees a part of himself, his femininity, in the external world. In other words, he reacts to the trauma of the circumcision with projection of his femininity. With this reaction he obviously still tries to protect his masculinity, as if to say: "In spite of all threats I am yet a man; what I lost is only my femininity; even castration cannot deprive me of my masculinity."[8]

It seems, moreover, that this fantasy or myth represents an attempt to master the bewilderment and anxiety evoked by the sight of the female genital, the sight of a human being without a penis. By denying the existence in the external world of a being without a penis, man attempts to undo the castration (circumcision) and creates for himself a new, a psychic reality which is less unpleasant and frightening. It also becomes less bewildering as it satisfies his primitive need for causality (Nunberg, 1930). It is as though man said to himself: "No castration occurred, only a separation of man from woman." After all, men and women are separated beings. Reality—Freud sometimes calls it "truth"—cannot be totally suppressed, even in fantasies (Freud, 1937b, 1939). It seems as if man was always aware of his bisexuality and perceived his inner sexual structure by projecting it into the outside world.

Both myth and individual fantasy thus seem to offer a simple solution for infantile curiosity about the creation of man. But as they also deal with the need—I should rather say, compulsion—of

---

[8] In this attitude may lie the source of the idea that the man must be brave, courageous and able to endure hardships and pain—"a boy does not cry." According to general opinion, it is not necessary for a girl to be courageous and bear pain without showing her suffering. Psychologically she has nothing to lose; on the contrary, she gains when she gives birth to a child. In fact, however, she is often more courageous than a man and can endure pain more stoically than he.

man and woman to join and love each other, we may ask ourselves, what explanation for this attraction is offered by the myth.

In the Bible the Lord says: "It is not good that the man should be alone; I will make him a help meet to him." To comfort Adam in his solitude, God cut out a part of his body, made a woman of it, and led her to him. From then on Adam had a companion; he was no longer alone. According to the Bible, it was, therefore, loneliness which produced in man the wish for union with a mate. As she (the mate) was a part taken from him, this union was rather a reunion with mother. And, obviously, this reunion nullified the separation from her brought about by circumcision.

Plato says that after the hermaphrodite had been cut in two, each half developed a longing for the other half: "... and then would they fling their arms about each other and in mutual embraces yearn to be grafted together.... Thus anciently is mutual love ingrained in mankind; reassembling our early estate and endeavoring to combine two in one and heal the human sore. ..."[9] The individual, our patient, thought that marrying a "good girl," his sister, would get him back his foreskin, heal his wound.

It is evident that the original motive for the attraction of the sexes is more transparent in the Platonic version than in that of the Bible. In the latter loneliness appears first, and then castration occurs; in the *Symposium,* castration occurs first, then loneliness is felt. This loneliness stimulates the longing of the sexes to be grafted together to "heal the human sore" inflicted upon humanity by the separation, i.e., circumcision.

It is as if love could nullify not only the separation of man from woman (as is, for instance, practiced in the puberty rites of primitives), but also circumcision itself.

According to the myth related here, the castration trauma can evidently be mastered in two ways: first, by projecting femininity into the outside world, and secondly, by mobilizing the heterosexual libido. This libido obviously stimulates the desire to unite both sexes in one, to restore the original identity of man. If our

[9] Plato, *Symposium.* The fact does not, of course, escape our attention that Freud saw in the myth as related by Plato an analogy to his theory of instincts, namely, that love, Eros, tries to unite human beings, to restitute the previous state of complete oneness (Freud, 1920).

assumption is correct that the prepuce symbolizes the feminine part of the man, then the restoration of the unity of both sexes in the myth may signify the restoration of the penis as it appeared before circumcision.

Our patient coped with the trauma of circumcision in a similar way and yet went beyond the reactions already related. We remember his fantasy that the doctor who performed the circumcision kept the foreskin for himself and that the patient felt tied to him by marriage. We further recall his idea that his analysis would be incomplete unless he recovered his lost foreskin and that, besides, he considered the end of his analysis as the beginning of complete, uninhibited sexual freedom. The idea of sexual freedom was thus coupled in his mind with the expectation of regaining his prepuce. The fulfillment of this expectation would, therefore, have removed his homosexual dependence on, or his submission to, the doctor, just as it would also have liberated his desire for heterosexual gratification. For, as has been pointed out in connection with one of his dreams, he had been unhappy and excited when, after his circumcision, his mother declined to continue taking care of his penis as she had previously done. Analysis of this dream showed that he identified the loss of his foreskin with the loss of pleasure derived from his mother's touching his penis. Thus restitution of his foreskin was to him tantamount to regaining his mother, who would, as formerly, provide him with sexual pleasure. The restitution of both, the mother and the foreskin, therefore had for him the same significance as nullification of the circumcision. The circumcision, which had at first caused homosexual dependence and disruption of heterosexual attachments, soon provoked rejection of this submission to the castrating father, and stimulated re-establishment of heterosexual strivings for the mother, by whom he felt deserted. He was, so to speak, lonesome like Adam in the Bible. And, as in the Bible or in the *Symposium,* heterosexual love healed the "human sore" of circumcision.

Loneliness readily produces feelings of insecurity and fear, both of which intensify the need for protection. It is difficult to determine whether our patient was aware of a particular loneliness after the circumcision, but he could definitely recollect his fear that the glans penis would fall off because it was no longer protected by the foreskin. He felt himself at a disadvantage beside his sister, whose "little penis" was, according to his imagination, hidden behind and very well protected by what he called her foreskin. This "foreskin" was in a psychic sense his own foreskin because, according to his previously related fantasy, his sister represented a part cut out of him and endowed with his foreskin. As we know, he had the obsessional idea of marrying his sister, which we interpreted as a wish to rejoin her, to undo the circumcision and to recover the foreskin. The possession of the foreskin meant to him protection of the glans penis. Later, when he learned of the existence of the vagina, he craved it as a place of security for his penis. The fact that the idea of security and protection provided by the vagina turned out to be a variation of his mother's-womb fantasies is not surprising.[10]

The need for protection of his penis developed into the need for protection of his whole body and adopted different forms. One of them was an interesting sleeping habit. He called my attention to this habit by complaining about profuse perspiration at night. When I learned that he covered himself, head and all, with a number of blankets, I understood the reason for his perspiration, but not for his habit of covering his entire body with so many blankets. The discovery that he could not fall asleep when prevented from covering himself in this manner indicated that the habit represented a protection from insomnia. He had, in childhood, suffered from a conditioned insomnia: he could not fall asleep unless the window was wide open. This symptom had developed in the following way: His mother used to put him to bed every night. He was probably afraid to remain alone because he tried, by the use of certain tricks, to induce her to stay at his bedside as long as possible. Among the tricks was the asking of various questions to which he demanded an answer. Once, after his circumcision, he asked her what death is, and was told that it is sleep forever. At that time he was already familiar with the nursery tale that children are angels in heaven before they are born, and become angels again when they die. As a consequence of this knowledge he kept himself awake, afraid that his angel might fly away from him while he was asleep

[10] Freud (1923b) says: "The vagina thus is highly praised as an abode for the penis, it is the heir to the mother's womb" (p. 244).

and never return if the window were closed. He therefore insisted that his mother leave the window open.

I do not think it necessary to try to prove to analysts that the angel symbolized a penis; the angel has wings, goes up into the air, flies away and comes back. Besides, the circumcision had taken place under narcosis, which is an artificial sleep. As he lost his foreskin in this artificial sleep, he was afraid to fall asleep again unless he had made sure that after awakening he would still have his penis.[11]

When, after the circumcision, he was afraid that his unprotected glans penis might fall off, he tried to find manifold ways of protecting his penis, and when one method failed, he soon invented another one. Immediately after his operation he asked his mother to put ointments, bandages and dressings on his penis, as she had done before. When she refused, he masturbated and tried to pull the skin of the shaft of his penis over the glans. In this connection he remembered that, when he used to expose his penis, his mother told him to hide it. His sister was able to hide her penis, as he imagined. Therefore, he tried to push his penis into his pelvis so as to make it disappear and to protect it from all accidents. Hardly had he done this, when he became afraid that he might really become a girl and definitely lose his penis. So he gave up all these attempts and started to wrap his body in blankets, as if enacting his fear.

The circumcision disturbed his masturbation and forced him to abandon it temporarily. When he resumed, he disguised it more carefully than before because of the frightening experience. The techniques of hiding his penis thus served two purposes: protection of his penis and disguise of his masturbation. Hence, from protecting his penis he derived sexual pleasure. Before his circumcision he associated sexual pleasure to a great extent with an object—the mother. After the circumcision this pleasure became autoerotic because the mother refused to touch him and he was thrown completely on his own resources for gratification. However, he did not entirely renounce his mother; he tried to change into her, a woman, who, according to his idea, could protect her "penis" better

---

[11] It is an interesting problem why children are so deeply impressed by narcosis, frequently even more than by the actual operation.

than a man does. The identification with mother thus created a form of protection for the penis, such as the prepuce had offered before the circumcision. It seems that this specific identification substituted for the lost foreskin.

Reviewing our material, we find that the trauma of the circumcision released forces aimed at overcoming its effects. All of the fantasies, thoughts, and habits served a single purpose: preservation of the phallus, protection of the genital. The hermaphroditic fantasy, i.e., the fantasy about the origin of man and the sexes, the marriage fantasy, the mother's-womb fantasy, the obsessional ideas, and, paradoxical as it may seem, the fantasy of becoming a girl, had the same aim: integrity of and safety for the penis.

As we have seen, the urge to maintain the phallic organization mobilized a series of defense mechanisms, which included undoing, denial, projection and identification. The initial success of these defenses, however, was inevitably followed by failures, which in turn were replaced by new efforts. The patient encountered failure in whatever he undertook to counteract the trauma of castration, and was repeatedly compelled to invent new ways of protecting his masculinity. These alternating successes and failures resembled a vicious circle. It seems as if a *vis à tergo* existed, an inertia, a form of stabilizing factor, a force trying to fixate the effects of the trauma. Perhaps the repetition compulsion was at work here (Freud, 1920). And yet this principle seemed to be opposed by another, which counteracted the trauma and tried to nullify its effects. In a sense it represented the self-healing tendencies of the ego (Nunberg, 1925).

As a result of these opposing tendencies, the trauma of the circumcision brought on a *short* standstill of genital activities, such as a temporary inhibition of masturbation. In addition, it caused a *partial* withdrawal of libido from the genital with subsequent cathexis of pregenital drives. This process, as is generally known, is called regression. Since the regression deflects the attention from the injured organ to other erotogenetic zones, and since the ego is thereby enabled to avoid displeasure, pain or anxiety, the regression may, as we have learned from Freud, also be considered, in this relation, a form of defense mechanism.

The painful sensation around the glans after circumcision drew narcissistic libido to the penis (Freud, 1920; Ferenczi, 1919). As a consequence, the patient became more aware of his genital than heretofore. The experience of circumcision increased penis consciousness as if it were a demonstration of the organ's importance. In addition, the anal region acquired new importance. Immediately after the circumcision the patient felt pain not only in the tip of his penis but also in the anal region. It spread—obviously through a reflex mechanism—from the glans penis to this region where it produced a spasm of the sphincter ani. Other patients, even after the sensation of pain around the glans has passed, still feel pain, irritation, tension in the anal region, or experience the sensation of having a foreign body in their rectum which provokes an irresistible urge for evacuation. This will be demonstrated by another case. The specific anal pain draws narcissistic libido to the anal region, just as the pain in the penis draws libido to that organ. As a consequence, the region becomes hypersensitive and hyperactive. The trauma of the circumcision therefore sensitizes anus as well as penis. Both regions were confounded in the patient's mind where they became interchangeable.[12] Circumcision lays bare and fixates earlier existing conditions.

We remember that after the circumcision our patient had asked his mother to handle his penis as she had used to do. Since she refused to comply with his wish, he asked her to clean his anus and to put Vaseline on it, just as she did whenever she gave him an enema. When she denied him this gratification, too, he grew furious and developed temper tantrums, but soon tried to comfort himself in his own way. After the circumcision, as indicated in another connection, he tried to pull the skin of the shaft of his penis over the glans, as though making an artificial foreskin and providing himself with protection for the denuded glans. As this protection did not seem adequate he tried to push his penis back into the pelvis and to hide it there. When he was discussing these manipulations, the recollection came to him that before the circumcision he would close his prepuce by pressing the edges of his foreskin tightly together with his fingers and urinate into the sack

---

[12] As early as 1913, Dr. Paul Federn, in his remarkable paper, "Beiträge zur Analyse des Sadismus und Masochismus," called attention to the fact that pain in the penis stimulates anal and sadistic impulses.

thus formed. Furthermore, he remembered that during childhood he believed that animals have a tail for the purpose of putting it in their rectum to fertilize themselves. In accordance with this fantasy, he tried to imitate animals by pushing his penis toward his anus. However, he achieved nothing but bed-wetting. Would it not seem that all of these efforts were but dramatizations of his bisexual or hermaphroditic fantasy, already cited above: "a man is a man in front and a woman in back, a woman is a woman in front and a woman in back; only a man can fertilize himself"? It appears as if within this game he had been demonstrating to himself the "real" situation as he perceived it in his childhood: the man has a penis, the woman none, the male organ is separated from the anus, it is clean, the female organ is not separated, it is a "cloaca," dirty. If we take into consideration his fantasy that a woman has a penis hidden and well protected in a place corresponding to a man's foreskin, a place from which she seems to urinate and defecate, when we keep in mind, furthermore, that, after circumcision, he tried to hide his penis, first in his pelvis, then in his rectum, we may conclude that, in his mind, not only prepuce and vagina were equivalent, but that both were also equivalent to the rectum and that all three could be substituted for one another.

This conclusion was confirmed by numerous details. For instance, he would play with his smegma, smell his fingers with great pleasure, but later become disgusted. This behavior is reminiscent of that of some girls who stop masturbation because of disgust with their genitals and for fear of being discovered through the smell of their fingers. Like so many other circumcised boys, he used to look down on uncircumcised ones as dirty and disgusting. The orthodox Jew has the same attitude: he considers unclean whoever is not circumcised. So does the Mohammedan. I wondered whether in the Bible an indication may be found of the relationship between anality and circumcision, and I am indebted to Dr. Paul Friedman for the information that the Hebrew word *arel*, which as a noun means "prepuce," in its verbal form means "to be not circumcised," "not to be open," "to be stubborn," "to be constipated." The word *arel* (uncircumcised) is used synonymously with the word *tameh* (unclean) (*Jewish Encyclopaedia*). This is confirmed by Fuerst in his *A Hebrew Chaldee Lexicon to the Old Testament,* according to which the word *arel* means uncircumcised, with foreskin, unclean, obstinate. Stubbornness, according to psychoanalysis, is a typical anal trait. The word *tameh* in Fuerst's Lexicon, is explained as meaning guilty, dirty (also used for uncircumcised), unclean body.

In this connection one detail of the hermaphroditic fantasy deserves more attention, the idea about self-fertilization and giving birth to children. The fantasy about animals fertilizing themselves by inserting their tail into the rectum shows clearly that the patient had anal birth in mind. But how can this be reconciled with the fantasy that children are born from the penis through circumcision? In addition to the fact that two contrasting fantasies dealing with the same subject can exist independently of each other, these two fantasies have one point in common. The genital birth fantasy signified becoming a man by getting a new penis. However, the patient, afraid of losing the unprotected glans after the circumcision, tried to hide his penis in his rectum, but then, again afraid of losing it, tried to expel it, which could be effected only by defecation. Thus it seems that the anal birth fantasy was a counterpart to the freeing of the glans penis by the circumcision. Consequently, our patient had two birth fantasies: a phallic one and an anal one. The latter was revived by the regression following the circumcision and persisted by being combined with the phallic fantasy.

Since this explanation may seem too theoretical, I should like to demonstrate the relationship through the analysis of one of the patient's numerous habits. He had the compulsion to pull scabs off from his head or face; any protuberance on his skin irritated him so much that he would scratch it until it bled. For a long time it remained utterly impossible to understand why he tried to mutilate himself. At last a phrase came to his mind that started a new chain of associations. It was the phrase: "I will beat him until he jumps out of his skin." At first he was himself puzzled by the sudden emergence of this phrase, but soon he remembered that his father used it when angry. When I asked him—rather rhetorically —what connection there was between this phrase and his pulling off the scabs, he answered promptly that it meant birth. Since I did not even try to hide my astonishment at this bold interpretation, he went on, again discussing his childhood fantasies about his father beating his mother (on the basis of overheard parental intercourse), and then remembering his mother's statement that he (the patient) had caused her pain at birth. When he heard his father angrily saying: "I will beat him until he jumps out of his skin," he combined the impressions, fantasies and ideas which revolved around beating, pain, and birth, into the single fantasy that his mother had been beaten by his father until he (the patient) jumped out of her skin, *until he was born*. The birth fantasy thus acquired a sadistic or masochistic character, depending on the point of view. The fantasy about "being beaten" (Freud, 1917a) is a fairly frequent one, but it could not have taken this particular form, had our patient not been afraid of losing his glans penis after the circumcision. The fear was specific, namely, that his glans would "jump out of the skin" enveloping the shaft of the penis. We know that he tried to protect his penis by pushing it back into his pelvis, quasi into the rectum, imagining that he was thus undoing the circumcision. But by pulling off the scab of his skin—we may now as well say by pulling off the foreskin from the head of the penis— he performed just the opposite act, as though repeating the circumcision on himself that the doctor had once performed on him. Inasmuch as the doctor is a substitute for the father, we are justified in concluding that the trauma of circumcision brought about a masochistic fixation to his father, manifesting itself in numerous repetitions of the event. By giving birth in pain to his new penis or himself he identified himself with his mother as "being beaten by his father." Taking into consideration the fact that he was afraid of losing his unprotected, denuded glans penis, we see that by repeating actively in a symbolic way what he had previously suffered passively—i.e., the circumcision—he tried to control, and to master, the castration fear, and at the same time to gain masochistic gratification.

However, he was not always afraid that his glans penis would fall off, "jump out." There was a period when he even wished his glans to "jump out" of his foreskin. He had this wish before the circumcision. In order to realize it he would squeeze the penis until the glans "jumped out." Although this was painful, he felt gratified by having freed his glans. Pain seemed to be compensated for by the satisfaction of having a penis like father's. The unconscious traces of this pain obviously still persisted after the circumcision in his masochism which—paradoxical as it may seem—helped to maintain the craving for a larger penis. In other words, masochism entered the service of the castration complex not only by its destructive, castrative tendencies, but also by its help in preserving the genitalium.

This masochistic birth fantasy was superimposed upon or coupled with an anal sadistic fantasy.

Whenever he tried to describe his masturbatory practices before circumcision, he expressed himself as follows: "I squeezed the head [of the penis] until it jumped out of the skin." He repeated almost the same sentence when he was discussing his evacuations in childhood. Then he would say: "I squeezed stool until it came out." I called his attention to the similarity of these expressions. Immediately after that he had a very short dream about a snake in his belly. To this dream he associated first a penis (which, of course, was not surprising) then feces. Finally the image of a snake changing its skin appeared before his inner vision. This image was rather a screen memory, replacing recollections of snakes, of which one was outstanding: as a child he was fascinated by the idea that snakes change their skin. The fascination culminated in a fantasy game where he himself, as a snake, changed his skin. Since snakes, changing their skin, symbolize birth and rebirth in many myths, we have here a symbolic equation: the appearance of the freed glans penis equals feces after evacuation, and both equal a new-born child.

Thus it is not surprising that the "squeezing out" idea brought to the surface a number of recollections concerning the patient's anality. For instance, his mother checked his evacuations strictly. Never satisfied with his performances, she always urged him to give more, to "try hard." He tried hard and pressed and squeezed. When he succeeded in "squeezing out" a large lump, his mother praised him. "Squeezing out," therefore, was a way of gaining mother's love.

In summarizing the patient's ideas about birth, it is, I think, not superfluous to point out that the initial need to retain mother's love, fulfilled by obeying her demands to defecate, transformed itself into the wish to give birth to a new penis, to be reborn and, finally, to give birth to a child (Freud, 1917b).

The following example may show how grotesque became our patient's wish to have a child. When he was first married he squeezed his wife's belly so vehemently that he hurt her. Only much later, in the last stages of his analysis, did he become aware of the unconscious meaning of this violence: he had tried to squeeze a baby out of her. His actual passive and narcissistic wish for children had activated the then repressed unconscious urge, surviving from childhood, to squeeze feces out of himself or to squeeze out the glans penis. Hence, in squeezing his wife's belly he was identifying himself with her and projecting his own strivings onto her, thus acting out on her his own repressed fantasies. His own masochistic fantasies, attached to another person, a sex object, took the shape of sadism.[13]

Ruth Mack Brunswick (1940) says: "In the anal phase, with its new concept of giving and receiving and of increasing object relations to the mother, the wish for a baby acquires a second root: both boy and girl then desire a baby from mother. The originally passive wish, like every other, acquires an active form: the wish to present the mother with a baby. The boy gives up the passive baby wish when his activity predominates." This activity, however, becomes obvious for both sexes in the phallic stage.

If we compare what we have learned from our patient in regard to the boy's fantasies of giving birth to a child, with what we know from Freud (1933) about the girl's birth fantasies, we may state unhesitatingly that they are not essentially different. When the boy first fancies giving birth to his penis or himself and then to a child, he has almost the same ideas as the girl. For instance, when the girl plays with her doll, the doll represents first herself and then her child. In view of the masturbatory character of this fantasy, the analogy carries even further. Freud (1925) says ". . . the peculiar rigidity of the monotonous formula [in the fantasy] a child is beaten, possibly admits of a special interpretation. The child that is beaten, i.e., caressed, in fact may be nothing else but the clitoris itself. Therefore, this sentence contains in its deepest layer the

---

[13] "If babies can be born through the anus, then a man can give birth to a child, just as well as a woman. A boy can therefore fancy that he too has children of his own without our needing to accuse him of feminine inclinations" (Freud, 1908b).

confession of masturbation which is attached to the contents of this formula from the beginning of the phallic state till late in life." Since the clitoris represents the feminine equivalent to the penis and since the boy feels his penis as a child in a similar way as the girl probably feels her clitoris, or *vice versa,* it seems that the birth fantasies of both, boy and girl, are essentially identical. To both, the child is primarily a narcissistic object. If it is true that the boy's fantasy of giving birth to a child is as genuine and general as the girl's, we might perhaps conclude that this fact forms the psychobiological foundation of the social institution of paternity which originated in the dim past of mankind.

Still another dream shows that our patient reacted to circumcision with regressions which went beyond the anal-sadistic stage. The dream was: "I was given ice cream and strawberry shortcake. The ice cream was better because you could put out fire with it. The strawberry shortcake, I thought, is very good, but I prefer ice cream because of the fire." This dream combined his circumcision with his tonsillectomy which had occurred some two and a half years earlier, when he was about two and a half years old. After the tonsillectomy, he remembered, he was given as much ice cream as he wanted; it soothed the pain and the burning. After the circumcision he was also given ice cream which, however, did not quite satisfy him. He asked for more and more and wanted— or even actually tried—to pack it around his penis to soothe the pain, the burning. But he felt pain and burning also when he irritated his penis by excessive masturbation. Then he would ask his mother to take care of it, to touch it, to soothe it with her soft hands. Is it not significant that just after having remembered the frustration of his wishes to be comforted by mother, he dreamed about ice cream, which once before, in his early childhood, actually had relieved him of discomfort and pain?

Ice cream not only symbolized his mother, rather milk of her breast, it also symbolized smegma, the substance secreted by the lining of the foreskin. The patient never referred to this substance as "smegma," but as "cheesy substance" or "cottage cheese." When asked why, he said that it was perverted milk, a "cheesy milk." It was unclean, he said, dirty, malodorous, disgusting and yet fascinating; he had, indeed, stuffed it enjoyably into mouth and nose. We can easily see why he was repelled and attracted by it at the same time: its psychic representative, the idea of the smegma, symbolized mother's milk and fecal matter as well. It paralleled the equation mentioned above, according to which the prepuce represented mother and cloaca, vagina and rectum. In the dream he tried to comfort himself and overcompensate the loss of the prepuce and all that it represented, by making a regression to oral and anal ways of gratification.

This interpretation, however, does not exhaust the meaning of the dream. The dreamer was also given strawberry shortcake. The cake to him meant mother's breast. The strawberries reminded him of the nipples as well as of the tip of the penis when the foreskin is slightly retracted (before circumcision). With this association he evidently expressed the idea that his own glans penis and mother's nipples were the same, in other words, that his mother had a penis in common with him. The idea that they had something in common indeed facilitated his identification with her and implied that she had a penis like his and that he had breasts and nipples like hers. As far back as he could remember, he had always wanted to have breasts like mother. In the dream, however, he did not care much for the strawberry shortcake; he cared for the ice cream. One does not crave what one has, but what one has not. In fact, he had his glans penis, but no foreskin. He substituted unconsciously the glans for the mother's nipples, as we have seen, and the foreskin with the smegma (cheesy substance) for mother's breast and milk. The former represented to him the masculine principle, the latter the feminine one. Thus, by getting ice cream which he craved so much, he regained his lost foreskin with its cheesy substance, in other words, he restored the unity of his masculine and feminine parts, of himself and his mother; he became bisexual again, a man and a woman in one person. If the ice cream really symbolized mother's milk, and the glans penis her nipples, then the idea of putting ice cream around the glans penis may mean, in the deepest psychic layer, sucking at mother's breast with a mouth full of milk. This kind of gratification would nullify all separation from mother, it would radically undo the circumcision. The infant, the son, would be reborn and united with his mother—an idea which is of such great importance in many religions.

Moreover, if this interpretation is correct, we can better understand two slight perversions that occurred in our patient's puberty. First, he tried to drink his semen, but soon stopped because he was disappointed by its taste; it did not fulfill his expectation. He could, however, not say what he had anticipated. It was not the "cheesy substance" that he had expected because he had a definite recollection of its taste and smell. Since there are other boys who in puberty drink their semen or urine and are disappointed, although they had not earlier tasted their smegma, it may be assumed that our patient's anticipation of a definite taste of his semen corresponded to an unconscious memory of the taste of mother's milk, of something that unfailingly gave him complete comfort. Since it was no longer actually possible to obtain mother's breast whenever he felt in distress, he very soon resigned himself to abandoning this autoerotic gratification. The second perversion was not so soon abandoned. While ejaculating at the climax of his masturbation, he would aim with his semen at his nipples. When he succeeded in hitting his nipples with the semen he became ecstatic, intoxicated by an incomparable pleasure. It is not difficult to see that in this perversion he again acted out his hermaphroditic fantasy, becoming a man and a woman in one person. In so far as he possessed a penis and imagined himself possessing his mother's nipples, he felt himself a man; in so far as he had semen, smegma, and imagined himself to have milk, he felt himself a woman. Thus, at times, the trauma of the circumcision threw our patient so far back in his sexual and ego development that he craved the most primitive comfort one can get, the restoration of the erstwhile real infantile situation where he could suck at mother's breast. As this was in actuality impossible, he identified with the object that, in his childhood, had never failed to comfort him, his mother. The identification enabled him to play two parts in one person, those of a man and a woman.

MASCULINE, FEMININE?

A dream which occurred near the end of our patient's analysis shows to what degree bisexual ideas dominated his unconscious thinking: "Ann's navel protruded in three shapes: first, it protruded like a dog's penis with a sort of head stretching out, but more like a dog's penis protruding from a sheath; it was long, red and looked like the neck of a clam; the whole thing was flesh-colored. I got great satisfaction from taking the navel in my mouth, sucking it. Secondly, the sheath disappeared. The head remained like the pistil of a flower, without the shank. Third, the navel protruded in the form of a cone, the point of the cone touching the belly. In the opening of the cone was a white, cheeselike-tasting substance. I ate it. The pistil looked like a cherry. I buried my mouth and nose in it and ate it and had its taste in my mouth and its smell in my nose. At the end of the dream I had the feeling of having completely satisfied myself. . . ."

This dream speaks for itself. It contains, as if in a nutshell, most of the fantasies that occupied our patient's mind from childhood on, throughout his entire life. In the dream these fantasies were centered around the navel; and the navel, in the minds of children, is the place of birth. In the Platonic myth, it symbolized the scar caused by the separation of man from woman. In our interpretation it meant birth through circumcision.

The navel at first resembled a penis with a sheath around it. It may be assumed that the sheath replaces the foreskin; therefore the kind of navel represented in the dream symbolizes an uncircumcised penis. In that case, circumcision does not deprive the human being of the penis, does not change his sex character.

The second version of the same dream shows how difficult it was for the patient to accept the existence of a human being without a penis. In this version the navel assumed the shape of a clam, with a red, flesh-colored neck. No doubt, this symbolizes the female genitalia, the neck of the clam replacing the clitoris, and the red flesh-colored clam itself representing the vulva, which looks like a wound. Although in this form of the navel the female genitalia are depicted as a "wounded" organ, a symbolic penis is nevertheless retained in the shape of the clam's neck. No matter what happens, in fantasy man remains a bisexual being.

In the third variation of the dream the sheath disappears and the head of the penis emerges like the pistil of a flower. Since our patient's mother, like so many other mothers, had explained the so-called "facts of life" to him by using the comparison with the growth of flowers and planting of seeds, we may assume that the head of the penis standing out like the pistil of a flower symbolizes the birth of a child. If the sheath symbolizes the foreskin, then the disappearance of the sheath and the reappearance of the head of the penis in the shape of the pistil of a flower represents birth, rather rebirth of a man in the shape of a penis. This interpretation is again in full accord with the meaning of the circumcision as expressed in the patient's fantasies as well as in the puberty rites of the primitives.

The navel or pistil protrudes like a cone containing a white "cheesy-tasting" substance, and looks like a cherry. It is not difficult to guess that this version of the dream again symbolizes the bisexuality of the dreamer. For the cherrylike cone with the white cheesy substance represents his penis and mother's nipples condensed in one picture.

The fantasies as reflected in this dream were indeed of a highly narcissistic nature. In all of them the patient not only retains his penis but also equips the woman with a penis, an organ of enormous value to him. By attributing his organ to her, he makes her equal to himself.

In the course of development, however, the boy is forced to restrain his narcissism and to adapt himself to *sexual reality*. Then he renounces the conception of "the woman with a penis" and accepts her as a human being like himself and yet different as to her genitals. This difference makes her appear to him as a "castrated boy." Evidently, "boyishness," "masculinity" are, in his mind, closely associated with the bodily image and sensations of his penis. Since the girl's clitoris is an equivalent of the boy's penis, we assume that from the image of her clitoris and from its sensations she derives sexual feelings which are analogous to those of the boy. It therefore seems quite logical that in the phallic phase of the libido development one sex chiefly should be known to the child, whether boy or girl, the masculine sex, as characterized by possession of the penis and its equivalent, the clitoris. Freud (1905c, 1925) says that the libido is always masculine, and that, furthermore, in the phallic phase of libido development the masculine element prevails in the sexual life of both boy and girl. Expressed in anatomical terms, this phase is characterized by the penis in the boy and by the clitoris in the girl. In addition to the clitoris, the girl also possesses the vulva, the center of sexual sensations which probably originate very early and then subside. Since the clitoris is considered a masculine organ and the vulva a feminine one, the external female genitalia seem to be of bisexual nature. Do the boy's external genitalia also display signs of bisexuality? It is difficult to give a simple answer to this question. However, we remember that our patient identified his foreskin with the vulva; it represented the "woman" in himself; in his fantasy it was a symbol of his "femininity."[14]

The problem of bisexuality persistently occupied Freud's mind, and was to him rather a biological problem. He said that "a certain degree of anatomical hermaphroditism is normal" (Freud, 1905c) and "all human individuals because of their bisexual *Anlage* and crossed heredity comprise male and female characters, so that pure masculinity or femininity are theoretical constructions with vague contents" (Freud, 1925). Finally, in the posthumously published *An Outline of Psychoanalysis,* which is somewhat of a summary on the subject, he says: "We are faced here by the great enigma of the biological fact of the duality of the sexes; for our knowledge it is something ultimate, it resists every attempt to trace it back to something else. Psychoanalysis has made no contribution toward solving this problem, which clearly falls entirely within the province of biology. In mental life we find only reactions of this great antithesis; and their interpretation is made more difficult by the fact, long suspected, that no individual is limited to the methods of reaction of a single sex, but always finds some room for those of the opposite one, just as his body frequently bears, alongside the developed organs of one sex the stunted and often useless ones of the other" (Freud, 1940a).

Having recognized very early the importance of the psychic manifestations of bisexuality, he wrote as follows in his basic work on sexuality: "Since becoming acquainted with the aspect of bi-

---

[14] Perhaps the prepuce is an equivalent of the vulva. According to Bailey and Miller (1909) the labia minora correspond genetically to the prepuce. Herman Braus (1924) is even more explicit. He says that the prepuce (its external surface), the skin of the penis, and the scrotum correspond embryologically to the labia majora, and that the membrane covering the glans penis (the inner lining of the prepuce) corresponds to the labia minora. *Hence the external genitalia themselves seem to exhibit signs of bisexuality.*

sexuality I hold this factor as here decisive, and I believe that without taking into account the factor of bisexuality it will hardly be possible to understand the actually observed sexual manifestations in man and woman" (Freud, 1905c).[15]

We have reached a point where we can no longer evade the question: what is masculinity and what is femininity? Freud's contention that psychoanalysis did not contribute much to the solution of this problem is true, but psychoanalysis, by making important contributions to the psychological understanding of man and woman, increasingly delimits the biological problem of masculinity and femininity.

The analysis reported here and other cognate material seem to support the statement made above that masculine feelings are to a certain extent dependent on the sensations perceived from penis and clitoris respectively. Women derive their feminine feelings from the bodily image of, and sensations in, the vulva and vagina. According to our patient, men derive their feminine feelings from the sensations in the prepuce. But he identified his prepuce not only with his sister's vulva, but also with his anus, as if prepuce were a link between his rectum and her vulva. We recall that the concept of anality served to characterize, for him, the "femininity" of both man and woman in the phallic phase. In other words, femininity was to him identical with anality. Adhering longer than is usually done to the "cloaca theory" of the female genitalia, he found particularly disgusting the fact that the woman, according to his conviction, urinated and defecated from the same "hole." His own genitals, his penis, seemed comparatively clean to him, particularly after the removal of the foreskin, which had been malodorous and dirty. He was proud of his genitals. Thus it seems as if he had enjoyed the idea that the circumcision not only liberated his glans penis, the symbol of masculinity, but also freed him of the dirty prepuce, the symbol of femininity. Hence, the circumcision made it easier for him to project his own anality onto his sister's, the girl's genitalia. As men generally consider the female genitalia more or less unclean and ugly, and their own clean and attractive, we must assume that projection of a certain quantity

[15] Only S. Rado (1940) is fortunate enough to understand sexuality of man and woman without taking these factors into consideration.

of man's anality onto the woman belongs to his development to full masculinity.

However, it is not only the man who considers the female genitalia dirty; the woman herself looks on them as on a kind of "cloaca" and is disgusted with and ashamed of them. She does not, however, project her anality onto the man, but shifts it, instead, from the anal erotogenic zone to the genital zone. Freud says that the excitability of the vagina is mainly of anal derivation, and adds that "the vagina is, in the admirable phrase of Lou Andreas-Salome, 'hired out' from the rectum" (Freud, 1933, p. 139). Ruth Mack Brunswick (1940) was also of the opinion that there exists an early vaginal sensitivity of anal origin. The fact that the female genitalia retain more anal libido than the male ones is of great importance for the further development of the girl into a mature woman. It influences her attitude toward her own genitalia and toward sexual intercourse as such; it is reflected in her reactions to the man before and after sexual intercourse (i.e., she is grateful to him for loving her in spite of her "disgusting" genitalia); it predisposes her to take care of the infant, particularly in so far as cleanliness is concerned.

Summarizing, it may be stated that the feelings of femininity in both sexes have partial origin in anal sensations. After maturity, the sensitivity of the clitoris shifts into the introitus vaginae. As a result of this shift the libido of a "male" organ (clitoris) increases the sensitivity of a female organ (vagina). A similar displacement, in the opposite direction, takes place in man's development to full maturity.

The clinical fact that anal stimulation produces genital excitement, and *vice versa,* is in accordance with the other familiar observation that one part instinct can easily be replaced by another and that they are, therefore, often taken one for another. Ruth Mack Brunswick thought that it is more difficult to separate the strivings of the anal phase from those of the oral one than both from the phallic phase, and she was right. For the deeper we delve into the id, the less organized is the instinctual life, the less are the aims differentiated and the more easily can one aim be supplanted by another. In the unconscious, for instance, anal drives are confused with oral ones. At the end of his navel dream our patient buried his mouth and nose in the vulva and enjoyed its taste and smell.

As our patient demonstrated, in his unconscious, mother's breast and milk were replaced by smegma and fecal matter, while on the other hand, her nipples were replaced by his penis. At the same time he established a cross-identification which is to be understood as follows: the "cherry," as a symbol of mother's nipples and his own glans penis represented a bridge between himself and mother: *imagining that he possessed her nipples, he identified himself with her.* The "cottage cheese," symbolizing mother's milk and his own smegma, formed another bridge; *in so far as he fancied himself in possession of her milk and breast, he identified himself with her; in so far as he imagined her having his prepuce and smegma he identified her with himself.* As a result of this cross-identification there was no difference between himself and his mother, between a man and a woman; they were both the same and bisexual, both had traits of the other sex.

It has thus become evident that some erotogenic zones represented themselves to our patient in two series: first, as penis, clitoris, nipples and other similarly shaped organs, symbolizing masculinity; second, as rectum, foreskin, vagina and its secretions, breast with milk, and the like, symbolizing femininity. Here it is strikingly demonstrated that the symbolic meaning of the erotogenic zones coincides with the meaning of symbols in general (Freud, 1916-1917). May we perhaps take one further step and ask ourselves whether it might not be true that the biological representation of masculinity is a solid erectile organ, and that of femininity a hollow organ, a cavity, a sort of container?

At this point we may recall a theory about instincts which Dr. Ludwig Jekels (1913) attempted to formulate more than thirty years ago. According to him, the aim of the sexual instinct depends on the shape of the erotogenic zone, that is, of the organ functioning as such. In other words, the morphology of the erotogenic zone determines the nature of the aim of the sexual drive. As we know, this aim is either active or passive. Jekels assumes that activity coincides with masculinity and passivity with femininity.

Independently, Dr. Paul Federn expressed almost identical ideas, published in two exceptionally stimulating papers in 1913-1914.

Referring to the terms "activity" and "passivity," he says: "We want to determine the ideas 'masculine' and 'feminine' in relation to the libido according to its aim, i.e., whether the sensation is in a primarily masculine or feminine organ [Federn, 1913]. The sexual aim is, however, neither exclusively active in the man nor exclusively passive in the woman..." (Federn, 1914, p. 119). Then he continues: "In general one may say that, when a sexual desire can be gratified by a tactile stimulus applied to a sensitive spot, a passively directed sexual component appears. When, however, a movement or a muscular action of the organ effects gratification, an active sexual component develops.... In contrast to the penis are vagina and vulva—the organs from which the strongest passive libido emanates.... Also the anal zone has ... an individual meaning in each case.... In some individuals voluptuous-active sensations are attached to the function of the sphincter ani, hence in these cases one may speak about muscle eroticism. In other individuals the anal mucous membrane is highly erotogenic even without muscular contractions, sometimes to the extent that these passive lust sensations reach primacy before the sex organs.... Thus the anal zone makes passive as well as active contributions to the total libido..." (Federn, 1914, p. 120).

Federn's ideas are confirmed by clinical observation. For it is true that the aim of the instincts is alternately or coincidentally active or passive. It can, therefore, easily be understood how difficult it is to differentiate between masculine and feminine character traits. Antitheses of "masculinity" and "femininity" do not exist in the early libido development. Then, according to Freud, particularly in the anal-sadistic phase, the equivalent of the contrast between "masculinity" and "femininity" appears as a contrast between activity and passivity. In the next, the phallic phase, there is still no complete differentiation between boy and girl. For in the sexual life of both an exquisitely male organ plays the decisive part, the penis in the boy, the clitoris in the girl. Even after puberty, when the definite differentiation of sexes has been established, it is still difficult to state with certainty what is "masculine" and what is "feminine." This uncertainty may result from the distribution of active and passive strivings in the libidinal structure of the personality (Freud, 1931b). If activity prevails in the boy's personality, his sexual drive takes the form of a clear-cut urge to conquer and take the girl. If passivity prevails in the girl, she develops a wish to have and keep the boy. Since the words "have" and "keep" imply some kind of activity, we must conclude that "femininity" is not completely devoid of activity. Yet, clinical experience shows that complete passivity exists in certain stages of relaxation and is enjoyed.

The problem of activity and passivity is closely related to anality. Toward the end of his analysis, our patient described the relationship rather accurately. I quote him literally: "I noticed that when I get angry I protrude my stomach like a child pushing out his stomach in anger, like puffing in temper tantrum, getting red in the face; he inhales a lot of air throwing out his stomach; the stomach is distended like making stool; the child gets round, blows up his stomach trying to squeeze out stool." As the patient was the youngest child in his family and had little opportunity, even later, to watch children in the nursery, this description must apply to himself when still very small, trying to have bowel movements and getting angry automatically. Evidently he described an unconscious process which occurred in his childhood: the stimulus to the mucous membrane of the rectum set in motion, by a kind of reflex, the whole muscular apparatus of the abdominal press; the latter expelled the fecal matter—removed the stimulus—at the same time producing the effect of anger.[16] It need not be stressed that this is the same patient who squeezed his wife's belly during cohabitation, in order to get a child. We remember, besides his circumcision birth fantasy, he had two other fantasies about producing children, an anal one (squeezing out stool) and a sadistic one (father beating mother until a baby jumps out of her). In symptoms and habits, he acted out these fantasies on himself as when he scratched his head until it hurt and bled. Or, when trying to squeeze out a child from his wife's stomach, he identified himself with her and projected his anal and passive masochistic tendencies onto her while he himself assumed an active and sadistic role.

[16] The analysis enabled him, obviously, to reproduce ideas and attitudes of his childhood, to connect and express them in words, thus giving them a conscious meaning. In my opinion patients unconsciously know much more about the anatomy and physiology of their body than we are ready to admit.

Anal-sadistic and passive trends, stimulated and fixated by the trauma of circumcision, were even more apparent in the following case. Only a few pertinent facts from this very complicated analysis will be related. The patient was circumcised three or four months before his fourth birthday. Immediately after the operation he felt an urge to urinate and defecate, but could do neither. He suspected that the doctor had "plugged" him up. In the course of time he developed a chain of fantasies, of which the following proved to be the most important one. A horse was standing on the ground and the patient or someone else covered its genitals with a strainer wrapped in cheesecloth; this strainer "plugged up" the horse so that it could neither urinate nor defecate; the patient himself cupped one hand over his own genitals and pressed the palm of the other hand against his anus, imagining that he was suffering in the same manner as the horse. The cloth-covered strainer reminded him of the gas mask put on his face for the circumcision. This mask over his mouth and nose before he fell asleep and the awakening with the painful sensation in penis and rectum were almost the only memory he retained of the whole operation.

It is evident that the horse represented himself. Even without detailed analysis, it is easy to see that in this fantasy he repeated fears and sensations centered around the circumcision, though he was not aware of this. At the time of the operation he had not attributed his pain and discomfort to the operation, but to a sty on his eye, for his mother had told him that the doctor was going to "open" it. The idea of being "open" played a very important part in his life, as we shall see.

The structure and history of the horse fantasy are very interesting, but it will suffice to say that its variations and ramifications accompanied the patient throughout his life. In many ways, he repeated and enacted its contents. In childhood, while playing Indians with other boys, he suffered tremendous fear, almost panic, that they would "impale" him, drive a spear in his rectum and turn it around. As a mature man he broke a leg, which necessitated a surgical operation. When he had returned to his room and a young attractive nurse asked him how he felt, he answered: "Do you know how it feels to have a red-hot poker turned around in your arse? That's how I feel."

Whenever he had sex relations, he would grow restless, tense, feel "plugged up," become angry; at times, he even had temper tantrums. Simultaneously, he felt guilty for having "plugged up" the woman.[17] The sexual component of the anal reactions as well as of the anger is obvious. The best comment I can make here is to quote Ruth Mack Brunswick (1940, p. 308): "Rage appears to be the motor expression of anal eroticism, the equivalent of orgasm."

The spasm in his rectum, which he felt as a "plug," gradually took the form of stubborn constipation which was accompanied by very unpleasant, annoying sensations all over the body. He felt full, bloated, tight, closed, stiff, strained—sensations which seemed to perpetuate those released by the circumcision. He was not able to endure their strain for too long. Believing that his constipation was the source of all his troubles, he tried to control his bowel movements, and did so in fantastic ways. His aim was to have "soft" evacuations, to be "open," "relaxed." However, when he happened to be "open" and "relaxed," he became afraid that he would become weak and faint, fall to the ground and be disgraced. It is noteworthy that just when his wish to be "open" and "relaxed" was going to be fulfilled he was seized by the attacks of anxiety. The fact, however, that this anxiety occurred in public toilets, when he knew or believed that a man was near, may throw some light on this paradox.

He referred the fear of disgrace to constant criticism by his father. From early childhood on, he deeply resented being constantly teased and laughed at by his father. Unable to defend himself, he felt humiliated and embarrassed, and had similar feelings when he was teased for not behaving in a manly way, when he was afraid to ride a pony, to fight with other boys, etc. The one outstanding fear of his childhood, however, was impalement by his playmates. The same idea, but without fear, was reflected in the fantasy about the horse, which was "plugged up." Both fears, the actual one of being "open" and "relaxed" and the infantile one of

[17] The following example may be mentioned as a female counterpart to the sensation of being "plugged up": When one of my constipated female patients finally succeeded in having evacuations, she did not feel relieved nor relaxed but still continued to have the sensation of a foreign body in her rectum. Only after having masturbated at her clitoris, did she feel relieved and lose the sensation of the foreign body.

having a spear driven into his rectum, thus point to a danger threatening his masculinity. Even his fear of fainting belongs in the same category. He himself connected it with fear of loss of consciousness when taking anesthetics for surgical operations, such as he was given for the first time before his circumcision. But he could not remember having been afraid on that occasion, although he did remember that he was afraid on other such occasions. His last operation was delayed for some time because he refused to sign the routine form empowering the surgeon to operate on him. He maintained that, rendered unconscious by the anesthetics, he would have no control over the surgeon who might then cut more than necessary. It seems thus as if the actual fear of fainting was a new edition of the infantile fear of "castration" (circumcision) during narcotic sleep. The fear of relaxation, obviously, was a reaction to his infantile idea that something had been inserted in his rectum ("plugged up") while he was helpless in an unconscious state.

When he had the sensation of a foreign body in his rectum, he became tense, restless, angry, and, according to his own words, had the feeling of "cutting to pieces" the stool, of "grinding it to a pulp." It looks as if he was in this way living out his aggression against the contents of his bowels, without producing anxiety. If we substitute penis for feces—which is constantly done in the unconscious—we may conclude that he lived out his aggression against a penis, namely, his father's, as the analysis of this very involved material showed. In other words, he lived out his aggressive homosexuality in these unpleasant sensations (Nunberg, 1936).

His alternately sadistic and masochistic attitude toward his father may perhaps best be illustrated by the development of one of his behavior patterns. As already mentioned, he resented his father's teasing and felt humiliated by it. Although it often made him angry, he did not react visibly. But one incident stood out in his memory, when he could no longer control his anger. It happened in his early teens, when his father once again criticized and reproached him for something he had done. In a rage, he asked his father to stop lest he "break his neck." The father glanced at him and—without uttering a word—left the room. The patient remarked that his father obviously realized that he meant what he said and the incident burdened his conscience whenever he thought of it. His self-consciousness and sensitivity to criticism increased; he was always on the defensive. He became repeatedly involved in conflicts, particularly with his superiors. It looked as if he had a persecution mania. According to Freud (1911b) persecution mania indicates repressed passive homosexuality.

We have learned before that when he happened to defecate in presence of men, he would first feel "open," "relaxed" and "relieved," but then be overwhelmed by anxiety. From Freud we know that anxiety is a signal of danger. The source of this danger in our case seems to be fear of being plugged up and circumcised (castrated). In puberty this danger took a new form. Following a burglary in his parents' home, such fear of robbers gripped him that for many years he kept a loaded shotgun beside his bed when he slept. It is easy to see that sleeping with a loaded gun at his side signified protection against homosexual persecutors. To be prepared for aggression against an anticipated homosexual attack helped him to overcome his anxiety in the same way as did his oversensitivity to criticism. The circumciser (doctor, father) is certainly considered the persecutor, but so is fecal matter, the scybalum, according to Van Ophuijsen (1920). Our patient had no anxiety when he was tense with the sensation of a foreign body in his rectum. His anxiety appeared when he freed himself of this sensation and was relaxed, open. Thus one can see that he was afraid of men who might try to insert something into his rectum at a moment when he was unable to defend himself. Since there was no actual external danger requiring protection, the danger could only be internal and projected. In fact, it presented itself as an unconscious wish or urge to yield to his own passive-masochistic and homosexual tendencies, which may have been stimulated and fixated by the trauma of the circumcision. This may explain the lack of anxiety when he felt tense and "plugged up" and the release of anxiety, almost panic, when he felt relaxed and "open."

There is, perhaps, another reason for the release of anxiety by relaxation and relief. As seen above, the patient's only vivid memory of the circumcision was the mask on mouth and nose before he fell asleep and the awakening with painful sensations in penis and anus. Obviously he telescoped the experience immediately before the operation with the sensations afterward. Since he was unconscious during the operation, he did not consciously experience the circumcision, the symbolic castration. When, after awakening from the narcotic sleep, he felt the spasm in his rectum, he thought that this had been done to him in his deep sleep. His later attempts to relax and feel nothing made him afraid of fainting, i.e., of losing consciousness again. Thus it may be assumed that he produced the effect of anxiety to force himself to stay awake and to experience the emotions which he had missed because of the narcotic sleep. In this light, the anxiety may also be considered a belated reaction to the circumcision. The original, normal reaction to the circumcision—anxiety—seems to have been inhibited by the narcosis, but later on reactivated and consciously experienced over and over again. It seems as if this anxiety, once reactivated, helped him repress his passive homosexuality and thus to protect himself from yielding to his own dangerous drives.

Not only anxiety protected him against passive homosexual drives, but also certain fantasies and habits. The cheesecloth wrapped around the strainer (gas mask) in the horse fantasy reminded him of a suspensory. His considerably older brother, a great athlete, used to wear one. As far back as he could remember, this intrigued him immensely. When he himself started to participate in athletics, he bought a suspensory and wore it constantly, even at night. The strainer wrapped in cheesecloth thus represented not only the gas mask, the instrument which deprived him of his consciousness, i.e., security, and which "harmed" his genitalia; it also represented protection for them. Since it covered the rectum as well, the protection was extended to the anal region. While in his fantasy he protected the horse's genitalia and rectum with the cheesecloth-covered strainer, in reality he covered his own with his hands. The position described above, one hand pressed against his penis and the other one against his rectum, became a habit with him. In this way he would fall asleep and wake up. There is no doubt that this habit was some kind of magic gesture by which he protected himself against sexual attacks by men. It was also somewhat of a compromise because he derived masturbatory pleasure from this protective gesture. If we take into account, furthermore, that in sexual intercourse he identified himself with the woman—he believed that he "plugged up" her vagina with his penis while he felt his own rectum "plugged up" with feces—we must assume that the trauma of the circumcision stimulated not only passive homosexual strivings in him, but also anal and feminine drives. It therefore seems that this patient confirms the conception that femininity is characterized by an admixture of passive, masochistic and anal traits (Freud, 1911b; Deutsch, 1944).

In childhood, female genitalia are looked upon as a "cloaca" and therefore identified with the rectum. Both vagina and rectum are usually considered exclusively passive organs, which is not true, however, in all circumstances. The rectum is unquestionably also an active organ. Freud (1905c) pointed out that anality has a particular affinity to sadism, and Federn maintains that passive as well as active impulses emanate from the rectum (Federn, 1913, 1914). The same may be said about almost all other organs, for instance, the mouth (Abraham, 1924). Jekels (1913) believes that the shape of the organ determines the activity or passivity of its aims. This, however, seems to be valid only to a certain extent, for all of these organs possess both an active motor and a passive sensory apparatus. For instance, the mucous membrane of the rectum is in part a passively perceiving organ while the muscles of its wall perform actions (Federn, 1913, 1914). Sucking with the mouth on mother's breast is an active as well as a passive process (Abraham, 1924). The penis, though a solid organ and as such an exquisitely active and penetrating one, is nevertheless in certain parts a passively receptive sensory organ, the sensations of which spread all over the body. The glans is in many cases less sensitive than the posterior parts of the penis (Abraham, 1924; Federn, 1913, 1914). The vagina, as a cavity, is an exquisitely receptive organ, to such an extent that when it relaxes and opens, it renders the woman helpless (like the male patient when his rectum opened); and yet when she reaches the climax in intercourse the vagina performs contractions; she behaves then like a man. To many a woman, especially the frigid one, the orgasm signifies being a man. (She often thinks: "Without a penis one cannot have sexual pleasure.")[18] Thus the male organ is not exclusively active nor the

---

[18] These facts look like a confirmation of Freud's contention that libido is always masculine. Sexual sensitivity of the vagina is dormant until it is brought to life by cohabitation with the male, thus in an indirect way, maybe by identification.

female one exclusively passive. For this reason both man and woman seek to gratify their sexual needs in both a masculine and a feminine way. The man is a man in so far as he is active, he behaves like a woman in so far as he is passive; with the woman the same is true. In other words, the male sexual instinct sensitizes active aims, while the female one sensitizes passive aims. Full masculinity is characterized by the prevalence of active aims, full femininity by the prevalence of passive aims. To take a striking example: when a man is submissive, inactive, and confines himself to hoping when he is expected to be active and aggressive, we say that he behaves like a woman; when a woman is active and aggressive when, according to our expectations, she should be inactive and just hoping, we say that she behaves like a man.

Freud says that psychoanalysis gets along with only one kind of libido, i.e., energy of the sexual instincts. He stresses, however, that the libido "knows active and passive aims, i.e., ways of gratification. In this antithesis, first of all in the existence of libidinal strivings with passive aims, is contained the unresolved part of the problem" (Freud, 1931a). Hence the problem of masculinity and femininity is simplified, or reduced to the conception of activity and passivity. But what is activity and what is passivity? The answer to these questions is enormously difficult. While it seems possible to a certain extent to express the idea of "activity" in the more definite terms of muscular innervations, motions and actions and their psychic representatives, we are at a loss when we try to formulate the idea of "passivity" in somewhat more familiar terms. As Freud pointed out in the sentence quoted above, the passive aims of the instincts present the main problem. But when, in spite of the difficulties, we attempt to define the concept of passivity, some kind of inertia comes to mind, tardiness, a tendency to submission as if man were trying to perpetuate his infantile dependence or to repeat this dependence over and over again, we recollect that women expressed hopes, expectations and longing, in situations in which men acted. The best example of feminine inactivity seems to me the woman in pregnancy. The fetus grows in her, takes nourishment from her, kicks her, makes her feel uncomfortable; she wishes it to develop in a certain way, to be a boy or to be a girl, yet, having no power over nature's course, she accepts her helplessness, even with satisfaction; she merely waits and enjoys her pregnancy. Similar passivity, though less marked, is displayed by the woman in suckling the infant. Although she derives passive pleasure from being sucked (sexual pleasure, as many women admit), yet she has to be active in bringing the baby in touch with her breast. It is worth mentioning at this point that the woman loses her passivity and becomes active when she takes care of her child. As paradoxical as it may seem, she then becomes masculine —if masculinity means activity.

How difficult it is to discern between activity and passivity may best be illustrated by the example of a patient with an extraordinary faculty for self-observation. On the surface this patient seemed active, while in fact she was very passive. Her sexual life was centered around masochistic fantasies.

I shall repeat here almost literally what she told me on various occasions in her prolonged analysis: "I learned to make my legs *tense* and *relaxed* . . . this tension and relaxation of the inside of my thighs and of my buttocks produce sexual sensations. . . . The genitals get tense and relaxed and that excites the vagina. The tension presses on the rectum and draws it in, and at this moment the genitals start to vibrate."

We remember the constipated woman who, after evacuation, still felt pressure in her rectum, as though a foreign body were stuck there, and could not relax unless she masturbated. We also remember the man who felt "plugged up" and to whom defecation meant to be "open" and "relaxed." Occasionally he was afraid to defecate, lest he should be exposed to sexual attacks by men. When he felt relaxed, he felt helpless, passive. "Tension" he felt as rigidity. This rigidity immobilized him, made him inactive. In many cases this inactivity is mistaken for passivity.

"As you know," the patient now under discussion said once, "I am often so sleepy. There is pleasure in this sleepiness. My body, my eyes, tend to fall, to drop as after sexual intercourse. I feel tensions and relaxations keeping my eyes closed and open, but the pleasure is a different one when I feel my eyelids over my eyeballs or when I feel my eyeballs touched by the eyelids. The feelings in the eyeballs are inactive feelings and yet they are not quite inactive, they only seem inactive to an outsider."

In her attempts to understand those feelings, to explain them to herself, she repeatedly referred to her past. She would then remember being afraid to cry in front of her mother. Mother did not permit crying. "So I tried to control myself. Then I got these tensions in my body, in my eyes, in my lips, in my throat—and these tensions were pleasurable. For example, by enough tension I could control the trembling of my lips, I could press them together against my teeth. I was nine months old when my mother stopped my crying by beating me on the buttocks with a hairbrush." She had no direct memory of these experiences; she had, however, indirect evidence. She would remember that she was repeatedly told by her mother how she used to cry as a baby, how nervous that made her and how she, the mother, beat her with a hairbrush on the buttocks and how the patient stopped crying when she got "black and blue." Father also told her of the beatings by mother. Besides, she had direct memories of her mother beating her brother, who was considerably younger. Later, when the children grew older, their mother beat them less frequently, but then it was no longer necessary because they were completely "cowed."

"The beating," she continued, "produced considerable passivity in me—I imagine this was a general reaction to the beating. I know that this is rather a guess, but I have a feeling of truth; when a baby cries, he is tense, he has tears in his eyes, beats around with his arms and legs. When I was nine months old and my mother began beating me for crying, I did not know that it was particularly for the noise. Therefore I had to inhibit the activity going with the crying, my eyes had to be open instead of pressed closed, my mouth closed instead of open, my legs quiet instead of drawn up. Then I could not move, I could not eat, then I became inhibited in every respect. You know, I became a feeding problem. Since, I have this difficulty in movement, in action, when something has to be done. So, for instance, I had to send a telegram yesterday, but I could not, I stared in the air; to send a telegram is not difficult, what is difficult is the initiative."

Mother made many references to beating when talking to her children. She would say "eat the potatoes or I'll spank you," "put on your coat or I'll spank you," "have your bowel movements or I'll spank you," etc. The patient would often not know whether her mother's threats were a way of speaking or real threats. She could remember a certain kind of caress, called by her mother "love pat." That was a slight spank on the buttocks, her mother's only form of tenderness; a kiss disgusted her. When her mother threatened that she would take off the child's clothes, tie her to the bedpost and beat her with a yardstick until it broke, she could clearly see the picture of the naked body of this child tied to that brass bedstead. "I would stiffen in immobility and yet in tension"—she added— "and in particular the buttocks would be held so tense that at the end the genitalia would tremble and I got absorbed in this picture."

It does not matter very much whether the beating actually occurred or not. The important fact is that the patient grew up with the idea that she had been beaten by her mother almost from birth on.

The mother's will clashed with the daughter's. The more she inhibited her, the angrier the daughter became, feeling an impulse to argue with her, to speak harshly to her. Instead of doing so, she "controlled" herself and became tense and rigid. She "pressed her lips together, pressed the tongue against the cheek, and that was a great pleasure; it was such a great pleasure not saying the words I would like to say." Anger, aggression toward the mother, she thus turned against herself and changed them into "self-control" (Freud, 1915, 1923a). She derived pleasure from this self-control, from this self-imposed inhibition which resulted in inactivity.

The "inactivity" had, however, still another root. This was not the fear of mother, but her hyperactivity, that produced inactivity on the part of her children. In the mother's opinion, the children could not do anything right; she had to do everything for them. It seems that they had no chance to develop any degree of activity. "My mother always decided for me what I should do," the patient stated. The result was that she always procrastinated and expected everything to be done for her. She became immobilized. For example: "I should telephone, I don't do it, I delay, my lips won't telephone, they get kind of stiff, and I feel a pleasure in my lips; I get something to read, I stare in space and forget to read. . . ." She became so passive that she often did not know whether she was hungry or thirsty and whether she should eat or drink. If food was given her, she ate it. After mother's death she gradually started to decide what to do, to make plans and to become aware of her physical needs. However, only in recent times, obviously under the influence of her analysis, was this process speeded up considerably.

Her mother showed her so little tenderness that she would be surprised whenever she saw a woman showing tenderness to a child. And yet, she remembered mother's way of expressing affection, the "love pat." When the mother gave her that slight spank on the buttocks, she was confused. She did not know how to take it, as a sign of love or a sign of aggression. Whatever it meant, she accepted it without any external reaction.

Judging from numerous habits, character traits and fantasies, which can be classified only as "oral," the patient must have been exposed to various oral stimulations and deprivations on the part of her mother. The repeated frustrations which, later on, probably she herself often provoked, put her in an almost constant state of expectation. This state which grew out of her passivity, rather immobility, inactivity, was accompanied by pleasurable sensations in her body. Asked for an example, she gave the following: "One of my present fantasies is that of being somewhere in the evening with this man I love. There would be a cocktail but I would not take it; only if he handed me the cocktail would I take it and then feel a great pleasure in receiving it. If he gives it to me, my whole hand becomes pleasurable."

In puberty her dependence upon mother and submissiveness to her shifted first to her father and then to men in general. Her attachment to her father again developed out of her passivity. For when she grew older and began to have more contact with him, her inactivity was strengthened by him, but in a different way than by her mother. He himself was an unaggressive person with old-fashioned ideas about women. In his opinion they should be guarded constantly, dependent. He wanted them to do nothing, to be obedient, submissive, to love and adore him. He forced his daughters to listen to his endless talks, admonitions, recitations of poetry, quotations of philosophers, etc. "Prepared by mother in my inactivity, I could be inactive towards my father," she once exclaimed. "Mother acted for me, father thought for me."

This passivity, naturally, was also reflected in her fantasy life. When, in her perverse fantasies, she saw herself loved by someone, she always wanted to do what he desired of her. She had no wishes, no will of her own, but felt that she had to carry out the other person's wishes and to live his life.

Her father's language was very vivid and imaginative. So she would listen for hours and experience in her fantasy all the things he told her. She stopped talking to her friends and instead listened to them, and became a good listener. She loved to read and developed a faculty of seeing so vividly with her inner eye what she read, that when traveling she found some places quite familiar because she knew them from her reading.

She was so full of her father that in the transference situation she expected the analyst to behave exactly like him. She expected him to guess her thoughts and feelings and tell them to her in absolutely the same way as her father would have done. As, for obvious reasons, her hopes could not be fulfilled, she not only became utterly aggressive, but stopped talking and kept the relevant psychoanalytical material to herself (Nunberg, 1928). When she finally revealed this material, she concluded with the following statement: "I always wanted to be quiet like a baby who drinks milk all the time." I, on my part, should like to add: a baby who drinks milk at mother's breasts. That was possibly the deepest root of her infantile, passive dependence, not on her father, but on her mother.

Leaving aside the problem of masochism, we recognize with extraordinary clarity two forms of passivity in this case. One is caused by tension and results in rigid immobility, inhibitions. This is by no means passivity; it is rather *inner activity*. The second form is *genuine passivity*. It seems to be rooted in the infantile fixation to the mother, where gratification may be achieved in a quasi magical way without any action; it may stem from the prenatal state in the mother's womb. It seems as if it were governed by the compulsion to repeat previous states of low tensions. These two forms of passivity seem to be corollaries to primary and secondary masochism as expounded in Freud's *Beyond the Pleasure Principle*.

In view of all these considerations it seems that the interpretation "you are passive" or "you are feminine" frequently given the patient cannot be fully understood, unless the analyst is able to show the patient clearly the specific significance of his passive or feminine attitude in each situation.

The answer to our question was virtually given in advance, and the result of our survey may, therefore, not seem very fruitful. It would seem that, no matter how we tried to attack our problem, we always arrived at the same conclusion; we could not help but agree with the popular view that masculinity is characterized by activity and femininity by passivity. Nevertheless it is logical to ask: what is activity and, even more, what is passivity? This is a problem which cannot be solved by psychoanalysis because it is a biological problem. Yet our investigation was not superfluous, since it enabled us to recognize clearly, from the psychological point of view, that active and passive instinctual aims are inherent in the sexual life of both man and woman and for this reason form the basis of their bisexuality. The problem of masculinity and femininity is thus the problem of the aims of the sexual instinct. Therefore, it seems that the object choice, i.e., the hetero- or homosexual choice, is determined by the aims of the sexual instinct.

Whatever the essence of passivity may be, clinical observation shows that femininity is represented in the man by the passive aims of his sexual instincts. Circumcision activates these aims and brings to the surface the feminine homosexual trends. But circumcision also stimulates masculine or active aims. The ensuing contrast between the opposed sexual aims forms the background of a conflict that crystallizes in the castration complex. It is a conflict between hetero- and homosexuality which may be solved in various ways. These ways determine the state of health or sickness of the individual and, in the past, were largely responsible for the creation of myths and religious systems.

The most important fact, however, is that similar conflicts can be found where there has been no actual circumcision. Observation of the female genitalia at a certain susceptible age may have the same effect. Threats to the genitals evoked by masturbatory habits, prohibition of masturbation, and other frustrations—inhibition or inability to satisfy instinctual demands—produce similar reactions. It would seem that frustration had the same effect upon the ego of

the individual as does the trauma of circumcision (castration).[19]
It must, however, be stressed again at this point that frustration,
deprivation, and loss of mother's breast are not identical with
castration; they can substitute for castration only symbolically. It
cannot be repeated often enough that the term "castration complex" should be reserved for these occasions only when the idea of
deprivation becomes associated with the loss of the male organ.[20]
Circumcision "magnifies" certain reactions of the ego, bares their
hidden meaning and, in the manner of an experiment, makes the
whole castration complex more accessible to direct observation
than does mere frustration. It can then be seen that the conflict
between homo- and heterosexuality forms the psychobiological
basis for neuroses as well as for primitive puberty rites and the
religious systems of more civilized peoples. The circumcision forced
upon the initiate under primitive compulsions by the medicine
man (father), liberates and sets in motion forces in the son which
endeavor to master the eternal struggle between son and father.
This conflict ends either with submission to the father's power or
with rejection of his authority.

ATTEMPTS TO REJECT THE CIRCUMCISION

It has been demonstrated that the acceptance of circumcision as
a token of submission to father's will is overcompensated for by the
fantasy of rebirth as a mature man and is rewarded by the fantasy
of giving birth to a child, a son. When the young man becomes a
father, his love for the son is a narcissistic love. It is, therefore, very
difficult for the father to sacrifice his son and permit him to be
circumcised. The resulting conflict and its outcome is illustrated by
the following case.

During the analysis of an orthodox Jew, a son was born to him
who, according to the Jewish tradition, had to be ritually circumcised. Our patient displayed some unusual reactions to the birth of
his son. He feared that the child would take his wife's love away

---

[19] We find here an analogy to the relation of a trauma to the typical fantasies
as described by Freud. He says that where reality fails, one of the typical
fantasies emerges.
[20] Cf. Freud, 1923b, p. 247.

from him. He became envious when he saw the infant suckling at his mother's breast and fantasied biting off the boy's penis. On the other hand, he felt compassion for him, expressed in the fear that the approaching circumcision might harm the boy for the rest of his life. He anticipated that his son would take revenge on him. He felt uneasy, as if he, and not the boy, would have to undergo the operation. And yet, he saw no escape from the compulsion to carry out the family tradition.

In the following dream he attempted to find a solution to his inner conflict: "I had to take a drink out of a cup. I put a hat on to say a blessing, but I did it surreptitiously, so nobody would see me doing it. I was ashamed. Two nurses from the hospital [where his wife was confined in childbirth] saw me; they came over to me. They did not realize that I was doing anything to be ashamed of. They asked me about the cup. I pointed out to them that it has to be done according to a certain ritual; the rim has to be metal, so it won't chip. The wine cup was made out of a piece of metal which was S-shaped. It was an innovation. There was another cup of silver that I had to use. It was like my father's cup. I said to the nurses: 'It is best not to force a person to do things, not to force him to use the silver cup when he wants the other cup.' "

Putting on a hat to say a prayer reminded the dreamer of the Jewish custom of covering the head while saying prayers, and also of the mohel—the pious man who performs the circumcision ritually and who prays during the ceremony. These associations indicate that the patient, in the dream, was substituting himself for the man saying prayers, a kind of priest, who was going to circumcise his son. But the prayers had to be performed in a surreptitious way because he was ashamed before the nurses. Actually, he was ashamed to tell his analyst about the approaching ceremony because he would thus betray his religious superstition. Yet, in the dream, instead of the anticipated ridicule by the nurses, he received encouragement from them. In fact, they represented his sisters who not only encouraged, but emphatically urged him to have his son circumcised. To this he associated the fact that his mother, then already dead, had always insisted that he observe all the Jewish rituals and ceremonies, and that his father had been less strict in this respect. In the dream he seems not only to be indifferent in regard to religious customs, as his father was, but even reluctant to carry out the circumcision of his son.

Since his conflict about this situation was conscious, it is not surprising that it was repeated in the manifest dream. We are surprised, however, that women, not father, encourage him to carry out the religious ceremony. It seems as if he needed their sanction in order to relieve his feeling of guilt toward his son. This attitude leads me to a recollection of the passage in the Bible which tells us that because Moses neglected to circumcise his son, his wife Ziporah performed the religious ceremony, thus protecting him from the wrath of God. The instrument used was a flint knife. Commentators[21] assert that the use of such an ancient instrument testifies to the antiquity of the custom.

The episode of the abduction of the daughters of Laban by Jacob may be regarded as another example of the adherence of women to ancient customs and beliefs. When Laban overtook the fugitives, he asked only for the Teraphim, the house gods, which his daughter Rachel had carried off with her. In this connection the Vestal Virgins of ancient Rome may be mentioned. It was their chief duty to watch over the family hearth and to preserve the entity of the family. Vesta, goddess of the hearth, was intimately connected with the Penates, the house gods, and Frazer (1925b, pp. 125-206) stresses her conservative traits in regard to the family. In modern history we can find further examples of the woman as guardian and bearer of the family tradition, as a conservative factor in society. This conservative trend in the woman seems to be in conformity with her passivity and tardiness, as shown in the foregoing chapter. Our patient was ready to subject his son to circumcision only when authorized by mother, the guardian of tradition.

However, the dreamer tells the nurses that he does not want to drink wine from the silver cup but from the cup with the S-shaped rim. In his first association he refers to the Jewish religious custom, according to which the mohel sucks blood from the penis after the circumcision, and drinks wine from a cup. We recall that this dream was preceded by the fantasy of biting off the son's penis. Assuming that the mohel represents a substitute for the dreamer's

[21] *Jewish Encyclopædia.*

father, we may interpret the unwillingness of the dreamer to drink from the father's cup as an attempt to reject his identification with his father and to suppress the wish to bite off the son's penis. The meaning of this part of the dream is simple: it reflects the patient's reluctance to do to his son what his father had once done to him. In other words, he does not want to be as cruel as his father, because he feels not only hate for his son but also love.

The analysis of the first case demonstrated that it is not only the little girl who wishes to have a baby but also the little boy, and that this wish is contained in the oedipus complex. The birth of a son, therefore, fulfills an infantile wish of the mature man. Why, then, is he afraid of his son and why has he aggressive impulses against him? Our first patient was afraid that he would die as soon as his child was born. It seems as if he feared that his life would pass from his own body into the body of the newborn. Apparently he still believed, like the primitive man, in transmigration of souls, or reincarnation of the ancestors in their progeny (Frazer, 1925a, 1925c). Orthodox Jews, at the circumcision ceremony, usually name their son after their deceased father. Theodor Reik (1914), supported by considerable anthropological material, maintains that in his feelings for his son, a father revives his feeling for his own father, as if the grandson reincarnated his grandfather. "The fear of retaliation," says Reik, "is the real motif in the teaching of the migration of souls" (Reik, 1914, p. 76). It was, however, Otto Rank who first recognized the meaning of the fear of retaliation. He says: "The son who feels hostile impulses against his father and must repress them will, as soon as he himself becomes a father, fear, out of the same unconscious complex, the same attitude on the part of his son" (Rank, 1912, p. 89). This fear is expressed in contemporary savage customs, in ancient religious rites, and, in a mitigated form, in Greek mythology, when, for instance, Cronos castrates his father Uranos and eats his own children for fear of retaliation (Frazer, 1925c).[22] Both our patients had fantasies about castrating their respective fathers and swallowing their genital organs. We know that such fantasies reflect not only aggressive impulses, but also love, craving for identity with the father, a communion with him

---

[22] Jekels (1917, p. 372) says: "...obviously the relation to one's son appears to be strictly conditioned by the relation to one's father."

(Nunberg, 1936). It is quite evident that the birth of the son re-activated all these impulses in our patient. However, in reality as well as in the dream, he tried to deny them; he did not want to drink from the father's cup. The meaning of the refusal is obvious. He did not wish to repeat the primal sin, he did not wish to kill or castrate his father in his son (Freud, 1912-1913, 1939).

Recognizing the fact that the father's initial hostility against his son is neutralized by his fear of retaliation, we must still ask whether no other factors inhibit our patient from yielding to his compulsion to perform the religious ceremony of circumcision (Freud, 1907). Love is certainly another factor; we have seen his conscious compassion for his son in his identification with him. In the manifest dream we did not discern either fear of castration or any compassion, but uneasiness, shame and almost fear that the nurses would catch him doing a wrong. Through the analysis of that part of the dream we discovered that he wanted authorization from his mother to perform the bloody operation. Theodor Reik says: "Among many peoples the father has to undergo expiation and atonement after the birth of a son. On the other hand, if the child dies prematurely, he is accused of causing its death and punished by the women" (Reik, 1914, p. 63). Otto Rank (1909) mentions that Freud believed that it was the mother, the woman, who gradually accustomed the primal father to spare the son and to accept the younger generation.

Our dreamer vividly remembered incidents when his mother became very angry at him because he criticized his father or attacked his brothers. Through the fear of arousing her anger, which was tantamount to the fear of losing her love, he sought to avoid repetition of such actions. Asking mother's permission to circumcise his son thus expresses the wish to remove his rival without losing her love. To the fear of retaliation by his son-father is added the fear of losing mother's love. These were the factors responsible for his reluctance to perform the religious ceremony.

He did not want to drink from father's silver cup but from mother's metal cup. Its nonchipping rim symbolized a sharp knife, since he remembered that the "shochet," the man who performs the ritual slaughter of animals, is required to use a very sharp knife in order to spare them pain. Thus it seems as if the patient was saying:

"If the circumcision is unavoidable, it has to be performed by mother, or in her way, rather than by father, because it hurts less."

He wanted mother's approval of the circumcision for three reasons: first, because she was the bearer of the family tradition; second, because he was afraid of losing her love; and third, because in identification with his son, he expected that circumcision performed by her would be less painful.

The rim of the cup had the shape of the letter S. When the patient was studying art, his teacher told him that the S-shaped figure, the spiral, is a perfect one, as it represents the woman's body. Our patient agreed with him, adding, however, that the S-shaped figure reminded him of a snake. It seems that to him the combination of a male symbol—the snake—with a female symbol—the cup —formed a perfect figure. In the previous chapter we saw that the foreskin symbolizes a female organ which, like a cup, envelops the male organ, the glans penis. Thus the cup with the S-shaped rim symbolizes a bisexual person, a hermaphrodite, the mother with the penis. The desire to be circumcised by mother rather than by father now acquires an even deeper meaning. Utilizing the insight gained by the analysis of a fantasy reported by the patient some time following this dream, we may interpret the drinking of wine from mother's cup as the drinking of blood from mother's penis. And further, since in reality mother has no penis and the penis is often used as a symbolical substitute for nipples, the idea of drinking blood from mother's penis means drinking milk from her breast. Since the patient also identified himself with his son, the deepest meaning of this dream is: even biting off mother's breast does not cause loss of her love. This interpretation may seem too daring, but it is completely confirmed by the aforementioned fantasy, which will be analyzed later.

It is significant that there is hardly any action in this dream; nothing happens. The patient drinks neither from father's nor from mother's cup; he cannot decide whether or not to circumcise his son; the dream simply reflects his inner conflict. The following night he resumed the same topic in another dream, trying again to solve his painful problem.

The dream is as follows: "I am talking to my chief. He shows me the figure of a person lying on the floor with the face up in a very uncomfortable position. He says that is the position which certain Catholics assume in prayer. I think to myself: what an uncomfortable position. Sure enough, I am attending a Catholic prayer."

In anticipation of the circumcision which was to be performed the afternoon of the next day, he intended to ask his superior to substitute for him in the office while he himself attended the ceremony. However, he hesitated to ask this favor because he was ashamed to reveal to the chief—who was Catholic—that he still adhered to his old religious customs. And yet, he thought, a Catholic is not ashamed of his religion; only a Jew is ashamed of it because he has a strong feeling of guilt. Of course, it is not correct to assume that the Jew is ashamed of his religion because of his exaggerated sense of guilt. We know that our patient had an increased feeling of guilt on account of the forthcoming circumcision of his son. When, in the dream, his chief, a Catholic, a man who does not circumcise his son, shows him the uncomfortable position which Catholics assume in prayer, it seems as if this painful position, in the mind of the dreamer, is a substitute for the circumcision. The conclusion of the dream report with the words: "Sure enough, I am attending a Catholic prayer," may be understood as follows: "I am a Catholic and I would rather assume the painful position of Catholics than circumcise my son."

As the patient was also ashamed to talk to his analyst about his "religious superstition" of circumcision, we may assume that in his dream his chief was a substitute for the analyst. In fact, the patient was convinced that his analyst, though a Jew like himself, would not subject his son to such an operation. In the eyes of an orthodox Jew a man who does not perform all ritual is a lawbreaker. The notion that his analyst was a freethinker, a man who had broken away from the Jewish religion, reflected, to some extent, his ideas about his own father. Until late in puberty he would watch his father closely to see whether he performed properly all the prayers and ceremonies prescribed by religion, spying on him in order to discover some oversight or transgression. At one time it seemed to him that his father had smoked a cigar on the sabbath, at another time, that he was making advances to the maid. As heretofore mentioned, his mother reproached him severely when he tried to talk about his father's "immoral" conduct. To him his father was an apostate, a Gentile.

The nature of the prayer as a repentance and as psychologically identical with the circumcision is expressed in still another detail of the dream, not yet mentioned. The person praying on the floor reminded the dreamer of the pious Jews who, on the Day of Atonement, fall on their knees, prostrate themselves before God, and beg his forgiveness. Thus the day of the circumcision of his son had become the Day of Atonement for him.

According to the rabbinical tradition, Abraham was circumcised on the Day of Atonement.[23] Arthur Feldman (1944) says that the Day of Atonement is intended to bring forgiveness for the primal sin, and continues: "The two, the circumcision and the Day of Atonement, are the product of the same mental complex. ... Among many Jews, circumcision is a 'Korban,' a sacrifice. The father says a prayer to that effect during the rite." On the second of the ten days of Penitence (Rosh Hashanah), the tenth of which is the Day of Atonement, the "Akeda," the story of the binding or sacrifice of Isaac, is read to the praying congregation. When Abraham, despite his great love for his son, obeyed the Lord's command and was ready to kill him, a miracle occurred. The Lord showed mercy and in place of Isaac, a ram, caught in the thicket, was sacrificed by Abraham. Theodor Reik says: "This particular narrative in Genesis xxii, 1-18, can be traced back to various sources, and is preserved in a strongly modified form to which different periods of time have contributed. The original meaning of the narrative shines through all the elaborations and super-impositions of the ages. It corresponds exactly to the puberty rites which students have described among the Australians.... [In both,] the part played by the unconscious hostility of the fathers is unmistakable; for, although they pretend that they are sorrowfully executing a higher command, in reality they wish to offer their sons as victims..." (Reik, 1919, p. 282).

In Reik's interpretation the father was killed instead of the son. But according to the Apocalyptic writers, the son, likewise, did not remain unharmed, since the following happened: "When Abraham finally held the knife over his beloved son, Isaac seemed doomed, and the angels from heaven shed tears which fell upon Isaac's eyes, causing him blindness in later life."[24] From our psychoanalytical

[23] *Jewish Encyclopædia*, Pirke El. 9.
[24] *Jewish Encyclopædia*.

experiences we know that blindness often symbolizes castration. King Oedipus gouged out his own eyes after killing his father and sleeping with his mother. The killing of the father and the castration of the son are hidden, removed from consciousness. The conscious meaning of the story of Abraham's sacrifice is that God forgives. Submission to His will obtains His mercy: this is in conformity with the meaning of the Day of Atonement.

The person in our patient's dream is not only humbly prostrate on the floor but at the same time raises his head. The dreamer, curiously enough, was very much impressed by the raised head. He remarked that a snake raises its head when it is going to strike. A few days before the dream he had watched a cat playing with a mouse. The mouse raised itself on its hind legs as if to frighten off the cat. It is easy to see that the little mouse represented his newborn son to him. This son challenges the cat, obviously the father. Moreover, since he was thinking a great deal about his son in those days, it came to his mind that he was probably rearing a viper and that one day in the future this child would resent him and take revenge. The thoughts called to his mind the parable about the man who killed his parents. Brought before the judge, he was condemned to carry a basket of stones on his shoulders. In the basket was a growing snake that began to threaten him. But the judge, refusing to relieve him of his burden, said: "Your parents did not know that they were raising a viper that would kill them, now you yourself have one."

It is obvious that the person on the floor represented the patient himself as a repentant son in relation to his father, but also as a rebel against the humiliation of circumcision.

As dreams are overdetermined, certain elements being condensations of many strivings and ideas, it is not surprising that the person with the raised head, associated in the dreamer's mind with a snake raising its head, also symbolized a phallus. The snake, however, is not only a male symbol, it also represents a woman; and is therefore a bisexual symbol. The fact that the patient is not certain whether the person on the floor is a man or a woman, serves as further evidence of its bisexuality. He felt that there was a woman around all the time, and for a moment it seemed to him that this person was a woman, his mother-in-law, "And she has such a poisonous tongue," he concluded. The person raising its head from the humiliating position is protesting not only against circumcision but also against its femininity, as if attempting to say, "I am not lying flat on my back like a woman; I can raise my head and have an erection like a man."

At this point I took the opportunity to call the patient's attention to the fact that in his preceding dream the woman with the penis was symbolized by the cup with the metal rim and that the cup somewhat resembled a foreskin with a penis hidden in it. He then recalled a circumcision that he had once witnessed. "When the foreskin was cut and a lot of blood gushed out," he said, "I could not look at it. I got sick and fainted." Yet, he noticed, and since then had always remembered, that the head of the penis stood out as something of particular importance (the raised head of the person on the floor, which impressed him so much). He added: "When I saw this gaping wound around the head of the penis, I thought that the bleeding vagina must look like that." Hence, the person on the floor with his head raised symbolizes the man-woman with the "glans penis" sticking out from the "foreskin-vagina," as described in the first section. He could not look at the bleeding penis, he fainted; in a sense, he died. This is reminiscent of the legend of the terrible monster Medusa, at the sight of which men turned into stone.

Freud says that the terror of Medusa is a terror of castration which arises when the boy sees the female genitals, essentially his mother's. "The symbol of horror (the decapitated head with snakes instead of hair) is worn upon her dress by the virgin goddess Athena. And rightly so, for thus she becomes a woman who is unapproachable and repels all sexual desires since she displays the terrifying genitals of the mother. Such a representation of woman —who frightens away because of her castration—was inevitable among the Greeks who were in the main strongly homosexual" (Freud, 1940b).

If Medusa's head takes the place of a representation of the female genitals, or rather if it isolates their horrifying effects from their pleasure-giving ones, it may be recalled that displaying the genitals is familiar in other connections as an apotropaic act. What arouses horror in oneself will produce the same effect upon the enemy against whom one seeks to defend oneself. We read in Rabelais of how the Devil took to flight when the woman showed him her vulva.

Our patient displayed the same attitude. His reluctance to circumcise his son was caused not only by love for him and identification with him, by fear of retaliation and by opposition to his father, but also, and perhaps chiefly, by the fact that the circumcised penis reminded him of the awful genitals of the woman (the mother), the sight of which is repellent to the son. He closed the analysis of this dream with the following words: "When I witnessed the circumcision and saw this gaping wound around the head of the penis, I wondered how it could ever heal."

His concern about the healing of the wound caused by circumcision became a topic of discussion, not immediately, but some months later. Then it was apparent that his concern was about himself rather than about his son, although he could not, of course, remember his own circumcision. At that point he confessed, to my great surprise, his main masturbatory fantasy, which he had guarded as his greatest secret. In this fantasy he saw himself lying on his back while a woman was sucking his penis.

Strikingly enough, the first thought that came to his mind in association to this fantasy was the mohel sucking blood from the boy's penis after circumcision. Arthur Feldman stresses the fact that wine and food are essential at the ceremony of circumcision and that this ceremony can be performed only in the presence of ten initiated males (minian). He maintains that this sacramental communion where blood is sucked and wine drunk, points to the totem meal (Feldman, 1944). According to Freud (1912-1913), the animal eaten at the totem meal symbolizes the primeval father, and circumcision represents a mitigated castration, which is a substitute for death. Since the son is a reincarnation of his father's father, sucking blood from his penis at the circumcision ceremony is a relic of the totem meal.

Since our patient identified himself with his son, the mohel sucking blood from his penis was also a revengeful father. Nevertheless, when the patient talked about the mohel in association with the woman of his fantasy, he was no longer the sinister character of the person behind the first dream. On the contrary, sucking now meant to him the alleviation of pain, healing. Recollections emerged reaching far back into childhood, of which one was especially vivid in his memory: when he was definitely less than three years old, he had a severe earache. His father, carrying him in his arms, held his head with the aching ear over a pot with steaming water. Mentioning this recollection repeatedly, he never failed to stress his feeling of great fear and relief on that occasion. He remembered also that his father was strict and although he at times inflicted punishment, he was always forgiving and just. The thought of father's forgiveness stirred great emotions in him. His confidence in father's forgiveness filled him with a sense of security and comfort incomparable to anything else in the world. His great emotion brought to his mind two passages from the Bible, one concerning Cain and the other King David. He quoted: "... when Cain confessed his sin, and accepted the punishment, the Lord set a sign for Cain, lest any finding him should smite him" (Reik, 1917). Thereupon, he took a wife and had children by her. In the opinion of our patient, Cain's confession of his crime and accept-ance of the punishment of the mark (castration sign, according to Reik) was of supreme importance since it induced the Lord to forgive him and to permit him to have children. In the same way, he thought, the Lord forgave King David. When King David sent Uriah to his death and married his wife—an obvious allusion to the oedipus complex—the Lord sent the prophet Nathan to admonish him. However, when David said to Nathan: "I have sinned against the Lord," Nathan replied to him, "The Lord hath put away thy sin; thou shalt not die." The patient concluded, reassuring himself, that although God punished David by bringing disaster upon his house, he was nevertheless merciful with him and let him have an offspring and a successor in his youngest son, the great King Solomon. Thus, confession of the sin of Oedipus and acceptance of punishment—both of which seem to be equivalents of circumcision—saved the transgressor from death and secured his issue.[25] The punishment deprived neither Cain nor David of

---

[25] Confession is an ancient Israelitic institution. According to Frazer, some savages also take recourse to confession as a means of expiating sins. By confes-sion they seem to visualize the crime and to revive the killed person (*The Golden Bough*). See also Nunberg (1926).

their masculinity; on the contrary, they could have children and continue to live through them. We have learned that circumcision symbolizes rebirth, as do confession and baptism (Reik, 1925). Thus the faith in the father remains unshattered. Even if he punishes, he forgives, he loves his son and makes a mature man out of him. When the patient understood these connections, he said: "That explains to me why I am always touched when I see a father who is kind to his child and has pity for him . . ." He could not finish the sentence because he started to weep, so overcome was he by deep emotion.

In the first dream the patient could not decide whether or not to have his son circumcised. After the circumcision had been performed, he adjusted himself to the accomplished fact in this fashion: I did not circumcise my son, the reincarnation of my father, but my father circumcised me. Instead of harming my son-father, I took the punishment upon myself.[26]

The next day I resumed discussion of the same topic with the patient, asking him whether he was aware that his associations to the woman of the fantasy concerned only men. The question stimulated two mental pictures: a snake, and a woman with a shawl around her head.

When a snake bites, he said, you suck out the blood, and that is a healing procedure; when your finger is bleeding, you suck it; when a child injures himself, the mother kisses the injured part of his body. The woman sucking his penis in the fantasy thus seems to represent his mother, healing him after the circumcision. Here she seemed to have the same function as the healing mohel-father. (Hygieia, the daughter of Aesculapius, is represented as feeding a snake from a jar.)

The fact that he saw in the woman with the shawl a kind of healer is further evidenced by his complete description of the mental picture. The woman was sitting beside a boy, doing something of a very intimate nature to him, without showing any dis-

---

[26] Here we find once again a confirmation of Freud's idea about the development of the superego. Submission to father's will equals acceptance of punishment by him. In other words, the son's aggression against the father turns against himself which, in conjunction with certain further identifications, leads to the emergence of the superego as the heir of the oedipus complex.

gust; she was either licking him, or taking care of his bowels; the boy was sick and helpless. At this point his wife came to his mind; if he were sick, she would take care of him and would not be disgusted. He stressed the fact that this was, unquestionably, how his mother used to behave. When his boy was circumcised, he did not want to approach and look at him, because, in general, he did not want to see injured people. His wife, however, had no repulsion whatsoever about taking care of his penis after the operation. His mother was never repelled by anything that had to be done when someone was sick. It seemed to the patient that he could not stand the sight of a penis that had just been circumcised, that only a woman could stand it. The man cannot handle it so well, he might hurt it, etc. When sick, he wanted to be taken care of by mother rather than by father. It had been made apparent to him long ago, he added with something of relief, that he got along much better with women than with men.

Combining all this material, we find that the woman with the shawl represents, first, his wife taking care of the circumcised penis of his son, then, his mother, who took care of him when he was sick as a child. She was a "good" woman, she healed his wounds and seems to have been counterpart of the healing father.

That this woman with the shawl really represented the patient's mother is further shown by the fact that during the patient's childhood, the mother used to wear a shawl around her head, which resembled a hood. Actually, she also wore a cape with a hood on it. "It protected your head, ears and neck," he said, describing it. As a child he used to play with it, putting his head in it, always feeling that it was very cozy. I don't think that it requires much imagination to guess what is symbolized by a hood over a head—a penis with its foreskin. The woman with a hood over her head therefore represents a woman with a penis hidden inside her. We have already heard that a woman with a penis is a beautiful woman; we now learn that she is also a good woman, a healing mother. It is interesting to note that the ancient god of medicine, Aesculapius, has a serpent as his emblem, a typical phallic symbol, as if it were the phallus that protects from evil.

In summation, we may say that the patient seems to express the following ideas: the father forgives, if you submit to circumcision

—which is equal to a healing process—but it is the mother who really heals the wound.

When, as a child, he put mother's hood over his head, it felt cozy, like something he had known long before. It hung in the closet, and even when he was not playing with the hood, he liked to be in the closet, saying that the closet was as cozy and safe as the hood. In his mind they were interchangeable. An incident that occurred when he was less than five years old stressed the importance of this closet to him. Opening its door, he found his cat with kittens to which she had just given birth. It seemed as if reality were confirming his fantasy in which the hood and the closet symbolized mother's womb; the closet seemed "really" to be a place where children were born, a cozy and safe place. He was impressed by the sight of the kittens lying "cozily" around their mother, and especially impressed by the fact that, although blind, they found the nipples; "they were feeling around and found them," he repeated over and over again. It seems to me that this fascination with the blind kittens finding their mother can be understood only if we refer to our knowledge that blindness, like any other mutilation of the body, symbolizes castration. His fascination may, therefore, express the unexpected gratification and feeling of comfort evoked by the discovery that, even if castrated, one can find his way to mother and not be rejected by her. When this was discussed in his analysis he started to cry bitterly, as if something very painful had come to his mind. He then remembered that the cat did not move, as if tired from nursing her kittens, who did not release the nipples; they sucked and bit the nipples, which were already bleeding.[27] This recollection reminded him of his mother telling him repeatedly that he used to bite her nipples until they bled. And when she scolded him for some mischief she would say: "Even when you were still an infant, I was worried that you might become a murderer."

---

[27] Another recollection: The kittens were already half-grown, but nevertheless insisted on nursing at the nipples. The cat, however, refused to allow them to nurse and kept driving them away. The patient felt that the cat was being "inconsiderate" and held her down while the kittens took hold of the nipples and began to suck. At first the cat struggled to get away, but finally she became exhausted and lay motionless, no longer able to resist. The patient then felt remorseful for having hurt her and bundled the kittens away.

No doubt, he identified himself with the kittens, and his crying was an expression of his feeling of guilt toward his mother, which obviously goes back to the biting of her nipples, although he could recollect this only through her reproaches, and not directly. The first dream said that he would like to drink wine from mother's cup; the wish to bite her nipples still existed. When we compare this wish with the fantasy of the woman sucking his penis, we are confronted with two contradictory fantasies, on different levels of consciousness, of course. The fantasy of biting off mother's breasts was unconscious; the other, about the good woman sucking and healing him, was conscious. It is evident that the conscious fantasy replaced the unconscious one, and that they express opposite ideas. The unconscious one translated into conscious language reads: I want to suck and destroy my mother's breasts. The conscious one does not need much translation; it reads simply: my mother is good, she sucks my (injured) penis and loves me. Our theoretically well-founded assumption is that since the first fantasy was too contradictory and too painful to the patient's moral standards, it had to be repressed at all cost. One of the best methods of defense is to change the contents of a fantasy into its opposite. That done, the fantasy is: it is not true that *I* bit or wanted to bite my mother's breasts and to suck her blood, *she* sucked blood from my sore penis and healed me. Such an idea could be accepted by the patient. Moreover, it expressed the conviction that, no matter what happens, whether father castrates, circumcises you, or whether you bite off mother's breast, she will always love you and take care of you. That is a grandiose conception of mother love. Yet, this kind of love is not only fantasy, it is also reality. And we know that when a fantasy is nourished by reality, the illusion is almost indestructible.[28]

It is difficult to hate a person whom you love and who loves you. These two feelings come very easily into conflict with one another, forming the basis of the "feeling of guilt." Our patient's feeling of guilt toward his mother seemed to be coupled with the castration

---

[28] The Hebrew verb *räkham* means to glow inwardly, to have mercy, compassion. The noun *räkhäm* means womb, original seat of glowing. The word *rakham* means the womb, fig, a maid, a woman (engl. woman = womb man). The plural *rachemim* signifies compassion, tender love, mercy (Breslau).

complex, as it was in relation to his father. During the discussion of the feeling of guilt connected with his aggressive impulses against her, he said suddenly: "When this woman in the fantasy sucks my penis, I have a peculiar feeling that I must not move, that I must not do anything to her, that I must not hurt her; and I wonder whether this 'head-dress' had something to do with a bandage, with something that heals a wound—Kotex." Is it not striking that at this moment he disclosed the fact that the shawl had still another feature, one that made it similar to a "dressing," to a bandage which heals wounds? By the association "Kotex" the type of wound which he had in mind is indicated: menstrual bleeding.

The shawl that he now called "head-dress" had a floral design, which stimulated the following recollection: As a child, he once saw a woman suckling her infant, and was fascinated. When she noticed him staring at her breasts, she was embarrassed and covered herself with a kerchief decorated with a floral design, similar to the one of the shawl in the fantasy. While he was reporting this incident he felt a peculiar chill along his spine (probably of sexual nature). Yet, the breast and the sexual excitement had been completely forgotten, repressed. He remembered, however, the floral design of the kerchief which had obstructed his view of the breasts, and which reappeared as a detail on the shawl. Now a similar design emerged, as a recollection of one of his mother's dresses that he had liked very much as a child and had always urged her to wear. With a dress one covers one's body, with a kerchief one's breast, as with a loincloth one's genitals. We know that a woman's breasts are a secondary sex organ *par excellence*. Accordingly, they are easily substituted in fantasy for female as well as male genitals, and *vice versa*.[29] Since the recollection of the cat's bleeding nipples was the point of departure for this entire chain of associations, we assume that our patient unconsciously fused the picture of the bleeding nipples with the picture of the bleeding genitals. With the analysis of the second dream we learn how he reacted to this sight; he was horrified, like the youth in the myth about Medusa. It has now become clear that he overcame his horror of the female genitals by denying their existence and by converting them into

[29] The first patient substituted genitals for breast very easily.

something quite different in the fantasy of the woman with the shawl. They were made to appear not horrible and repulsive, but attractive, like flowers adorning the shawl on the head. If the "perfect" woman was the woman with the penis, the attractive and immaculate woman is a woman who has no genitals.

But what has that idea to do with feelings of guilt? The answer to this question is fairly simple: the recollection of the bleeding nipples brought into the focus of our patient's consciousness his repressed aggression against his mother and the feelings of guilt attached to it. The latter released the associations of the head-dress, the Kotex and the floral design. These, in turn, were allusions to the sight of mother's bleeding genitals. We may, therefore, infer that this sight caused not only horror, but also the same feeling of guilt as was aroused by his aggressiveness against his mother, specifically the aggressiveness directed against her breasts. On the phallic stage, he considered himself, unconsciously of course, responsible for the woman's lack of a penis; in other words, he felt as if he had castrated her.

This feeling of responsibility throws some light on his attitude toward women, for instance, his great pity for, as well as cruelty toward, them.[30]

But how can this feeling of guilt, based on the fantasy of having castrated mother, be brought into accord with the fantasy of the "mother as castrator"? In connection with the first dream we learned that, submitting to his sisters' importunities, he carried out the family tradition and permitted his son to be circumcised. That meant to him that women are cruel. Besides, he had numerous dreams in which women castrated him. A striking counterpart to these dreams is the fact that those of my patients who had been circumcised in childhood blamed their mother for the operation, hated her and, in turn, felt guilty themselves. There is no doubt that all these patients are highly ambivalent toward their mothers, loving and hating them. These two emotions are patently incompatible. One of them has to be eliminated from consciousness.

---

[30] I should like to call attention to the fact that one source of feelings of guilt toward his mother was also the conviction that he injured her at his own birth. By injuring himself he repeated his own birth and punished himself. He recalled an old Jewish saying that man would be punished in the next world for sucking his mother's blood with her milk.

The feeling of hostility and aggression is projected onto the mother, whereupon she appears as castrator. Then the idea of the mother as castrator has the following meanings: It is not I who injure my mother; she is injuring, castrating me. It is most interesting to note that the pregenital aggression toward her appears in the phallic stage and is reflected in the castration complex.

However, the castrating mother is not simply imagination, not purely a fantasy that has its origin only in man's mind. Aggressive mothers did and do exist, and a great number of sisters are very aggressive. The sons or brothers are aware of their hostility and are generally afraid of them. Moreover, history reports aggressive mothers. The opinion has been expressed that in prebiblical times Jewish women circumcised their sons.[31] Elderly women of maternal type are represented on Egyptian sculptures assisting in the circumcision of the boys (Bryk, 1941). Most important, however, is the fact that in the religions of the ancient Middle East, the cradle of Western civilization, men castrated themselves in religious ecstasy and offered their genitals on the altar of the Great Mother, the goddess Astarte, also known under other names. What men really did in ancient times, they dream and fancy in modern times. Why man of antiquity actually offered his genitals to the Great Mother is difficult to guess, and why modern man carries out this wish in fantasy is equally difficult to explain.[32]

In our patient's fantasy the face of the woman was blotted out. We know that she represented his mother, whose identity as a sexual being had to be completely disguised. She had no face, but

[31] *Jewish Encyclopædia.*

[32] Perhaps the feeling of guilt toward woman with its feeling of responsibility and compassion may account for it, as already indicated. The meaning of this specific sacrifice then could be as follows: what I have taken away from you, i.e., the penis, I am restoring to you. If this interpretation is correct, we can understand certain traits of the relationship between man and woman; on his part the inclination to make sacrifices for her, on her part, even on the part of very independent women, the demand for sacrifices coupled with a deep feeling that all that man does and gives to her is not enough, which may be due to her resentment over the lack of a penis. As a man's son is a reincarnation of his father to him, so is he a reincarnation of her father to the mother. Then the unequaled love of the mother for her son and her admiration for him seem directed also toward the reincarnation of her father with his penis. It must, of course, not be forgotten that, basically, the boy equips the woman with a penis for narcissistic identification.

she had a mouth. Taking into account the defense mechanism of libido displacement from one erotogenic zone to the other—here from "below upwards"—we must draw the conclusion that the mother's mouth symbolized her vagina. Then the patient was carrying out, in his fantasy, incestuous relations with his mother. In order to conceal the incest from himself everything had to be changed: the mother's face was blotted out; she had no vagina; he was not active; he remained passive while she was the active one. It seems as if by retreating from activity to passivity and depriving mother of her sex organs, he saved his own genitals. His sexual relations with her took on an oral and passive character. A relationship like that acted out in the fantasy had, of course, never existed in reality between him and his mother, but another relationship had once been real; he had, as an infant, sucked at his mother's breasts and bitten them.

The unconscious wish to bite her breasts, as expressed in the first dream in drinking from her cup, was completely repressed. There was left in the fantasy only her sucking of his penis, a reversal of his actual sucking at her breasts as an infant.

The analysis of the fantasy leads to the same results as the first dream, where the dreamer did not want to drink from father's but from mother's cup. Both dream and fantasy showed how the patient tried to cope with the threatening danger of circumcision.

It must be stressed again that this fantasy existed before the son's circumcision and before the dreams. He behaved in the fantasy as if he himself were being circumcised, or rather as if he remembered his own circumcision, and reacted to it in a way similar to that in the dream. It looks as if, in a sense, these reactions were pre-existent, and as if all that was needed to bring them to the surface was an actual stimulus.

Indeed, the expectation of the son's circumcision had a traumatic effect upon him which he tried to master by mobilizing similar traumatic experiences of his life (Freud, 1920). Some of them were fantasies, some actual events that could no longer be remembered as such, as for instance, biting mother's breast or his own circumcision.

His reactions were, however, not individual ones exclusively; they repeated, in a sense, experiences of preceding generations.

We may say that his attempts to solve the conflict of circumcision reflect in many respects the religious and sociological development of mankind; in his efforts to master this trauma as an individual, he repeated history. Were it different, we could hardly understand his struggle with the age-old problem of circumcision. We can understand it only if we agree with the Freudian hypothesis that ". . . the archaic heritage of mankind includes not only dispositions but also ideational contents, memory traces of the experiences of former generations" (Freud, 1939, p. 157). He further says that "masses, too, retain memory traces of the past," as does the individual. Paraphrasing him, we may say, not only hysterics suffer from reminiscences, but also peoples.

The struggle between the two tendencies, to circumcise and not to circumcise, is, indeed, deeply rooted in the past of mankind. Ancient Judaism was aware of it, long before the advent of Christianity. In the Holy Scriptures we find: "Circumcise therefore the foreskin of your heart, and be no longer stiffnecked" (Deut. x, 5, 6). Similar ideas were pronounced by the prophets Jeremiah, Ezekiel, and others. In Arthur Feldman's (1944) opinion, Ezra the Scribe, and Nehemiah abolished circumcision. Furthermore, Feldman suggests that the Pharisees reintroduced it when they became more influential and more powerful than the Sadducees. However, they made a compromise between circumcision and noncircumcision by performing the ceremony eight days after birth, not at puberty as had been done before.[33] St. Paul, the founder of the Christian religion, himself proud of being a Jew and originally a zealous

[33] The fact that the circumcision was displaced from puberty to infancy may be due to a desire to mitigate the cruelty of the custom. But the choice just of the eighth day may be motivated by other factors. The Jewish year is a moon year, each month being divided into four seven-day weeks. The seventh day, the Sabbath, was observed by Israelites even before monotheistic times. The term *Shabath* is akin to the Babylonian *Shabattum*, the name given to the nefasti or evil days. On these days no work was done because no blessing went with it (See Georg Beer as quoted by M. Woolf in *Eating Prohibitions in Orthodox Jewish Law*). The eighth day, i.e., the first day of the second week, was considered the day of resurrection (*Jewish Encyclopædia*). Since the circumcision was regarded as symbolic rebirth, the choice of the eighth day seems to correspond to a regression to an older premonotheistic religious belief, which in disguised form could easily be adopted by the adherents to circumcision. Christ's circumcision on the eighth day after his birth coincides with New Year's Day, the rebirth of the year, indeed.

defender of the Judaic laws, after protracted inner struggles, put a
definite end to the custom of circumcision. It is evident that, wish-
ing to make the Jewish religion universal, he tried to convert as
many Gentiles as possible and, in order to achieve this goal, he had
to abandon the rite of circumcision. But the urge to proselytize
does not seem the only reason for breaking with such a deeply
ingrained national custom. The impulse must have its origin in the
unconscious. Freud says: "... Among the customs through which
the Jews marked off their aloof position, that of circumcision made
a disagreeable, uncanny impression on others. The explanation
probably is that it reminds them of the dreaded castration idea and
of things in their primæval past which they would fain forget"
(Freud, 1939, p. 144). In another passage he is more explicit:
"Circumcision," he says, "is the symbolical substitute for castration, a punishment which the primæval father dealt his sons long
ago out of the fullness of his power; and whosoever accepted this
symbol showed by so doing that he was ready to submit to the
father's will, although it was at the cost of painful sacrifice" (p. 192).
St. Paul did not accept this symbol demanded by the one and only
God. He rejected circumcision and also denounced a great part of
the Judaic law, attributed to Moses, the powerful father figure, who
introduced monotheism to the Jews, and, according to Freud
(1939, p. 141), also circumcision. By the removal of the sign of
man's submissiveness to God, he essentially undermined God's
authority. The substitution of God-Father by Jesus Christ, the
Son of God, seems to prove it. Freud (1939, p. 138) expressed the
result of this substitution in a simple formula: "The Mosaic religion had been a Father religion, Christianity became a Son
religion."

Paul, however, gave up not only circumcision and the ceremonial laws, he rejected the dietary laws also (Klausner, 1943).
No doubt their abolition tore down another barrier separating
Gentiles from Jews as did the abandonment of circumcision, but
here as there we must assume deeper reasons for this abolition than
merely the wish to bring in proselytes.

Among the dietary laws there is one strange yet very interesting
prohibition. It concerns mixing milk and its products with flesh,

and is based on the biblical command: "Thou shalt not seethe a kid in his mother's milk."

M. Woolf (1945) published a very interesting paper on this subject. Referring to Exodus, considered the oldest part of the Bible, he points out that this prohibition is only the last part of a series of other prohibitions and commands, which fully reads: "Thou shalt not offer the blood of my sacrifice with leavened bread; neither shall the fat of my sacrifice remain until morning . . .; the first of the first fruits of thy land thou shalt bring into the house of the Lord thy God. Thou shalt not seethe a kid in his mother's milk." This passage refers to the Passover sacrifice, and on Passover "The bread must not be leavened but dried upon the stones heated by the sun—like the kid roasted in the fire." Agreeing with scholars in that field, he says further: "Now Pesah [Passover] is a festival of spring, and spring festivals everywhere and among all peoples are festivals of sun and fire. The ancient Semites, as we know, were sun-and-fire worshippers, and the customs and usages here described are of very old origin, much older than monotheism and the exodus from Egypt." He adds that the excavations in Ugarit (Ginsberg, 1936), in Syria, established the fact that the chief deity of the nomadic Israelitic tribes was the Sun God and Fire God known as El, and that during the spring festivals the first-born were sacrificed to him.

The excavations in Ugarit yielded a large tablet with inscriptions about the worship rites of the goddess Astarte, among them an injunction to kill a kid and cook it in its mother's milk. The biblical prohibition against "seething a kid in his mother's milk" represents, in Woolf's opinion, a "struggle of monotheism against heathenism, of national Jewish faith against the religions of their heathen neighbors" (Woolf, 1945, p. 174). Knowing from psychoanalytic experience that boiling or cooking, in the symbolic language of the dream or in other expressions of the unconscious, often means maturing in mother's womb, he finds in the words "seethed in mother's milk" confirmation of the infantile fantasy that the child in the womb is fed by mother's milk until born. "It is for this reason"—Woolf says—"that seething the kid in his mother's milk became the symbol of fertility of Astarte. . . ." Thus, in the springtime festivals and mysteries of Western religions, as indeed throughout the cultural world around the Mediterranean, the chief part was played, not by the father, but by the son; the latter was adored by his mother, killed by his father, and rose again in the spring under such names as Tammus, Adonis and Dionysus.

The Bible veto, Woolf maintains, apparently seeks to destroy the matriarchal rite. And again referring to his psychoanalytic experience, he interprets the meaning of baking leavened bread in an oven as a symbol of pregnancy. Hence, he reasons, the prohibition of this custom, expressed in the command to eat unleavened bread dried upon a stone heated by the sun, means the same as the prohibition against seething the kid in mother's milk. He finds a confirmation of this assumption in the fact that preparing bread on a hot stone, and not in the oven with dough, was an old custom of the Israelitic wanderers in the desert, and formed an important part of the ritual at the feast of the Sun God. Therefore, the prohibition against seething the kid in his mother's milk and the command to eat unleavened sun-dried bread have the same meaning: not to come in contact with the mother's womb.

Why are all these prohibitions and commands not expressed in a straightforward way? Why are they veiled, distorted? There can be only one answer to this question. They are the result of a miscarried repression; in other words, when the repressed material tries to return to consciousness, it is at the last moment distorted by the defensive function of the ego. As these prohibitions and commands are directed at oral functions, i.e., to eat or not to eat, we may, in agreement with Woolf, infer that the repression took place through the mechanism of displacement from below upward, from the genitals to the mouth, as in our patient's fantasy. Thus the prohibition and commands referring to the eating ritual symbolize not only the underlying struggle between monotheism and polytheism or Mother-Son Consort cult, but also the prohibition of incest—which is essentially the same.

The idea that the Israelites worshipped a mother goddess and a son god in premonotheistic times is gaining more and more ground among scholars. Theodor Reik (1923) was one of the first to make this assumption. Arthur Feldman (1944) and others (Hooke, 1938) maintain that the popular Israelitic religion was the cult of the Great Mother Goddess and her Son Consort; that this religion was never completely replaced by monotheism; that it was only repressed and returned again and again in veiled shapes, distorting the newer monotheistic beliefs and rituals. He states that the name of the Jewish God reflects this struggle. As is well known, the Jews are forbidden to call their God by his real name, yet permitted to pronounce it Adonai—and that is the name of the son of the Mother Goddess. The real name of God was spelled Yahweh. But, according to Feldman, it was originally Yahu, the name of a Sun God, that appeared in the *Papyrus of Elephantine* (Meyer, 1912). From the name Yahu was formed the divine name Yahveh, by the addition of the Hebrew letter "H," according to Feldman. The letter "H," he explains, is the common feminine ending in Hebrew.

If we accept this thesis, we must conclude that the name of the Israelitic God is the result of a compromise between a male and a female deity, whereby the female part is removed from consciousness.

It seems that the dual name of the God portrays not only the struggle between monotheism and polytheism, but also between masculinity and femininity. A male with a female ending, or *vice versa,* is certainly a bisexual creature, a mother with a penis, which is regularly found in our analyses.

That our patient oscillated between father and mother, was obvious (like our first patient who saw a hermaphrodite in everyone). To establish an equilibrium in his relationship to them was difficult for him. At one time he had to repress one part of the oedipus complex, at another time another part. The working through of his ambivalent relationship toward his father, however, made him fully conscious of his hostility toward him, and enabled him to admit, in a sense, the "original sin." Only then did he obtain the freedom to confess his incestuous fantasy, to admit his sexual craving for his mother. The admission of the sin against the father apparently mitigated his anxiety and helped to remove the last barrier against incest.

The concept of the "original sin" was introduced by Apostle Paul. In *Totem and Taboo* Freud explains the deeper meaning of this sin. He says: "... In the Christian myth man's original sin is undoubtedly an offense against God the Father, and if Christ redeems mankind from the weight of original sin by sacrificing his own life, he forces us to the conclusion that this sin was murder. According to the law of retaliation which is deeply rooted in human feeling, a murder can be atoned for only by the sacrifice of another life; the sacrifice points to a blood-guilt. And if this sacrifice of one's own life brings about a reconciliation with God, the Father, then the crime which must be expiated can only have been the murder of the father" (Freud, 1912-1913).

Paul admitted the guilt of the original sin by accepting the sacrificial death of the Son of God as redemption (cf. Freud, 1912-1913; 1939). Although consciously he accepted punishment for this sin by identification with Christ, unconsciously, nevertheless, he still revolted against God, the Father. The external signs of the revolt were the rejection of circumcision, of the ceremonial laws of the Torah and of the dietary laws (Klausner, 1943). Since circumcision is a symbol of submission to father's will, the rejection of circumcision is a flight from father's authority. As acceptance of the Torah implies belief in the one God, rejection of the Torah implies the abandonment of monotheism and, therefore, negation of God-Father. Thus the rejection of circumcision and the Torah means essentially the same: renunciation of the father. Giving up the dietary laws, at least the law against mixing milk and flesh, means something different. Since it implies the prohibition of Astarte worship, hence of incest, its rejection signifies the reintroduction of the Great Mother and Son Consort cult, essentially the authorization of incest. One "crime" leads to another, the rejection of father, to incest with mother, to the fulfillment of the complete oedipus complex. As if horrified by his own deed, Paul says in his first Epistle to the Corinthians: "It is reported commonly that there is fornication among you, and such fornication as is not so much as named among the Gentiles, that one should have his father's wife" (v, 1). After his initial challenge, Paul apparently obeyed the higher law laid down by the primeval father whom he tried to reject, and in prohibiting incest, submitted to father's authority on the main issue. Now we understand more clearly what Freud means when he says that circumcision reminded peoples of things in their primeval past which they should like to forget.

Although living in a quite different world and so many centuries away, our patient seems to have had almost the same experiences as Paul. In spite of all his desires he could not face the idea of incest which was forcing itself upon him, and felt compelled to repress it repeatedly. Transforming his mother into an asexual being, he succeeded finally in freeing himself of the onus of incest. Although by abolition of the dietary laws by Paul, incest was facilitated, it was once again repressed by the transformation of the goddess of fertility and love into the Heavenly Mother who adores her son.

Here we touch upon problems that transcend the scope of our subject and the further discussion of which I should like to leave to others. But I should, nevertheless, like to say a few words in conclusion.

As has been stressed above—and I wish to repeat it here—the individual in his reactions to circumcision seems to reflect the reactions of mankind, to repeat them in a condensed form. They manifest themselves either in acceptance or rejection of circumcision, usually resulting in a compromise in which either one or the other form prevails. These contrasting reactions are the consequence of a basic conflict which, intensified by circumcision or the mere idea thereof, drives toward consciousness. The biological basis of this conflict seems to be formed by the homosexual attachment to the father. Man has always rebelled against this attachment. Some peoples and some individuals have succeeded in freeing themselves from this tie; not so the Jews. By accepting circumcision, they submitted unconditionally to the father's will, as represented by their God. Then they considered themselves his beloved and chosen children. A concurrence of historical circumstances seems to have favored the fact that monotheism, the new religion introduced by Moses, adopted the ancient custom of circumcision and made it the mark of the Jews' attachment to God. For the Jews had taken the custom of circumcision from the Egyptians, and Moses, who gave the Jews monotheism, was, according to Freud, an Egyptian. Out of love for their one and only God they sacrificed part of their genitals, thereby renouncing instinct gratification and at the same time initiating sublimation of their homosexuality. This sublimation resulted in a prohibition against depicting God, even in imagination, in visual form. That, in turn, forced the Jews into abstract thinking and impelled them to high performances in spiritual and moral spheres, with all the renunciations, restrictions and sufferings implied (Freud, 1939). During this process the idea of a material God faded. Christianity abandoned circumcision and loosened the homosexual relationship to God-Father; but the adulation of the Woman, the Mother, and the Son was reinstated. Herewith spiritualized monotheism lost its meaning and momentum. The earlier polytheism, hitherto abandoned, began to regain its previous importance and to express itself in its manifold forms. In comparison with the earlier polytheism, this was an advance, since the spiritual and ethical level of the new manifestations was higher than that of Jewish polytheism in premonotheistic times.

AFTERTHOUGHT

While working on topics like those treated in this paper, one is inevitably tempted to discuss a number of current problems. Though I endeavored to avoid them, there was one which forced itself upon me. It was the much-discussed "question of the German guilt." A comparison between the Jews and the Germans in regard to their respective sense of guilt may shed some light on this problem.

The Jews submitted themselves to the authority of their God unconditionally, and from this surrender they derived their moral laws. They considered the symbolic sacrifice of castration, the circumcision, the external sign of this submission. Circumcision was to them punishment and humiliation as well as elevation and nobility—and "noblesse oblige." In return for that sacrifice they expected recognition and love from their God. Circumcision symbolized, in addition, hope, promise of redemption and rebirth. Through circumcision the Jews entered into a covenant with God, which enabled them to identify with him. His laws and commandments became their own; they learned thereby to master their own aggression from within. However, the ritual of circumcision evidently was not sufficient for the complete control of aggression and rebellion against God-Father. For even the Prophets preached that the Jews should circumcise "the foreskin of their heart." Self-accusations and self-reproaches permeate Jewish history, from the very beginning up to the present time. It is as though being a Jew were identical with suffering.

Every year on the Day of Atonement the Jews confess their guilt
in public and expect mercy, forgiveness, redemption and rebirth
free from guilt. As we saw before, confession also implies an attempt to undo the crime, the primal sin.

St. Paul adopted the exhortation of the Prophets to circumcise
not only the flesh but also the heart, and gave up the mutilation
of the body. Instead he admitted the primal sin and accepted the
sacrificial death of the Son of God as the redemption of mankind.

It seems that in the past hundred years, among the peoples of
Europe, the Germans were least able to endure the restriction of
aggression as demanded by Jewish-Christian ethics. After the first
World War, the victors tried to make them accept their guilt, but
they vehemently rejected this charge. This attitude seems to explain the fact that they had no moral inhibitions against starting
a second world war. Then their unrestricted aggression knew no
limits. They rejected Christ, the Son of God, and murdered the
Jews, the Children of the God of Israel, as if they wanted to take
vengeance on them for having given Christ to the world—and still
do not feel guilty.

The grave question arises: are redemption and rebirth possible
without admission of guilt?

As the Jews submitted unconditionally to their God, so the
Germans submitted to their kings, and later to their Führer. The
Jewish God prohibited the killing of man as such; the Führer
ordered the killing of man, except for the Nazi. By licensing murder
the Führer relieved the Germans of the sense of guilt. They could
then feel: "Not I am killing, but the Führer is—and he has the
right to kill."

Man acquired his sense of guilt, as Freud indicated, through the
primal sin, the killing of the primal father. In primitive society the
tribal chief does not die a natural death; he is killed after the
expiration of his term (Frazer, 1925a). Every reign seems to have
ended in a kind of revolution.

In the last hundred years the Germans made several attempts at
revolution, all unsuccessful. The revolution of 1848 was a failure.
In the abortive revolution which followed the first World War,
they did not kill their leaders, the father substitutes. On the contrary, they emphasized with pride that the Germans had never

been *Königsmörder,* regicides. In a psychological sense they were, therefore, justified in not accepting the guilt ascribed to them by the victors in that war. After the last war they might have had a better opportunity to kill their leaders in a real revolution, had not the victors taken justice in their hands. Doing the job for the Germans, they prevented them from abreacting their pent-up aggression against their leaders and from developing a new sense of guilt. From a psychological standpoint they are therefore again justified in their refutation of guilt. Thomas Jefferson[34] said: "The tree of liberty must be refreshed from time to time with the blood of patriots and tyrants, it is its natural manure."

In primitive society the victorious tribe eats the dead enemy in order to incorporate his virtues. The psychic equivalent to physical incorporation is identification. After this last war, the victors seem more and more to identify with the vanquished. What will happen to the conscience of the victors if the identification with the vanquished continues?

---

[34] In a letter written to Colonel William Stephens Smith, November 13, 1787.

A COMMENTARY ON FREUD'S
AN OUTLINE OF PSYCHOANALYSIS

WHEN I UNDERTOOK to review this book (Freud, 1940a), I did not know how difficult a task it would be. A mere review can by no means do justice to this work; only a thorough commentary would be an adequate tribute to Freud's genius.

To get the full value of each single sentence, the reader should read this book over and over again. Then he will discover ever new thought-provoking formulations.

The *Outline* seems the last attempt of the Master to state the ideas of his lifework, an attempt, as it were, to convey to posterity the essence of his teachings. This, his last presentation, is not the only one in which he summarizes his doctrines. Such publications as the *History of the Psycho-Analytical Movement,* the *Autobiography,* the *New Lectures,* etc., were the result of his vigilantly taking stock of his findings and constantly giving himself critical account of his doctrines. Revising them, he never hesitated to admit and correct errors. Yet, whenever he modified previous statements, he could always point out new problems, open new horizons. Analysis was never static in his hands; it was always alive and growing. Even in this final work he pointed out with admirable sincerity all the problems which analysis had been unable to solve.

The *Outline* is of all his summarizations the simplest, clearest and yet most comprehensive.

In none of his works did Freud ever try to force his ideas upon others. He expressed them and waited patiently. In the concluding sentence of his introductory words he says of this book: "... Its

Reprinted from *The Psychoanalytic Quarterly,* 19: 227-250, 1950.

intention is naturally not to compel belief or to establish conviction"—just as, I should like to add, in analysis one should not try
to force conviction upon the patient.

The author proceeds systematically. He tries at the beginning to
examine the concept of "psyche" or "mental life." He states: "We
know two things concerning what we call our psyche or mental
life: firstly, its bodily organ and scene of action, the brain . . . and
secondly, our acts of consciousness, which are immediate data and
cannot be explained more fully by any kind of description." Everything that takes place between the state of initial action of the
brain and the emergence of consciousness is unknown to us.

On the basis of these facts and of innumerable observations of
the development of the individual, he makes the far-reaching
assumption that "mental life is the function of an apparatus to
which we ascribe the characteristics of being extended in space and
being made up of several portions."

Freud first offered this conception of the structure of the psychic
apparatus in the theoretical part of *The Interpretation of Dreams*.
The portions of this apparatus were then called the systems Unconscious (Ucs), Preconscious (Pcs), and Conscious (Cs). Although
this conception was discarded as utterly fantastic by some of his
followers of that time, especially those in Burghölzli, it remained
the fundamental hypothesis of his doctrines. Subsequently, when
the psychology of the ego began to take shape, these systems coincided to a certain degree with the division of the personality into
mental provinces or agencies, the id, superego, and ego.

The id is the oldest part of these psychic provinces, containing
everything that forms our constitution and is inherited, containing
"above all, therefore, the instincts which originate in the somatic
organization and which find their first mental expression in the
id in forms unknown to us." In other words, the first mental expression of instincts is *absolutely* unconscious.

At the beginning of life, the id is not yet differentiated from the
other psychic agencies; it is only surrounded by an external layer
equipped "with organs for receiving stimuli and with an apparatus
for protection against excessive stimulation." From this layer very
soon another mental province arises, the ego. Its main task is self-
preservation, mediation between the external and the internal

world, the id. For the first time, Freud gives here a full enumeration of all the activities to be performed by the ego in the service of this task; then he stresses that they "are governed by consideration of the tensions produced by stimuli present within it or introduced into it," that is, by the unpleasure-pleasure principle: the ego pursues pleasure and seeks to avoid unpleasure. Here he indicates that probably these feelings do not depend on the absolute degree of the rising or falling of tensions as much as on the rhythm of these changes.

The third mental province or agency is called the superego. Its function is to reconcile the demands of the id, the ego and reality. It is the result not only of the child's prolonged dependence upon his parents and the social milieu, "but also of the racial, national and family tradition." In this connection he says: "... the id and the superego have one thing in common: they both represent the influences of the past (the id the influence of heredity, the superego essentially what is taken over from other people), whereas the ego is principally determined by the individual's own experience...." It is thus very clear that Freud considers the id the carrier of the biological traits of man, and the superego the carrier of the tradition, i.e., of the experiences of past generations.

Here the author finds a connection between human psychology and the psychology of higher animals inasmuch as both have an ego and an id. He makes it very clear, however, that the superego, having as its precondition prolonged dependence in childhood, cannot be applied to higher animals.

After this brief discussion of the psychic apparatus, the author turns his attention to the theory of instincts. The instincts are those forces, he says, which "we assume to exist behind the tensions caused by the needs of the id. ... They represent the somatic demands upon mental life." All instincts are distinguished by two characteristics: first, by the mechanism of displacement, i.e., by the two facts that they can change their aim and pass their energy from one to another, a mechanism which, according to the author, is still obscure; secondly, the instincts are by nature conservative, which means that "the state, whatever it may be, which a living thing has reached, gives rise to a tendency to re-establish that state as soon as it has been abandoned."

The underlying principle is the repetition compulsion known to us since the publication of *Beyond the Pleasure Principle* (Freud, 1920), in which Freud first expounded his theory of instincts and assumed two basic instincts: the love instinct or *eros* and the *destructive* or *death* instinct. The aim of eros is "to establish ever greater unities and to preserve them thus—in short, to bind together"; the aim of the destructive instinct "is to undo connections and so to destroy things. We may suppose," he continues, "that the final aim of the destructive instinct is to reduce living things to an inorganic state. For this reason we also call it the *death instinct.*"

This theory of instincts has remained the most controversial part of Freud's teachings. Many of his pupils did not accept the existence of a death instinct.

The author stresses that the repetition compulsion can be applied to the death instinct since living things arose from inanimate ones; not however to eros, since that would imply "that living substance had once been a unity but has subsequently been torn apart and was now tending toward reunion." The deduction, in relation to eros, is certainly correct, but, as the reviewer sees it, only in the genetic sense, not in the economic sense. For the tendency to reduce "the tensions of the love instinct" and to return to the previous state of rest—of "no-tension," of "no-instinct"—seems to be governed by the same repetition principle, which, indeed is "beyond the pleasure principle." The pleasure-unpleasure principle is, to be sure, an economic one.

The two basic instincts almost never appear in a pure form. In their biological functions they either work against each other or combine with each other and form fusions. A disproportion in the mixture of these instincts results in psychic disorders. Both instincts display a certain amount of energy; the energy of eros is called libido, while for the energy of the death instinct there is no analogous term. It is easy to observe the manifestations of the libido because they are "clamorous." It is, however, difficult to see the workings of the death instinct because they are "silent."

In the early stages of psychoanalysis we talked about "sexual instincts" in contrast to "ego instincts" (*Ichtriebe*). Freud considered the latter "mute" as if he felt in advance what development psychoanalysis would take. At that time there was very little known about the ego. When Freud introduced the concept of narcissism, and ego love and self-preservation turned out to be of libidinal nature just as object love and the drive for the preservation of the species, there still remained a part of the ego that was "silent." The difficulty in understanding the "silence" of the ego was removed by the assumption of a death instinct. As long as this instinct works within the boundaries of the ego, it is silent. Only when it is turned outward, toward external objects, does it manifest itself as a *destructive* instinct. This instinct makes use of the skeletal musculature for its purposes, with action resulting in destruction or mastery of the external world, instead of self-destruction. When the superego, a product of civilization, begins to develop, it absorbs much of the aggression directed toward the external world and works thus within the ego.

As to eros, there is hardly anything known about the behavior of its libido within the id or the superego: "Everything that we know about it relates to the ego, in which the whole available amount of libido is at first stored up." This state is called *primary narcissism.* The ego libido is changeable into object libido. It can, however, at any moment be withdrawn from object representations and be reconverted into *ego* or *narcissistic* libido. The ego "remains the great reservoir" of libido.

Libido has two contrasting characteristics: mobility and fixation. (These characteristics obviously have a relation to libidinal types.) It has somatic sources and "streams into the ego from various organs and parts of the body. This is most clearly seen in the case of the portion of the libido which, from its instinctual aim, is known as sexual excitation. The most prominent parts of the body from which this libido arises are described by the name of *erotogenic* zones, though strictly speaking the whole body is an erotogenic zone."

The third chapter is devoted to the discussion of the development of the sexual function. In a few simple sentences the well-known basic ideas about sexuality are repeated: " (a) Sexual life does not begin only at puberty, but starts with clear manifestations soon after birth. (b) It is necessary to distinguish sharply between the concepts of 'sexual' and 'genital'.... (c) Sexual life comprises the function of obtaining pleasure from zones of the body—a function which is subsequently brought into the service of that of reproduction. . . ."

Reviewing succinctly sexual development, Freud stresses its *diphasic* onset: it starts at birth and continues until approximately the fifth year; a period of latency follows; this is succeeded by the second onset, the maturing sexuality of puberty. The diphasic onset of sexual life occurs only in man. *Infantile amnesia* is probably connected with it. "Our understanding of the neuroses and the technique of analytic therapy are derived from these views."

The meaning of the concept of "sexuality" is illuminated by the example of the sucking baby: "The baby's obstinate persistence in sucking gives evidence at an early stage of a need for satisfaction which, although it originates from and is stimulated by the taking of nourishment, nevertheless seeks to obtain pleasure independently of nourishment and for that reason may and should be described as 'sexual.' Physiology should not be confused with psychology."

The development of sexuality progresses through its four phases, each phase having a certain admixture of aggressive instincts. The first, the *oral* phase, during which sadistic impulses occur sporadically, is followed by the *anal-sadistic* phase. In this phase the aggression is increased to such an extent that the child exhibits pronounced *sadistic* tendencies. The author explains sadism by the assumption of a *fusion* of libidinal with destructive impulses and raises the important question, whether satisfaction of purely destructive impulses can be felt as pleasure. He answers this question in the negative.

In the third, the *phallic* phase, the fusion of destructive and libidinal impulses finds its expression in the *castration complex*. In this phase only the penis is known to both sexes (the girl's clitoris is analogous to the boy's penis). When infantile sexuality reaches its climax in the course of the phallic phase, the sexuality of boy and girl begins to develop in different directions. At this time the boy becomes subject to the *oedipus complex*: his libido is directed toward his mother and his aggression against his father; ". . . but at last, owing to the combined . . . threat of castration and the spectacle of women's lack of a penis, he experiences the greatest trauma of his life. . . ." He acquires the "castration complex."

Freud does not demonstrate the further relation of aggression to libido in both the castration and the oedipus complexes. Therefore I should like to add that the castration complex is ambivalent, positive and negative: it generally expresses castration fear, but in certain cases it contains a wish to be castrated; for the most part both forms are combined. The aggression which as a component part of the oedipus complex is usually directed against the father, turns subsequently against the child's own ego and is felt as a castration threat. If another part of the same destructive instinct has remained in the ego, it is felt as a wish to be castrated, to be feminine, and results in passivity and submission to the father.

The development of the girl is somewhat different. With her, masturbation does not lead to the fear of castration as with the boy. "The girl, after vainly attempting to do the same as the boy, comes to recognize her lack of a penis or rather the inferiority of her clitoris, with permanent effects on her character." In fact, this means that the girl in normal development resigns herself, within certain limits, to suffering and masochism. Often, however, the girl becomes aggressive and turns away altogether from sexual life.

In the phallic phase the organization, i.e., the coordination of all component instincts (emanating from the erogenous zones) into one sexual aim, begins to evolve; but only in the fourth phase, in puberty, is this organization completed, and only then do the genitalia become the central sex organ.

Frequently the development of the libido is disturbed, and inhibitions occur. Portions of the libido are fixated at earlier stages, while other portions progress to their normal aims. The genital organization may thus become unbalanced through the retardation of some sexual elements. The final result of such a sexual development is a weakening of the genital organization, whose degree depends on *quantitative* relations between the amount of libido that has remained fixated to pregenital objects and aims, and that which has progressed normally. "Such weakening shows itself in a tendency... for the libido to return to its earlier pregenital cathexes (i.e., to *regress*)."

The author closes this chapter with the following words: "During the study of the sexual functions it has been possible to gain a vrst, preliminary conviction, or rather suspicion, of two pieces of knowledge which will later be found to be important over the whole of our field. Firstly, the normal and abnormal phenomena that we observe . . . require to be described from the point of view of dynamics and economics. . . . And secondly, the etiology of the disturbances which we are studying is to be found in the developmental history of the individual, that is to say, in the early part of his life."

After the discussion of the psychic apparatus, and the description of the energies active within it, the author turns to the fundamental problem of the actual nature of mental life of which this apparatus is the stage. Many scientists have been deluded, he says, by the unique phenomenon of consciousness to assume that consciousness alone constitutes mental life. But simple observation shows that there are physical or somatic processes accompanying mental ones which are not conscious and yet prove to have mental qualities. Thus somatic processes have mental qualities which can easily be identified as conscious, and other mental qualities which are not recognized and can be identified by the psychoanalytic technique as unconscious processes. Unconscious and conscious processes form together a complete series. The somatic processes are thus broader than conscious ones because, as the author stated at the very beginning, the brain is "the bodily organ and scene of action of our mental life." On the basis of these facts, Freud arrives at the far-reaching conclusion that psychic processes are somatic. He says: "It thus seems natural to lay the stress in psychology upon these somatic processes, to see in *them* the true essence of what is mental. . . ." Although it may seem repetitious, the reviewer would like to stress that the hypothesis of mental processes being somatic includes the other assumption that not only conscious processes are mental but that all that is unconscious is also mental. Consciousness is only a transitory state of mental activity. This conception of the nature of mental life, Freud states, enables psychology "to take its place as a natural science like any other. The processes with which it is concerned are in themselves just as unknowable as those dealt with by the other sciences. . . ."

I think that the conception of mental processes as somatic contributes much to a better understanding not only of human behavior but also of some organic sicknesses and of the somatic neuroses. It is, for example, very illuminating in relation to the problem of conversion hysteria. The somatic symptoms of the neuroses (and some organic illnesses) are thus *direct* manifestations of unconscious mental processes. The "puzzling leap of mental states into physical ones"—as Freud expressed himself earlier—becomes less puzzling now than it seemed before.

The difficulties of psychoanalysis are very great as compared with those of the other sciences. While every other science is "based on the observations and experiences arrived at through the medium of our psychic apparatus," psychoanalysis has "as its subject this apparatus itself. . . ." Precisely with the perceptions of this apparatus we watch the events within it and even notice gaps in the series of conscious events; i.e., we notice some links to be missing, as a result of which we are confused and do not understand the mental process. Only by replacing these omissions with guesses, plausible inferences, and translating them into conscious language "we construct, as it were, a series of conscious events complementary to the unconscious mental processes" which we now can understand.

Using this method one soon learns that it is necessary to distinguish between three mental states: conscious, preconscious and unconscious. The most surprising and yet prominent quality of the conscious state is its instability, its "highly fugitive" condition. The preconscious state can become a conscious one at any moment. The unconscious mental processes cannot become conscious as such and are called the *unconscious proper*. As indicated before, they must be translated into conscious language.

Freud repeats here the warning given on many other occasions that mere interpretation and construction of the unconscious material presented to the patient is not sufficient to make this material conscious. He says: ". . . the material is present in his [the patient's] mind in two versions, first in the conscious reconstruction that he has just received and secondly in its original unconscious condition." It seems as if by stressing this fact over and over again, the author intended to indicate that correct analysis does not consist of mere "interpreting," and that the process of becoming conscious is a matter of emotional personal experience as well as of intellectual learning. It is, indeed, very difficult to transform unconscious material first into preconscious and then into conscious matter, but by persistent efforts we can succeed in causing both versions to coincide. (We estimate the resistance opposing this transformation by the amount of effort needed by the patient in order to overcome it.)

On the other hand, a spontaneous lowering of resistances to such an extent that unconscious material becomes preconscious and then conscious leads to psychotic states of mind. "From this we may infer that the maintenance of certain internal resistances is a *sine qua non* of normality." However, transformation of preconscious material or processes into unconscious conditions brings about numerous psychic disorders.

The qualities of the mental apparatus, the conscious, preconscious and unconscious states of mind, naturally are related to the provinces of this apparatus. Consciousness is a function of the perceptual organ of the ego which perceives external and internal stimuli: events taking place in the surrounding world as well as feelings and sensations originating in the body. Feelings and sensations are usually projected into the outside world so that it seems as if all perceptions of the ego were located outside. But a complication arises through the fact that one's own speech and thoughts bring other internal material into consciousness, for example, traces of visual or auditory memories and intellectual processes normally not easily projected into the outside world. The perceptual organ of the ego is thus a meeting place for external events and internal feelings, sensations, thoughts and ideas, a place where they become conscious. It is, therefore, easy for the subject to confuse them as to the place of their origin, i.e., whether they are located inside or outside the ego. In fact, such a confusion exists in early childhood, in dreams, and in psychoses. However, very early, a new faculty develops which differentiates between external and internal events. This faculty is called *reality testing*. If it breaks down, perceptions of the internal world acquire the quality of *hallucinations*. In dreams the weakening of this reality-testing faculty and the forming of hallucinations are normal phenomena.

Contents within the ego that are in an unconscious state, as for instance intellective processes, can be perceived by the perceptive apparatus of the ego and thus be transformed into a conscious condition. These states of mind are unconscious in a *phenomenological* sense and are called preconscious. The ego is, therefore, preconscious. According to Freud, the preconscious state "is characteristic of the ego and belongs to it alone ... large portions of the ego, and in particular of the superego, which cannot be denied the characteristic of being preconscious, none the less remain for the most part unconscious in the phenomenological sense of the word."

The mental qualities in the id are purely unconscious. "Id and unconscious are as intimately united as ego and preconscious. . . ." But developmentally the id consists of two kinds of unconscious material, the original part, its hardly accessible nucleus, and the repressed. The first, always present, is inherited; the second is acquired by repression of preconscious ideas and even conscious impressions.

Having established the fact that the ego is preconscious and the id unconscious, the author proceeds to investigate "What is the true nature of the condition which is disclosed in the case of the id by the quality of being unconscious and in the case of the ego by that of being preconscious, and in what does the distinction between them consist?" Although he cannot answer this question, Freud speaks again in guarded terms of his cherished idea about the two forms of psychic energy, an idea which might at some future time give a positive answer as to the nature of what is called "mental." Nervous or psychic energy seems to exist in two forms, one freely mobile and the other bound. In the id or the unconscious this energy is freely mobile; in the ego it is bound. It forms cathexes and hypercathexes analogous to electrical charges. A hypercathexis "brings about a sort of synthesis of different processes—a synthesis in the course of which free energy is transformed into bound energy."

The study of mental qualities has led to the discovery of certain laws by which the unconscious conditions of the id are distinguished from the preconscious conditions of the ego. The events in the unconscious id are governed by the *primary* process while the events in the preconscious ego are governed by the *secondary* process. For the first time Freud points out that thus the concepts "primary process" and "secondary process" express in terms of psychology the same ideas as do the concepts "freely mobile energy" and "bound energy" in terms of physics.

Freud tries to explain these processes through the example of the dream. Although the dream looks like a product of insanity it is a normal phenomenon. This fact makes the dream particularly suitable for the investigation of the unconscious id in its relation to the ego. The dream consists, as is well known, of the *manifest* dream material and the *latent* dream thoughts. The transformation of the latent into the manifest dream is called *dream work*. Its study "affords us an excellent example of the way in which unconscious material from the id . . . forces itself upon the ego, becomes preconscious and . . . undergoes the modifications which we call *dream-distortion.*"

The precondition of dreaming is sleep. In sleep the ego breaks off its relations with the external world and reverts temporarily to an earlier state in which it partially coincides with the id. "We shall be justified in saying that there arises at birth an instinct to return to the intrauterine life that has been abandoned—an instinct to sleep." The dream may be provoked by the ego or by the id: either a desire from the waking state is reinforced by an unconscious element, or an instinctual impulse finds its way into the dream; in the latter case an unconscious wish becomes so strong that it forces itself upon the ego during sleep.

As the ego is weakened in the dream, it is invaded by the unconscious id which helps to form the dream. The participation of the id in the dream formation manifests itself by many facts, among others by the following: the extensive memories in the dream, particularly those of early childhood (which are an indispensable help in the reconstruction of the patient's early childhood); linguistic symbols; and finally, material brought to the surface by the dream, which belongs to the *archaic heritage* of mankind. "Thus dreams offer a source of human prehistory. . . ." As we have no direct access to the id and can recognize it only through the medium of the preconscious ego, the dream is, in a sense, the best "experimental station" for observing how the unconscious id works. In the dream, preconscious thoughts in which the unconscious material expresses itself are treated by the ego as if they were parts of the id, and such preconscious thoughts which have attracted an unconscious instinctual impulse acquire likewise the characteristics of the unconscious id. "Thus dream-work is in its essence a case of an unconscious working-over of preconscious thought processes." As the ego organization is only weakened, not destroyed in the dream, it exercises also a certain influence upon the emerging unconscious material, which is modified by the ego, so that the dream finally represents a compromise between the demands of the ego and those of the unconscious id.

Thus the study of the dream work permits us to recognize the laws governing the processes in the unconscious id. They are first the law of *condensation* which expresses a tendency of the unconscious id to form new units of incongruous elements and, second, the law of *displacement* of mental energies from one element to another. On the basis of these two tendencies Freud assumes that in the unconscious id the energy is in a condition of free mobility. This condition defines the primary process as characteristic of the events in the id: that is to say, the tendencies in the id are in a chaotic state and their only aim is to discharge their quantities of excitation, no matter how and when.

The question arises: why does the ego make the effort to transform the unconscious material of the id into the manifest dream; why does it undertake the dream work? The unconscious id "makes a demand upon the ego for the satisfaction of an instinct," the solution of a conflict, etc. Since the aim of the individual, however, is to maintain sleep, it tries to ward off all disturbances. "The ego achieves this by what appears to be an act of compliance: it meets the demand with what is in the circumstances the innocent fulfillment of a wish and thus disposes of the demand. This replacement of a demand by the fulfillment of a wish remains the essential function of dream-work." To meet all doubts as to the validity of this formula, Freud enlarges upon it by explaining that all dreams are "an *attempt* to put aside a disturbance of sleep by means of a wish fulfillment."

The closing words of this chapter should be kept in mind: "... our study of the dream-work ... helps us to understand the puzzling symptoms which attract our interest to neuroses and psychoses. A coincidence of such a kind cannot fail to excite high hopes in us."

These hopes are stimulated by the fact that the dream exhibits all the characteristics of a psychosis and yet disappears spontaneously. Since this is the case, may we not hope to find a method for making a psychosis disappear? In the dream "the ego is detached from the reality of the external world" and invaded and overwhelmed by the internal world, particularly by the instinctual demands of the id. The weak ego of the psychotic corresponds to a certain extent to the sleeping ego of the dreamer. Unable to resist the pressure of the id and the superego it changes its organization, gives up one of its main functions, the testing of reality, and forms hallucinations and delusions.

Psychoanalytic treatment is guided by this insight. The psychoanalyst offers the weak ego of the patient help against the impact of the instinctual demands of the id and the moral demands of the superego. In exchange he exacts from the patient the promise of complete candor and confidence. Physician and patient form a pact with each other which constitutes the psychoanalytic situation. However, this pact can only be kept if at least a fragment of the ego is able to maintain some contact with reality—and the analyst. As the ego of the psychotic is unable to maintain such relations except for very brief periods, this pact will be ineffective with him "until we have discovered some other plan better suited for that purpose." (It seems to the reviewer that another such plan is now in the process of development.)

Since the ego of the neurotic is better able to maintain relations with reality than the psychotic, the neurotic can comply with the *fundamental rule* of free association and for a time be a cooperative patient. Soon, however, he will break this rule and complicate the psychoanalytic situation. This complication is caused by the phenomenon of *transference*. In transference the analyst becomes in the eyes of the patient a reincarnation of some important person or persons out of his past. The patient repeats his attitudes to them in his attitude to the analyst. The transference is *ambivalent,* positive and affectionate as well as negative and hostile. The positive transference is very helpful; at times it even stimulates a cure. The therapeutic success of the positive transference is probably due to the suggestive nature of this relation in the manner of hypnosis. This creates a great danger for the treatment since it might tempt the analyst to influence the patient according to his own ideals, "to make men in his own image." If he yields to this temptation he will repeat one of the mistakes of the parents, and will keep the patient in a state of dependence; "the analyst must respect his [the patient's] individuality."

Both the positive and the negative states of transference are repetitions of past relations to important persons. While positive transference brings about initial therapeutic success, negative transference undoes these successes. The danger of the states of transference lies in the fact that the patient mistakes them for realities and acts them out, instead of recognizing in them illusions reflecting the past.

Having established a positive transference, we try to obtain from the patient the unconscious material which "helps us to make constructions in regard to what happened to him but has been forgotten, as well as in regard to what is now happening in him without his understanding it." It sounds again like a warning against unfounded assumptions and "wild" interpretations when the author adds: "But we never fail in all this to make a severe distinction between *our* knowledge and *his* knowledge." The closer our constructions are to the forgotten real event and the nearer the patient himself has come to them through the preparatory work, the more easily will he accept them; ". . . *our* knowledge will then have become *his* knowledge as well."

The most difficult task in treatment is the overcoming of resistances. The *transference resistance* which has just been discussed arises during the treatment. The resistance which the ego has built up against the resurgence of certain elements of the unconscious id is inherent in the neurosis and is called *repression resistance*. It counteracts the aims of the analyst. Consequently a struggle ensues between the patient's ego and the analyst for admission into consciousness of the unconscious material and thus for giving the ego control over it. Whether the outcome of this struggle is acceptance of a hitherto repudiated instinctual demand or its definitive rejection after re-examination is a matter of indifference: "In either case a permanent danger has been disposed of, the compass of the ego has been extended and a wasteful expenditure of energy has been made unnecessary." Aside from the resistance opposing the aims of the treatment on the part of the ego, there are other resistances whose sources lie in the other provinces of the psychic apparatus. Among them appear two resistances which demand the closest attention. "They can both be included under the one description of 'need to be ill' or 'need to suffer'. . . ." Their sources, however, are different. One source stems from the sense of guilt and can be dealt with only by making it conscious and weakening the hostile superego; the second source of this "need to suffer" stems from the destructive instinct which becomes active and turns against the self when a defusion of instincts has taken place. This resistance is still very little understood.

After a masterly description of the neurotic's ego and of the changes brought about in it by psychoanalytic therapy, the author maintains that the final result of the treatment depends on *quantitative* relations, i.e., on the amount of energy which has to be mobilized in the ego in order to counteract the amount of energy represented by the various resistances, as well as on the degree of the inertia of these energies, the ability to sublimate, etc.

It is noteworthy that the author mentions, among other therapeutic factors, "order" which is established in the ego by psychoanalytic treatment. By order (and synthesis) is obviously meant the condition of bound energy which is active within the ego. In the neurotic, the free and mobile energy of the unconscious id has brought the processes within the ego down to the level of the primary process, as can be concluded from many signs. The ego behaves then in part as if it were the id. Treatment frees the ego from the primary process and transforms the freely mobile energy of the id into the bound energy of the ego, which corresponds psychologically to the *secondary process*. Order established in the ego means thus a solidified and unified ego, whose reactions do not occur at random any longer, but become intelligent, precise, clear and limited to a few but concentrated contents adapted to the exigencies of the actual situation.

Psychoanalysis began as a therapeutic technique, developed into a method of psychological investigation which opened new fields of research, and finally became a well-defined science dealing with the human mind.

The discoveries made with the help of this technique have shown that neurotics do not differ essentially from normal persons. Why, then, do they behave so differently and why do they suffer so much? In his preliminary answer to this question Freud says: "It is *quantitative disharmonies* that must be held responsible for the inadequacies and sufferings of neurotics." This explanation, however, is too general, since it "applies to every case of mental suffering," not to neurotic suffering specifically.

Analytic experience has taught that there is one particular instinctual demand and one specific period of life that must be considered in connection with the origin of neurotic sufferings. All neuroses are acquired in early childhood, up to the age of about six years, although there may be a prolonged period when they are latent. Traumatic neuroses alone are not acquired in childhood; or at least, as the author adds, their relation to infantile situations is as yet unknown. The origin of neurosis at such an early age may easily be understood if one considers the fact that the very young ego is weak and incapable of mastering traumatic events, i.e., certain external stimulations as well as internal excitations resulting from instinctual demands. Here again Freud calls our attention to the fact that "No human individual is spared such traumatic experiences; none escapes the repressions to which they give rise." These traumata and the various reactions to them, he further explains, are possibly necessary for the development of the primitive child into a civilized individual within a very short period. Although this development is made possible by hereditary disposition, it could not take place without additional parental influence, education which facilitates "the setting-up of repressions." Freud warns, "We must not forget, therefore, to include the influence of civilization among the determinants of neuroses. . . ." This warning refutes again the assertion that Freud neglects the cultural factor in the etiology of neurosis. He adds, however, that the cultural factor ought not to be overrated and that the biological factor of which it is a reflection, the prolonged dependence in childhood upon the parents, should not be neglected.

The predisposition of the ego to neurosis is thus determined by the interaction of three factors: its weakness and immaturity, the prolonged dependence of childhood, and parental (in a broader sense environmental) influences.

As to the instinctual factor, Freud states that theoretically it is conceivable that any instinct may be pathogenic, but experience contradicts this theoretical expectation and proves that it is the sexual instincts that play a predominant part in the etiology of neurosis. "The gap in our theory cannot at present be filled; and our decision is made more difficult by the fact that most of the impulses of sexual life are not of a purely erotic nature but arise from alloys of the erotic instinct with components of the destructive instinct." Having indicated a few factors which may be responsible for the pre-eminent role of the sexual instincts, he states briefly: "It is not psychology but biology that is responsible for the gap." He concludes: ". . . the weak point in the organization of the ego lies in its behavior toward the sexual function, as though the biological opposition between self-preservation and the preservation of the species there found psychological expression."

The specific nature of the sexual component instincts of early childhood is reflected in certain reactions of the immature ego to sexual experiences. Such experiences, which are more or less common, as seduction by an older child, witnessing parental intercourse, etc., force sexual impulses into certain channels. The ego becomes thereby oversensitized and represses those experiences immediately or as soon as they return as memories. The pressure of the repressed instinctual demands forms, then, the immediate precondition for a neurosis.

One or the other such experience may be accidental for the child, but not so the oedipus complex "which follows inevitably from the factor of the length of his dependence in childhood and of his life with his parents." This complex plays different roles in the boy and in the girl. Up to the period of the oedipus complex, there is almost no difference in the sexual behavior of boy and girl but "We are faced here by the great enigma of the biological fact of the duality of the sexes: for our knowledge it is something ultimate, it resists every attempt to trace it back to something else." However, each sex comprises some more or less distinguishable traits of the other sex which manifest themselves in psychological bisexuality. We do not know exactly what "male" and "female" are, but for the purpose of definition we consider everything that is "active" as male, and everything that is "passive" as female. Here again the reviewer believes it would be necessary to define what is understood by the terms "active" and "passive." In the oedipus complex "male" and "female" sex instincts meet, and the bisexual character of the love instinct finds expression.

The "prehistory" of the oedipus complex is very interesting. In the beginning of development there is no sharp differentiation between male and female; it evolves in stages. In the first phase, the oral, the mother suckles the child and takes care of its physical needs, thus becoming its first "seducer." "In these . . . relations lies the root of a mother's importance, unique, without parallel, laid down unalterably for a whole lifetime, as the first and the strongest love object and as a prototype of all later love relations—for both sexes." The author stresses here, as elsewhere, the fact that accidental experiences cannot change the phylogenetic foundations so "that it makes no difference whether a child has really sucked at the breast or has been brought up at the bottle. . . ."

When the boy—at the age of two or three—enters the phallic phase he acquires the castration complex. The castration threatened by mother or nurse in connection with the boy's masturbatory activities acts as a trauma which is immediately effective if he has already seen a female genital. If not, the trauma is latent and becomes effective when he first sees a female genital. In the acquisition of the castration complex the boy "experiences the severest trauma of his youthful existence." Never forgetting the influence of phylogenesis the author adds in a footnote: "The possibility cannot be excluded that a phylogenetic memory-trace may contribute to the extraordinarily terrifying effect of the threat—a memory-trace from the prehistory of the human family . . .," castration performed by the primeval father.

As a result of the threat of castration, the boy gives up the practice of masturbation, but not the fantasies which have accompanied it. In these fantasies he identifies himself alternately with father and mother. "Derivatives and modified products of these early masturbatory fantasies usually make their way into his later ego, and play a part in the formation of his character." The castration complex also determines the formation of the manifold neurotic symptoms. The severity of the neurosis will, however, again depend upon *quantitative* relations.

The "castration complex" of the girl is different. She has no fear of castration, of course, but has a "penis envy" which influences her whole development. The formation of her character or a neurosis may be determined by her efforts at compensating herself for her "defect." She resents her lack of a penis and holds her mother responsible for it. In her resentment, she rejects her mother as a love object and, in normal development, identifies with her and loves the father. She enters the oedipus complex as the boy does.

The difference between the male and the female oedipus complex is thus clear: in the boy the threat of castration brings the oedipus complex to an end; in the girl it is the lack of a penis that drives her into the oedipus situation.

Freud closes this chapter with the significant remark: "If we ask an analyst what his experience has shown to be the mental structure least accessible to influence in his patients, the answer will be: in a woman, her desire for a penis, and in a man, his feminine attitude toward his own sex, a precondition of which would necessarily be the loss of his penis."

In the first two parts of his book, the author combines experiment with logical thinking. He states empirical facts and draws from them logical conclusions. In the last part, he makes a most condensed summary of his doctrines.

The discovery of the unconscious, and the hypothesis of the psychic apparatus extended in space, made possible the understanding of the workings of the human mind, and put psychology on a scientific basis. The author compares the method of psychoanalysis to the methods of the scientists which never reach the ultimate reality hidden behind the phenomena accessible to our perceptions. As the physicist, with the help of his instruments, draws conclusions about the nature of the unknown reality, so does the psychoanalyst: ". . . we deduce a number of processes which are in themselves 'unknowable' and insert them among the processes of which we are conscious. And if, for instance, we say: 'At this point an unconscious memory intervened,' what this means is: 'At this point something occurred of which we are totally unable to form a conception, but which, if it had entered consciousness, could only have been described in such and such a way.' "

As to the psychic apparatus itself, he states he cannot give a complete picture of all its functions because not all of them have been thoroughly investigated. Recapitulating briefly the structure of this apparatus, he adds some details omitted before. Discussing the id and the organic instincts operating within it, he says that these "are differentiated from one another by their relation to organs or systems of organs." This seems to the reviewer to imply that the organs or systems of organs produce specific instincts or that the instincts are determined in their way of expression and in their aim by the structure of the organ through which they seek to express themselves. Furthermore, the id has no anxiety "or it would perhaps be more correct to say that, though it can produce the sensory elements of anxiety, it cannot make use of them." Up to the publication of *Inhibition, Symptom and Anxiety* (1926b), Freud had expressed the belief that libido can be converted into anxiety. In that book he dropped this theory and declared that anxiety can only be produced by the ego as a signal of danger. In this *Outline* he seems to assume that single sensory elements of anxiety can arise in the id, but that only the ego can integrate or synthesize all those sensory perceptions in the affect of anxiety and make use of it for self-protection. Thus the inceptions of anxiety are unconscious. It is in accord with this conception of the beginning of anxiety that, as the author states, the id "detects with extraordinary clarity certain changes in its interior, especially oscillations in the tension of its instinctual needs, oscillations which become conscious as feelings in the pleasure-unpleasure series." In fact, I have become convinced that the deeper the analysis penetrates, the more the analyst can see that the patient knows (perceives) more of the anatomy and physiology of his organs than we assume. Although it is not known by what means the perception of feelings—coenesthetic feelings and feelings of pleasure-unpleasure—comes about in the id, one thing is certain, namely, that the id is governed by the pleasure principle. Not only the id but also the ego obeys this principle. The ego can modify, not nullify, it. Here the author raises the important question whether the pleasure principle can ever be overcome. Then he continues: "The consideration that the pleasure principle requires a reduction, or perhaps ultimately the extinction, of the tension of the instinctual needs (that is, a state of *Nirvana*) leads to problems that are still unexamined in the relations between the pleasure principle and the two primal forces, Eros and the death instinct."

The reviewer suggested that the application of the principle of repetition compulsion to the sexual instincts as well as to the death instinct is possible from an economic although not from a genetic point of view. The satisfaction of the pleasure principle leads to reduction of tensions, which could also include the state of Nirvana (in Sanskrit literally "blowing out," "extinction"; in Buddhism Nirvana means extinction of all desires and passions).[1]

While the id is in no direct contact with the external world, the other agency of the psychic apparatus, the ego, is in direct contact with this world. However, it is not exclusively dependent on it, but it is also influenced by the id. The ego strives to free itself from this influence by "raising the processes in the id to a higher dynamic level (perhaps by transforming freely mobile into bound energy, such as corresponds to the preconscious condition)." This can only mean, the reviewer thinks, that the primary process of the unconscious id is changed into the secondary process of the preconscious ego when unconscious material becomes conscious, when the chaotic and unorganized id cedes some of its energies to the ego, thus contributing to its higher organization and order. When this transformation of energy occurs in the psychic apparatus, there develop several functions of the ego, such as the synthetic function of the ego, its selective function (perceiving and excluding certain stimuli), the reality testing (distinction between external and internal perception), the intellective activity, and anxiety as a signal of danger.

Danger threatens from the external as well as from the internal world. The defense against the dangers coming from the external world is a far easier task than that against the internal dangers. Danger is a relative conception dependent on quantitative relations between external stimuli or internal instinctual demands, on the one hand, and the strength of the ego, on the other. The ego of the little child is too weak to cope with the libidinal demands. It represses them, but the repression proves to be inadequate in later life when the "reanimation of sexual life brings a reinforcement to the repudiated instinctual demands. From the biological standpoint, then, it may be said that the ego comes to grief over the task of mastering the excitations of the first sexual period, at a time when its immaturity makes it incompetent to do so. We recognize the essential precondition of neuroses in this lagging of ego de-

[1] *The Shorter Oxford English Dictionary.* New York: The Clarendon Press.

velopment behind libidinal development...." Yet, these repressions in childhood seem indispensable for the cultural development because they enforce sublimations.

It is characteristic of Freud that he never loses sight of the implications of his findings: he sees the possibilities of both normal and pathological development from the same starting point.

When reality has become too painful to bear or the instincts have become excessively intensified, the ego withdraws from reality. This withdrawal results in a psychosis. The detachment from reality, however, is only partial. "We may probably take it as being generally true that what occurs in all such cases is a *split* in the mind. Two mental attitudes have been formed instead of a single one—one, the normal one, which takes account of reality, and another which under the influence of the instincts detaches the ego from reality. The two exist alongside each other."

Bleuler postulated a split in the ego for the Kraepelinian *dementia praecox* and therefore renamed it *schizophrenia*. Freud, however, maintained that a split in the ego is not characteristic of psychoses only, since it also occurs in neuroses and perversions. Having shown that there is no essential difference between what we call psychic "normality" and "neurosis," he now also lowered the barrier between neurosis and psychosis, both having in common the split in the ego.

This fact proves to be the basis for any therapy. For, if the ego were *completely* detached from reality there would be no possibility of establishing any contact with the patient and of influencing him. In psychosis as well as in neurosis the rejection of reality is only a half-measure. "The rejection [of reality] is always supplemented by an acceptance; two contrary and independent attitudes always arise and this produces the fact of a split in the ego." The treatment always takes advantage of that part of the ego which has remained untouched by the pathological process and accepts reality. With this intact part of the ego a contact can be established. The facility with which this can be done depends on quantitative relations. As the ego of the neurotic is less afflicted than the ego of the psychotic, it is easier to get in contact with the former than with the latter.

The split in the ego, naturally, is reflected in the behavior and the two attitudes of the patient: "... in that case, however, one of them belongs to the ego and the opposing one, which is repressed, belongs to the id. The difference between the two cases is essentially a topographical or structural one and it is not always easy to decide in the individual case with which of the two possibilities one is dealing."

This last remark seems to the reviewer particularly important for practical reasons. It is true that first the resistances or defenses of the ego should be interpreted. But as it is not always possible to say what belongs to the preconscious ego and what to the unconscious id, we are often forced to interpret the material in the order in which it presents itself. By interpreting preconscious defenses exclusively we run the risk of overlooking the unconscious id.

The relations within the structure of the psychic apparatus are more complicated than is apparent in the presentation up to this point. This complication is caused by the superego, which begins to develop at about the age of five years. Then the ego, in its function as a mediator between the external and the internal world, must also take into account the exigencies of the superego. Though the superego becomes an integral part of the ego, it represents in the latter a part at least of the external world, the parents. The severity of the superego "corresponds to the strength which is used in fending off the temptation of the oedipus complex. . . . During the whole of man's later life it represents the influence of his childhood." In the superego are accumulated the experiences of the cultural past. Faithful to his conviction about inheritance of psychic attitudes, the author states: "Some of the cultural acquisitions have undoubtedly left a deposit behind in the *id*; much of what is contributed by the superego will awaken an echo in the id; many of the child's new experiences will be intensified because they are repetitions of some primeval phylogenetic experience." It seems as if Freud saw and felt in one man all mankind.

At the end of the book we find a striking comment: "In the emergence of the superego we have before us, as it were, an example of the way in which the present is changed into the past. . . ." We cannot help but think here of the transference, in which the analyst is transformed into an object of the past.

The *Outline* was not completed; nobody knows how much more the author wished to say. But what he has said is enough to stimulate thinking for generations to come.

TRANSFERENCE AND REALITY

A PATIENT OF MINE was from the beginning of treatment very critical of me; whatever I did or said was wrong. She found fault with
everything. She corrected me constantly, trying to teach me what
to do, how to behave, what to think and what to say—not only
what to say, but also how to say it. Because I could not give in to
her attempts to re-educate me, she felt hurt and angry. Although
she soon recognized that she expected literally to find her father in
me, she did not change her attitude. The more conscious the attachment to her father became to her, the more she demanded that I
change to the likeness of his image within her.

What did this attitude express? Certainly, it did not reflect the
phenomenon that we call transference. It revealed merely her
readiness for transference. This readiness obviously produced two
attitudes in her: first, an expectation of finding her *real* father in
the analyst; secondly, the wish to change the *real* person of the
analyst into her father as she imagined him. As this desire could
not be realized, she suffered constantly from disappointments,
frustrations and anger. This situation led to conflicts with her
analyst on a *quasi real basis*. Thus it is evident that she did not
"transfer" her emotions from her father to her analyst, but rather
that she *attempted* to transform her analyst into her father. The
particular fixation to her father created the wish to find his reincarnation in the person of the analyst, and, since her desire to
transform the latter into a person *identical* with her father could
not be fulfilled, the attempts to establish a working transference
were futile. Thus transference often breaks down not because of
primary aggression, which is the driving force of the so-called nega-

---

Reprinted from *The International Journal of Psycho-Analysis*, 32:1-9, 1951.

tive transference, but because of disappointments and frustrated efforts at establishing an identity of present images with past ones.

What is transference? In spite of disagreement on the part of some of my colleagues, I still agree with Dr. de Saussure that transference is a projection. The term "projection" means that the patient's inner and unconscious relations with his first libidinal objects are externalized. In the transference situation the analyst tries to unmask the projections or externalizations whenever they appear during the treatment. What part identification plays in transference will be seen later.

As a matter of fact, the word "transference" is self-explanatory. It says that the patient displaces emotions belonging to an unconscious representation of a repressed object to a mental representation of an object of the external world. This object represented within the ego is the analyst, on whom emotions and ideas belonging to the repressed unconscious objects are projected. The repressed objects belong to the past, mostly to the patient's early childhood, and are thus unreal. Trying to substitute a real object (for example, the analyst) for the unreal one, the patient is bound to run into misunderstandings, to become confused and to suffer frustrations. The split of the personality and the resulting incongruity of the drives is obvious: the essential repressed wish is unconscious and belongs to the past, its preconscious derivatives having undergone certain rationalizations are projected on external objects and, when perceived, become conscious. If, for instance, a grown boy is excessively attached to his mother, he is not satisfied with the kind of gratification her substitute offers him in reality, but expects unconsciously those gratifications that he has experienced in the past.[1]

---

[1] In the discussion of this paper Dr. Hartmann and Dr. Loewenstein disagreed with me as to the role of the projection mechanism in the transference situation. They maintained that in transference only the mechanism of displacement is at work. The term "displacement," we know, means that the psychic stress or affect can be shifted from one element to another *within* the psychic systems. In transference the individual confuses the *mental* image of his father or mother with the real picture of the analyst and behaves as if the analyst were his father or mother. Of course, we recognize in this mechanism a displacement of affects; but, as the external object (the analyst) is treated like a mental image (father or mother), there is no doubt that the mental image is projected onto the analyst. Besides, Freud maintains that processes within the ego can be perceived (with a few exceptions) only with the help of projections.

If, in transference, projection of internal and unconscious images onto real objects is taking place, then the first patient's attitude can hardly be called transference. She did not project the image of her father onto the analyst; she tried to change her analyst according to the image of her father.

The next example is different. A patient was unable to understand me when she was lying on the couch with her eyes *open*. When she closed her eyes she could understand me; it then seemed to her as if she were hearing a ghost talking, and my voice sounded like the voice of her dead father. This illusion had almost the intensity of a hallucination.

The difference in respect to transference between this patient and the first one is striking: the first patient only *tried* to transform her analyst into her father, she tried to change a real person into an image of the past, she attempted to make the analyst conform with her memories of her father, to establish an identical picture of both; the second patient *succeeded* in getting an identical picture of her father through the medium of a real person, the analyst, to such an extent that the analyst's voice became her father's voice; she almost had a hallucination of her father. In the first case the effort to effect a transference failed; in the second it was successful. The second patient's feelings for the analyst in the psychoanalytic situation revived the repressed image of her father which she projected on the analyst, so that the two became almost identical. In fact, at times father and analyst became confused in her mind. The first patient tried unsuccessfully to transform the person of the present into the person of the past, whereas the second patient experienced the person of the past in the person of the present. Present objects and past images became identical in her mind.

The tendency to establish "identical pictures" is perhaps better illustrated by a fragment of the second patient's dream: water was pouring out through a hole in her refrigerator. *She held her hand under the hole in order to stop the flow but the hole sucked her hand in so that it hurt.*

The day residue consisted of the fact that the refrigerator was out of order and that the patient feared an overflow of water in her kitchen. The evening preceding this dream she had a visitor with whom she talked about sex education. The visitor told her that she forbade her little daughter to put her hand into her nose or mouth because a disease might enter her body. The patient was shocked and thought that this little girl later in life would think that a disease would enter her body when she had sexual intercourse. She herself suffered from severe phobias of touching, among them a fear of infection through the vagina during her pregnancy. Long before her marriage she was afraid of the pain during intercourse and at childbirth. She asserted that the pain in the dream was very *real*. In the same session she told me that on her way to my office she had thought she would even agree to my cutting off her arm if only I could help her to get well. At this point two childhood recollections came to her mind; first, that when she used to stuff her finger into her nose she felt pain, and secondly, that *a woman once told her of another little girl who put her hand in a toilet bowl and had her arm caught in the pipe of the bowl* because of the strong suction when the toilet upstairs was flushed. The patient stressed that the pain in her arm felt in the dream persisted when she was awake.

What happened here? The real and conscious fear of her kitchen being flooded by the leaking refrigerator, and the preconscious ideas and fears of her masturbatory activities stimulated by the conversation with her visitor revived a picture of her childhood which she dreaded because it reminded her of masturbation and the fears connected with it. In other words, a real expectation produced a regression and revived a picture from childhood which, in the dream, acquired qualities of reality. Freud calls this phenomenon the "identity of perceptions" (*Wahrnehmungsidentität*). This means that an actual perception of an idea revives old, unconscious, repressed ideas or emotions to such an extent that they are perceived as actual images although their meaning is not recognized by the conscious psychic apparatus; thus present and old ideas and emotions become identical for a while. This tendency to revive old ideas and perceptions and to make the present coincide with the past, forms the basis of the phenomenon which is called "acting out."

Another example may perhaps be even more instructive. About eight months after the conclusion of his analysis, a patient asked me to see him immediately because of sudden panic and insomnia.

I do not wish to go into the details of this complicated symptom. I wish only to say that the cause of this sudden panic and insomnia was his newborn son. When his wife came home with the infant from the hospital, she put it, as arranged in advance, in the room adjoining the parents' bedroom. For the night she wanted to close the door between the two rooms, but he wanted it open in order to hear every sound in the child's room. Since she, nevertheless, closed the door, he became frantic, overwhelmed by panic, and unable to sleep, trying to listen to all the sounds that seemed to him to emanate from the baby's room. This condition, which had lasted for several days by the time he came to see me, gave me the opportunity to remind him that he had had quite a number of fears in different periods of his life. I drew his attention to one particular fear of his childhood: frequently, when his parents were not home at night, he was seized by the idea that his rabbits out in the yard were being killed, and he insisted that his nurse go and find out whether they were still alive. When I mentioned this, he remembered another fear of his early childhood whose importance he could only now fully comprehend. This fear concerned the door of his room which faced his mother's room across the hallway. When his door stood open he could see whether his mother was at home; then he felt secure and could go to sleep. But when the door was closed, he felt alone, deserted by his mother, and therefore could not sleep and became panicky. Throughout his childhood he feared that his mother would leave him. About the age of five, he tried repeatedly to run away from home, pretending to leave his mother, thus reversing his fear of being deserted by her.

The panic caused by the closing of his child's door thus betrayed his infantile fear of being left alone by his mother. The urgent desire to keep the door open reflected the ritual of his childhood to keep his own door open. The difference between the actual and the infantile situation lies only in the fact that the subject is changed: instead of himself as a child being anxious about his mother's love, he was now as a mature man anxious about his son's safety and well-being. The situation was thus reversed; the insomnia and anxiety were, however, unchanged. It is obvious that the patient projected one part of his ego onto his son and that he identified another part with his mother. His son incarnated himself, and he incarnated his mother. Both these representations were, of course, unconscious. It is probable that his infantile wish to see what was going on in his mother's room was overdetermined; the actual panic might also reflect the one felt while overhearing the noises of the primal scene. This, however, would not change the meaning of our patient's reaction to his son; on the contrary, it would only broaden our interpretation.

For the purpose of our discussion the bare fact that our patient attempted to re-establish in the present a situation as it existed in childhood is more significant than is the meaning of the panic. What he wanted was simple enough: he wished to have the door open. The fulfillment of this wish would have repeated in actuality the infantile situation of the open door, and would have spared him anxiety.

This example shows—as do many cases—that the tendency to "transfer" infantile experiences into reality and to act them out can be observed not only in the transference situation but also independently of it. *An urge to establish identity of perceptions through repetition of past experiences is thus, in conformity with Freud's ideas, undeniable.*

Now we can see that the establishment of identical perceptions is an act of projection as well as of identification. Identification, as we know, has several meanings. One of them expresses a community of feelings and thoughts in a group formation. The analysis is a group formation of two persons. The common goal of analyst and patient is helping, i.e., curing the patient. This alone would suffice to establish an identification. Identification, however, is also a regressive substitute for love, if the love object in the external world becomes a part of the ego. In analysis the common goal of analyst and patient leads first to identification of the patient with the analyst and further to the revival of the deeper identifications with the parents. Hardly has this identification taken place when the patient tries to lodge with the analyst the reactivated residues of the infantile relationship with the parents. This can be accomplished only by means of projection. It seems thus as if projection helped to find the lost object in the outside world, as if the analyst were a screen on which the patient projected his unconscious pictures. In fact, when we reach certain depths in analysis, it is difficult to discern between identification and projection. It seems as if the boundaries of the ego were removed, as Federn would say, in which state the subject feels as if he were a part of the external world and the external world a part of himself. This corresponds to states of transitivism which Freud (1912-1913), in *Totem and Taboo,* ascribed to the animistic phase of human development. Later he referred to similar states as "oceanic feelings." States of this kind can, not too infrequently, be observed in those psychoanalytic sessions during which the patient is very deeply immersed in his unconscious id.

Although transference makes use of both mechanisms, identification and projection, one fact remains unchanged: the *tendency* to establish identity of old and new perceptions.

The tendency to bring about "identity of perceptions" seems to satisfy the repetition compulsion which, as is well known, is the driving force of many a psychic phenomenon. Compelling the individual to preserve the past, it is a conservative principle. And yet, as soon as it is coupled with the phenomenon of transference, it becomes a progressive element, in the sense, of course, of psychic topography. This statement may require some amplification. An actual event reactivates an old repressed one which, on its part, tries to replace the new experience; this can best be observed in dreams. The attempt to relive repressed experiences in actual ones is only in part successful, as the censorship of the dream or the resistance of the ego tries to disguise them. According to our theoretical conception of the psychic apparatus, this fact can be expressed also in the following way: certain perceptions and sensations produced by stimuli of daily life undergo historical and topical regressions to corresponding old, repressed, unconscious experiences. As soon as the cathexis (i.e., the charge of psychic energy) of the actual experience reaches the psychic representations of the repressed and fixated experiences in the unconscious id, it strengthens and reactivates them. These reactivated unconscious representations now manifest a tendency to "progression," i.e., a tendency to reach the perceptual and motor end of the psychic apparatus. Here they give the perceptions of actual events and the sensations produced by them an unconscious tinge; the ego behaves as if it were the id. Through this process the analyst, in the transference situation, becomes the representative of the objects of the unconscious strivings.

The readiness for transference exists, as indicated before, independently of the psychoanalytic situation. The mere fact that a patient decides to seek help from an analyst (or other therapist) furthers this phenomenon. Furthermore, the analyst's request for free associations stimulates reproduction of old memories, i.e., of mental repetition of repressed experiences. In addition, the repetition of old images stirs up emotions which once accompanied them. These old and yet new, actual, emotions try to attach themselves to the only real object available, the psychoanalyst, and to find an outlet in wishes, fantasies and actions directed toward him. It seems as if a new experience could not be assimilated—in the sense of the synthetic function of the ego—unless it found its way to the old patterns. Therefore it is not surprising that transference occurs also in other than psychoanalytic therapies. The psychoanalyst and the nonpsychoanalyst differ in their treatment and understanding of this phenomenon, in that the former treats the transference symptoms as illusions while the latter takes them at their face value, i.e., as realities.

The transference proceeds according to the need to assimilate actual experiences in such a way that their perception either conforms to or becomes identical with repressed unconscious ideas. What has been once experienced—particularly in childhood—seems to form an indelible imprint in the unconscious from which patterns develop. These patterns may be dormant for a long time and become active only under certain circumstances. The latency of these patterns, or their state of unconsciousness, is responsible for the fact that the meaning of the present experiences following these patterns remains unconscious. However, it must be added that complete gratification of the need for "identity of perceptions" is not achieved as a rule, except in dreams, delusions and hallucinations. In the transference situation the unconscious pattern overshadows the conscious perception of an actual event and produces an illusion, while in dreams or psychoses the same pattern or image forms hallucinations. Hence illusions can be reality-tested; hallucinations cannot, or can only in part.

It might appear as if the concept of transference and the concept of repetition compulsion had been confused here, but this is certainly not the case. In so far as a repetition of previous states takes place in the transference situation, transference is a manifestation of the repetition compulsion. In so far, however, as in transference the wishes and drives are directed toward the objects of the external world, though through the repetition of old experiences, transference is independent of the repetition compulsion. Repetition compulsion points to the past, transference to actuality (reality) and thus, in a sense, to the future. Repetition compulsion tries to fixate, to "freeze," the old psychic reality, hence it becomes a regressive force; transference attempts to reanimate these "frozen" psychic formations, to discharge their energy and to satisfy them in a new and present reality, and thus becomes a progressive force.

I would say that transference is like Janus, two-faced, with one face turned to the past, the other to the present. Through transference the patient lives the present in the past and the past in the present. In his speech he betrays a lack of feeling for the sequence of events, which is conceived as time. This lack, however, is not characteristic only of the transference to the analyst. Almost all neurotics are confused in relation to the element of time, whether they are in treatment or not. Many patients in analysis can identify recent events only after elucidation of childhood experiences; others condense experiences from different periods of their life into one event and can keep them apart only after thorough analysis, etc. The fact that the patient loses the sense of time in the transference situation is not surprising, as it corresponds to the phenomenon that repressed unconscious events, events of the past, are experienced in the present as if no time had elapsed. Indeed, we know from Freud that the unconscious is timeless.

That past and present flow together may seem an obstacle to recognizing the past in the present. But closer examination shows that through reanimation of the representations of repressed objects in the transference situation, the ego gains direct access to its childhood experiences; not the entire ego, of course, but only that part which has not been altered by the repression and has remained intact. This intact ego now has an opportunity to confront its feelings for and expectations from the analyst with the situation in the past, in childhood, and to compare them with one another as if the whole life were spread in front of the inner eye on a single plane. As soon as the patient becomes conscious of his transference, he gains the ability to assess his actual feelings in relation to the infantile situation. This helps him to distinguish between the images returning from the past and the perceptions of external, actual objects, and thus to *test reality* better than before. Some patients accept reality then as it is; others do not. The first patient discussed here did not accept reality; she could not give up the peculiar attachment to her father. She would rather have changed the world than change herself by accepting the analyst as an object of the outside world. The second patient was able to see that the analyst represented a new edition of her father, an edition which she herself created. The third patient became aware that his son represented himself as a child. It is evident that divesting the actual experiences in the transference of the influence of repressed images enhances reality testing. If, as often happens, in the course of free associations the patient produces images which have the intensity of real perceptions, or are hallucinations, the analyst may almost always be sure that he is dealing with actual memories. When the patient accepts such "hallucinations" as memories, he loses the incentive to project the memories (unconscious images) into the external world and then to perceive them as realities.

As indicated before, patients try to "act out" their repressed unconscious in the transference, by repeating certain patterns of their life. They bend reality, so to speak, in the transference situation. Sometimes the repetitions are helpful for the analysis; sometimes they make the analysis difficult. Then they form certain types of resistances. Freud said once that in the resistances the patient reveals his character. A very simple example may illustrate this fact. A patient showed from the very beginning an astonishing willingness for and understanding of the analysis. His associations flowed easily, he produced important recollections, and so on. He continued in this way for a fairly long period, yet the analysis did not make any progress, until we found that his mother used to ask him to tell her everything he thought and did during the day. Our patient confided all his thoughts to her until late in adolescence. It gave him great pleasure when she was talking with him at night while sitting on his bed, and he could see, through her thin nightgown, the contours of her body, particularly of her breasts. He pretended to tell her everything, but the secret of his sexual fantasies about her he kept to himself. Displaying similar behavior in his analysis, he pretended to tell the truth; in fact, tried to fool his analyst as he had his mother. In his behavior with other people he was sincere yet reserved and distrustful so that he never had really close friends. He was a lonesome man.

As soon as he became conscious of the fact that he was "transferring" his relationship to his mother into his relationship with his analyst, he understood that by doing so he defeated his own purpose, the success of his treatment. From then on he was sincere with his analyst, except at times when other resistances with different backgrounds arose. In other words, through the act of consciousness, i.e., through the perception of unconscious strivings of the id, the ego acquired the faculty to control the repetition of these strivings and to adjust itself to reality—which in this case was represented by the patient's will to recovery.

Not always, as in this example, is a character trait formed by a compromise between contrasting strivings. There are other formations of character traits. In this context, however, it is relevant to point out that contrasting strivings frequently remain separate, and alternately find expression. This alternation of feelings permeates also the patient's attitude to his analyst. At times, he is full of love for him, submissive, admires him; at other times he is aggressive, stubborn, defiant, etc. These alternating attitudes, this struggle between masochism and sadism, submission and rebellion, dependence and independence seem to repeat previous states representing a developmental pattern. One needs only to observe the development of children, from infancy to maturity, in order to gain the impression of the constant struggle between the retarding tendencies of the repetition compulsion, crystallized in fixations, dependency on the one hand, and the hunger, avidity for new experiences and impressions, for independence, on the other hand —a struggle which finally leads to adaptation to and mastering of reality and instinctual drives. In puberty the struggle between the strivings of the id and the needs of the ego becomes very intense and finally leads to the formation of a normal personality. However, if a disturbance has occurred in the course of this prolonged and complicated development, and the patient is in analysis, the same struggle continues in relation to the analyst in the transference situation, where the course of the development is accelerated and usually brought to an end. In other words, when the patient recognizes the attempts to relive the past in the present, he usually gives them up or modifies them. In this process the transference, which creates an artificial reality, is unmasked, and this amounts, in a sense, to a re-education. Indeed, from its very beginnings analysis was considered a kind of re-education.

Through transference the patient is re-educated not only in respect to the instincts and surroundings but also in respect to the superego. In order to understand this, we must again turn to the starting point of the analysis. Then the question arises as to why the mere decision to turn for help to an analyst (therapist or priest) creates, in advance, transference. The answer is very simple: in the unconscious id one asks only father or mother for help. The form of the transference is, therefore, predetermined by the patient's relations to his father and mother. The relationship between patient and analyst becomes very similar to that in hypnosis. In obedience to the hypnotist's suggestions the hypnotized person can even have hallucinations, positive as well as negative ones. The influence of the hypnotist is so overwhelming that he may force the hypnotized person to give up temporarily the reality-testing faculty. In the heat of transference the analyst has powers similar to those of the hypnotist, but uses them for opposite purposes: namely, to teach the patient reality testing. Originally, the hypnotist no more than the analyst possesses such power; it is only the patient who has invested him with it. And how did the patient obtain this power? From his father—through identification with him—would be the answer. This identification led to the differentiation of the superego within the ego. Freud says that the superego is the heir to the oedipus complex. According to him, the hypnotist is identified with the ego ideal of the hypnotized person. As later on the term "ego ideal" was replaced by the term "superego," we may say as well that the hypnotist is identified with the superego of the hypnotized. Similarly does the patient in analysis make his analyst identical with his father through the medium of his superego. But since the analyst is perceived as an object of the external world, now equipped with the father's attributes, the patient must have also projected onto him parts of his own super-ego. This could explain how the analyst obtains the enormous power over the patient. Through analysis of the transference the analyst, however, tries to divest himself of the power granted him by the patient.

There is much more to be said about the parallelism between the state of hypnosis and the psychoanalytic situation. I shall, however, limit myself to the discussion of a few points only.

The following is based on Freud's ideas about hypnosis. He maintains that hypnosis is a group formation of two persons. This group, like any other group, is held together by libidinal ties. In love, these ties are composed of directly sexual instincts and of sexual instincts inhibited in their aims, i.e., desexualized. In hypnosis these ties are only of an aim-inhibited nature. Hypnosis, therefore, corresponds to love with the exclusion of directly sexual instincts. The same humility, the same compliance, the same absence of criticism, the same overestimation in regard to the hypnotist can be observed as in the state of being in love in regard to the loved person. If directly sexual instincts get the upper hand, the group formation is destroyed. The same is true of the psycho-analytic situation as it is likewise a group formation of two. In hypnosis the identification with the hypnotist is a regressive sub-stitute for libidinal ties in the form of desexualized, aim-inhibited sexual attachments to the subject's parents. These ties form, ac-cording to Ferenczi (1909), the basis for the transference readiness or suggestibility. The hypnotist, Freud says, stimulates this readi-ness by claiming to be in possession of mysterious powers by which he can put the subject to sleep. In fact, as Freud stresses, there is something uncanny about hypnosis and hypnotist. We know from him that the uncanny represents something old and familiar which has been repressed but is on the verge of returning from the un-conscious (Freud, 1919). Upon the hypnotist's order to sleep, the subject withdraws his interest from the outside world and falls asleep. His sleep is, however, a partial one, a dreamlike sleep, be-cause the subject, though detached from the external world, never-theless concentrates his libidinal cathexes on the hypnotist. In this way the hypnotist establishes the *rapport* with the hypnotized person. In the psychoanalytic situation the patient is removed from contact with the external world but remains in contact with his analyst—conditions similar to those in hypnosis.

By putting the subject to sleep, Freud (1921) says, "the hypnotist awakens in the subject a portion of his archaic inheritance which also made him compliant towards his parents and which had experienced an individual re-animation in his relation to his father; what is thus awakened is the idea of a paramount and dangerous personality, towards whom only a passive-masochistic attitude is possible, to whom one's will has to be surrendered—while to be alone with him, 'to look him in the face,' appears a hazardous enterprise. It is only in some such way as this," Freud adds, "that we can picture the relation of the individual member of the primal horde to the primal father. . . ."

Hypnosis is thus a precipitate of archaic libidinal ties of mankind in the unconscious id of the present-day individual. Suggestion is a part of hypnosis and helps to establish the rapport (transference) between hypnotist and hypnotized. This archaic relationship seems to be repeated in the psychoanalytic situation. The analyst promises the patient help as if he were in possession of magic powers —and the latter overestimates and believes him. He is taboo to the patient as the primal father is to the primitive individual. The analyst is free and has his own will, while the patient has to submit to the psychoanalytic rules laid down by the analyst. The analyst sits upright, while the patient lies passively on a couch. The analyst is silent most of the time, while the patient tells him everything, gives him his unconscious material, as if performing a sacrificial act. The analyst is omnipotent, he is fearless and can look at the patient, while the patient is afraid of him and is not permitted to see him, like the primitive man who dare not look in the face of the primal father.

As the hypnotist represents the inner and historical reality of the hypnotized, so does the analyst represent the psychological reality of the patient. This relationship between hypnotist and hypnotized leads the latter to replace the external reality by the historical and psychic reality. The ego of the hypnotized person thus makes a regression to a primitive stage of development where indeed the psychic reality replaces the external reality and where the primary process replaces the secondary process.

A similar change occurs in the transference situation: while the patient is on the couch, his ego becomes temporarily weakened as does the hypnotized person's ego. As soon as the patient complies with the analyst's demand to give up selective, logical thinking and to abandon himself to free associations, the secondary process is supplanted by the primary one; an important function of the ego, reality testing, is temporarily suspended.

This, however, is valid only for the analytic session itself in which the patient is detached from external reality as is the hypnotized patient in hypnosis. In order to avoid any misunderstanding, it ought to be stressed that in the course of the analysis the patient's ego is strengthened, as the analyst endeavors to make the patient face the external reality and to free him of the dependence upon himself, in so far as he, the analyst, represents the patient's inner reality.

One can imagine what mastery over his narcissism the analyst must have gained not to be intoxicated by the powers granted him by the patient.

The fact that the patient's attitude toward reality is to a certain degree disturbed in neurosis—and in transference—is caused, among other factors, by an excessively strict and critical superego. Through the projection of his superego on the analyst, the patient frees himself in a sense from his superego which is now represented by the analyst. The analyst's superego is supposed to be neutral, usually milder than the patient's own restrictive superego. As the patient identifies at the same time with the analyst, he exchanges, as it were, his own superego—the father's moral standards—for the analyst's. The result of this exchange is that the patient learns not only to cope with the internal reality as represented by instincts and conscience, but also to accept the external world according to its full "reality value"; one is almost tempted to say "at its face value." The fact that "reality changes" are accomplished also under the influence of the superego, can be understood when we take the following considerations into account. In his *Group Psychology and the Analysis of the Ego,* Freud (1921) ascribed the reality-testing faculty to the ego ideal. In *The Ego and the Id* he retracted this statement and ascribed the reality-testing faculty to the ego (Freud, 1923a). In hypnosis this faculty is disturbed by the intervention of the hypnotist who is a representative of the patient's superego (or ego ideal). It is true that the hypnotized person seems in some way to perceive objects of the external world even in case of negative hallucinations, but this does not alter the fact that the hypnotist can at will suppress the reality-testing faculty of the subject's ego. I once made the statement, and this last fact supports it, that conscious perceptions of the ego must be sanctioned by the superego in order to acquire qualities of full, uncontested reality. This assumption could be helpful in understanding why, in addition to the undoing of repressions, changes in the patient's superego also enhance the reality-testing faculty of the ego.[2]

In conclusion: it seems to me that the tendency to establish identity of perceptions is illustrated in an impressive way by the phenomena of hypnosis and transference. Even the projection of the superego on the analyst proves this thesis. Through this projection the "father image" is externalized and then perceived as a quasi reality; in a sense, the father exists now in the external world (though disguised in the shape of the analyst) where he originally existed.

As long as the father is not recognized in the analyst, the identity of perceptions is latent. Through the analysis of the transference it becomes manifest. Then it diminishes in the same proportion as the repressed becomes conscious. However, it happens that people with successful, solid repressions are well adapted to reality. Their perceptions of actual events are not colored by repressed experiences, although they may appear emotionally inhibited. On the other hand, this tendency seems to gain control of the perceptive end of the psychic apparatus in dreams, hallucinations and delusions.

Further discussion of this topic would lead to new problems which exceed the scope of this paper.

[2] I would like to suggest the following: if hypnosis can really be considered an archaic heritage of mankind and suggestion (or transference) a part of it, then we are justified in assuming that the tendency to establish identical perceptions —i.e., to revive old experiences—can also be inherited. In this case we should have to agree with Freud's hypothesis that not only disposition but also content can be inherited.

DISCUSSION OF M. KATAN'S PAPER ON
SCHREBER'S HALLUCINATION

RECENTLY WE HAVE been hearing more and more about the psychological treatment of schizophrenia—and of cures. Indeed, we seem to be on the threshold of new developments—developments that may lead to a better understanding of schizophrenia. The psychological insight gained in relation to psychotics will probably influence our understanding and treatment of neurotics, as Freud predicted.

The scope of the problems of schizophrenia is enormous, and it is impossible to deal with them all at one time. In the present paper, Dr. Katan deals only with the problem of hallucinations. He brings us to the center of that problem by pointing out the fact that, when no longer able to master the influx of homosexual libido, Schreber developed hallucinations in which Flechsig talked to him.

We are accustomed to classify mental disorders into transference neuroses and narcissistic neuroses or psychoses. This classification suggests that transference neuroses develop transference and psychoses do not; in other words, that the psychoses show a specific disturbance in object relations. There is no doubt that, before Schreber's hallucinations set in, he was in a transference relationship with his doctor, the psychiatrist Flechsig.

Is it permissible to assume that all latent schizophrenias become manifest when the tendency to transfer emotions and ideas from a

---

Reprinted from *The International Journal of Psycho-Analysis*, 33:454-456, 1952.

This discussion pertains to a paper presented by M. Katan (1952), originally read at the 17th International Psycho-Analytical Congress, in Amsterdam.

person or a situation of the past into the present is thwarted? I have in mind not only the relationship of the patient to his doctor, but all those situations in which transference should or could be established.

What is the essence of transference? In brief, it is an attempt to relive or repeat old, repressed, unconscious experiences. With this tendency to repetition is coupled another, a tendency to establish an identity of perceptions between old and new experiences (*Wahrnehmungsidentität*). If there is too great a discrepancy between the new and the old experiences, or if the new ones are rejected, the old ones replace them, though in a distorted form, as we see, for instance, in dreams. We then call them *hallucinations*. It seems therefore that we have always a tendency to hallucinate, a tendency which is normally inhibited. The question, why we hallucinate, is therefore less interesting than the question, why we do *not* hallucinate; in other words, what is it that prevents us from hallucinating?

A first answer might be that, since we do not hallucinate in the waking state but do hallucinate in the dream, contact with reality may be the one factor which prevents us from hallucinating; or else that the patient is not quite awake when he is hallucinating, or is dreaming, which is essentially the same thing.

As long as we are dreaming we are convinced of the reality of our experiences; when we wake up we lose this conviction.

What is it, Freud asks, that makes the patient believe in the reality of his hallucinations or delusions?

Let us now return to Schreber. The quantity of homosexual libido mobilized in the transference situation was *relatively* too large to be mastered by Schreber: *then he simply denied Flechsig's real existence.* We assume that he withdrew the cathexis from the mental representations of Flechsig.

Since symptoms of transference are repetitions of infantile experiences, Schreber's denial of Flechsig's real existence must likewise be a repetition of an infantile denial. In this case Schreber must have denied the reality of his father's existence in some particular phase of his oedipus constellation.

It seems logical, then, to assume that, if Schreber had to deny his attachment to his father—his love for him and his submission—he could do nothing else but deny Flechsig's real existence when he felt his growing attachment to him. When he felt *helpless* in trying to master this attachment, he broke with reality and replaced the psychic representations of Flechsig by hallucinations, in which Flechsig or the father was represented in a symbolic, or some other, way. It is known that a weak father attachment is accompanied by weak ties with reality, or impairs the reality principle.

The structure of hallucinations is a very complicated one, as Dr. Katan shows. He demonstrates this complexity by the example of Schreber's hallucinations about the little men.

According to his interpretation, the "little men" represent: (1) Schreber's friends to whom he had been homosexually attached, (2) the sun and the rays of the sun, God with his sexual organs, (3) the little men dropping on his head also represent spermatozoa. Schreber warned the little men not to approach him, because the attraction he exerted on them was dangerous. Katan interprets this warning as a projection of his warning to himself as to the dangers of sexual activity.

Schreber's *hallucinations contained still other features; for instance, when an orgasm was threatening, he hallucinated voices which urged him to fight.* These hallucinations represent, it seems, projections of the patient's own urge to fight his masturbation or other sexual activities. Hence the voices can be interpreted as representations of his conscience. Conscience is a function of the super-ego which develops through identification predominantly with the father figure. Through the projection of the inner voices of conscience, the father figure was placed in the external world where the father originally belonged.

Thus we must agree with Dr. Katan's reconstruction concerning the origin of the contents of Schreber's hallucinations. He emphasizes that Schreber was dealing in his hallucinations with exactly the same thoughts that he had had in his prepsychotic period. Since, in the prepsychotic period, contact with reality was maintained, the hallucinations have their origin in that part of the personality which still maintains contact with reality.

This fact proves that schizophrenics retain the tendency to establish transference, which, at the same time, they consistently try to ward off. Furthermore, although hallucinations have their origin in actual reality, they tend to another, a psychic reality which has its origin in the past, a historical reality.

Hallucinations as well as delusions are formed of elements of real experiences, which are rearranged under the pressure of the primary process that prevails in schizophrenics much more than in neurotics. If I may use a simile, the schizophrenic productions look like a number of pages torn out of a book, mixed up, rearranged and then projected on a screen.

Hallucinations correspond to perceptions of certain elements of real experience, while delusions seem to correspond to perceptions of thinking processes which are degraded by the primary process to perceptions of *memory traces* of (similar or the same) past experiences. Often it is difficult to distinguish a hallucination from a delusion.

Rather than continue here, I would refer to Freud's (1937b) paper "Constructions in Analysis." He thinks that a general characteristic of hallucinations may perhaps be the fact that something experienced in infancy re-emerges into consciousness, perhaps distorted and displaced. He assumes, further, that delusions and hallucinations (which are constantly incorporated in delusions) have a common origin and that their *material* is treated in the same manner as that in *dreams*. From these assumptions he comes to the conclusion that hallucinations as well as delusions *always* contain a *fragment of a historic truth*. He adds: *"It is plausible to suppose that the compulsive belief attached to delusions derives its strength from infantile sources of this kind."*

The recognition of the kernel of truth in the hallucination or delusion would, as Freud states, afford a common ground for patient and doctor, and be of great therapeutic value.

Two objections might be made to the concept of "historical truth." One, which Freud himself raises, is that all neuroses have a kernel of truth and that in his original formulation he said that all hysterical patients suffer from reminiscences. The other is that, by introducing this concept, Freud came even closer to eliminating the barrier between neurosis and psychosis.

Instead of criticizing, we should perhaps rather try to find out what exactly is the difference in the manner in which the ego treats the "historical truth" in neurosis and in psychosis. Why can a neurotic accept the object of transference, the real object, and the psychotic cannot transfer on the object of reality?

At the end of his paper, Freud says: "If we consider mankind as a whole and substitute it for the human individual, we discover that it too has developed delusions which are inaccessible to logical criticism and which contradict reality. If, in spite of this, they are able to exert an extraordinary power over men, investigation leads to the same explanation as in the case of a single individual. They owe their power to the element of historical truth which they have brought up from the repression of the forgotten and primeval past."

Taking Schreber as a paradigm, are not the delusions of rebirth and reincarnation from which all psychotics regularly suffer, as well as their cosmic systems in which they personify the stars, the sun, the universe, and believe in them as gods, a "historical truth" in which in the past mankind really believed? But what the ancient man and the schizophrenic believe consciously, as it were, the neurotic believes unconsciously. It seems to me that our investigation should start at this point.

In order not to close with purely theoretical speculation, I should like to report a simple example, though one only indirectly experienced by myself.

Dr. John Rosen, who treats psychotics, once complained that he was not making any progress with one of his schizophrenics. He had had her in his care for more than a year, but he could not establish contact with her. One of her main symptoms consisted in her not knowing who she was. When addressed by her name, she did not react, as if she had a negative hallucination.

One day the psychiatrist thought of a possible connection with her castration complex that made the patient reject her name, and with it a part of her personality. He said to her: "You think that you are not good because you have funny genitalia; that is not true, you have beautiful, lovely genitalia; I love them, I admire them. Show them to me." The patient tried to lift her skirt, but stopped after a short while and turned away shamefacedly.

From the point of view of taste, this was a crude intervention, but it *worked*. From then on the patient knew who she was, answered when addressed by her own name, and a workable transference was established. She rejected a part of her personality as, obviously, she had in the past rejected her genitalia. Now, after her feminine genitalia had been accepted by others (the doctor, the father substitute), she was able to accept and integrate the hitherto split-off part of her personality.

The approach to the "reality core" used by my analysand is, of course, not the only one; there are still others; this approach is but one of many.

EVALUATION OF THE RESULTS OF
PSYCHOANALYTIC TREATMENT

IN ORDER TO EVALUATE any therapeutic method, it is necessary to compare it with other methods. But I know only one psycho-therapeutic method, and that is psychoanalysis. Being thus deprived of the opportunity to compare, I should perhaps stop here. However, having consented to participate in this symposium, I had to find some kind of approach to this problem. It occurred to me that the only possible way to ascertain the value of changes brought about by psychoanalytic treatment is to scrutinize these changes in the framework of Freud's concepts. (I shall refrain here from referring to the many contributions by other psychoanalysts to this subject.) In order to do so, one should first examine the problems of mental health and illness.

As to the first problem, we can be brief, because no one has been successful as yet in giving a clear-cut picture of the mentally healthy person. Whether a man is considered healthy or ill depends to a great extent on the milieu in which he is living. What, for example, would be considered as a heavenly revelation in a certain religious community, might be regarded as mental disorder in another community. When as a very young psychiatrist I discussed with my colleagues the problem of mental health or illness, we finally arrived at the conclusion that mental health ends at the gates of the mental hospital. Although definitions of mental health or illness are more refined nowadays, they are nevertheless no more precise.

How confusing mental illness may sometimes be for the observer may be illustrated by the following true story: A famous psychiatrist said after the examination of an insane man who had made an

Reprinted from *The International Journal of Psycho-Analysis*, 35:2-7, 1954.

assault on the life of the Emperor William II, that at the end he did not know whether he was insane or the patient was. Not infrequently similar ideas enter our mind when we talk with our patients. Sometimes a patient seems so disturbed that we are reluctant to accept him for treatment. But if, nevertheless, we have taken him, and begin to understand him after a while, we may find that he is not quite so ill, and sometimes think that in similar circumstances we might perhaps not have behaved differently. Had we not accepted the patient for treatment, we should have missed the opportunity to have the experience that initial understanding and temporary identification with the patient provide us with an access to the healthy part of his ego, which often paves the way for a regular and successful analysis. The analyst who has undertaken to treat such a patient will have an opinion about the value of analysis as a therapeutic method quite different from that of the analyst who did not even try to start the treatment and thus to understand the patient.

Let us take another example, also from real life: One analyst dismisses a patient as not curable, or the patient leaves him dissatisfied and turns to another analyst who cures him. Why is one analyst successful while the other is not? *Certainly, the reason must rest with the analyst and not with analysis.*

It is obvious in this connection that the evaluation of analysis as a therapeutic method depends on the environment as well as on the personality of the analyst. Besides, let us not forget that in all psychological evaluations the personal equation plays a very important part.

As it is difficult to define mental health, so it is difficult to define mental illness. If we turn our attention to an extremely pathological case, a schizophrenic, we are impressed with his awareness of certain ideas, strivings, or wishes which, in a neurotic or a normal person, are hidden under a heavy crust. What a schizophrenic reveals without inhibitions, we can see in a neurotic only after prolonged analysis. What is unconscious in a neurotic seems to be conscious in a schizophrenic.

As is known, the analytic method uncovers the unconscious wishes, fantasies, and strivings of the id.

The unconscious exists in the id in two conditions: in a repressed and in a nonrepressed state. Neither is pathogenic by itself. Only when the repression fails does the repressed unconscious become pathogenic. Since repression is a function of the ego, failure of repression seems to be due to a weak ego. A comparison of narcissistic and transference neuroses may shed some light on this question.

In the preneurotic or prepsychotic stage, the repressed material in both types of neurosis, though latent, not active, is nevertheless endowed with a certain quantity of cathexis or psychic energy. If the cathexis increases, the repressed material acquires such a momentum that it invades the ego and breaks down its main defense, the repression. As a consequence of the weakening or breaking down of the barrier between id and ego, the repressed material returns from the obscurity of the id and takes possession of a part of the ego or of the whole ego. At this point either a psychosis or a neurosis begins to take shape. In the narcissistic neuroses, the libidinal cathexes are withdrawn from the object representations of the external world; the latent fantasies become conscious and replace reality. The reality-testing function of the ego is thus immobilized or destroyed. In the transference neuroses, the repression is likewise broken down and the repressed material also returns from the obscurity of the id, but the results are much less devastating. The libidinal cathexis is not withdrawn from the external world; the sense of reality is practically not much damaged.

In both cases, then, the repressions are broken down, but in psychosis the ego loses contact with reality; in neurosis it does not, or does so only in a very limited way, namely, as far as the neurotic complex is concerned. The first therapeutic task, then, would appear to be the establishment of a contact between the patient and reality, for instance, the analyst. In neurosis this task is comparatively easy; in psychosis very difficult, if not impossible. *In neurosis such a contact will not be considered a remarkable achievement. If the analyst is able to establish such a contact in psychosis, it will be considered a great success.*

Establishment of contact with the patient is not, of course, identical with a cure. It is merely a vehicle for the treatment, and signifies the beginning of a transference relationship. In an ideal case the transference is completely resolved when the patient becomes free and independent at the end of analysis. This goal can be achieved—sometimes sooner, sometimes later, sometimes not at all. In fact, there are patients who need treatment for a very long time, and yet that does not say anything about the therapeutic value of psychoanalysis. A diabetic needs medical supervision for the rest of his life, and nobody would blame medicine for not having cured him at once. *It is obvious that the time element cannot be used as a criterion for the evaluation of psychoanalytic results.*

Perhaps examination of the concept of consciousness will give us more certainty.

The same material which in schizophrenia is conscious, in neurosis requires a great effort to be brought into consciousness. If it is true—and it is—that the first therapeutic task is to convert the repressed unconscious into conscious material, one may think it is easier to achieve this goal in schizophrenia than in neurosis. However, clinical experience shows the opposite.

When the ego of the schizophrenic breaks down and loses contact with reality, it behaves as if it were the id. In order to make it easier for myself at this point, I should like to remind you of a few theoretical concepts. In the id, all psychic material is subject to the primary process. This process means that the psychic energy in the id is mobile, shifting easily from one psychic element to another; in brief, the id is chaotic. In the ego, the condition of the mental energy is quite different. The ego is preconscious; its contents are therefore subject to the laws of the secondary process. Under its influence the psychic energy becomes bound, stable, not shifting from one element to another. In other words, the psychic processes in the ego are logical, not contradictory, orderly. When id material is going to become conscious, it has first to enter the ego where it acquires the quality of being preconscious; in the ego it undergoes changes according to the laws of the secondary process. If the material thus transformed satisfies certain demands of the ego, as for instance, those of the superego or of reality testing, it enters consciousness. In other words, it is then perceived by the perceptive apparatus of the ego, and, possibly, expressed in words and actions.

In schizophrenia, the ego is altered; to a great extent it has lost contact with reality. It has lost also the reality-testing function, the faculty of discerning between external and internal experiences. In addition, parts of the superego are dissolved, and with them the faculty of self-criticism. If we consider the fact that the ego of patients of this type is invaded by the unconscious material of the id which has eluded the elaboration of the secondary process; if we further consider the fact that the schizophrenic treats the external world as if it were his internal world and *vice versa*, it becomes obvious that his consciousness, though apparently the same, is not really the same as that of a normal or a neurotic person. His language is not our language; there can hardly be mutual understanding. If the difficulties of transference are added, it seems almost impossible to transform the schizophrenic's "consciousness" into that of a normal person. Sometimes, however, one does succeed in freeing the preconscious material from the domination of the primary process. Thus purified, it comes under the domination of the secondary process and enters consciousness. At the same time the overflow of the repressed material, which is a projection of the unconscious onto the ego, is pushed back into the id and repressed again. *If the "miracle" of such a transformation happens, it represents an enormous achievement of psychoanalytic endeavors.*

The ego of the neurotic treats the onrush of the repressed unconscious material in a different way. When the repressed material threatens to overflow the ego and to force itself upon its consciousness, this ego, though relatively weakened, is still strong enough to reinforce the original repression and to push the repressed material back into the id. In support of the original repression, the ego then mobilizes countercathexes which activate various kinds of defenses (after expulsion). Out of the conflict between the repressed unconscious id and the ego with its defenses, symptoms and character changes evolve. As a rule, the ego succeeds in keeping the id drives from consciousness.

Analysis, on the contrary, endeavors to lift the repressed unconscious material into consciousness. If it is successful, the infantile amnesias are filled in or the first five years of childhood are reconstructed. It is known how difficult a task this is. As some of the recollections are screen memories, others confused with fantasies, or displaced and condensed as to time and milieu, the material thus obtained is still in a state of chaos. It has to be complemented and rearranged; briefly, through the process of working through, order has to be established in the mind of the neurotic. Some patients lose their symptoms only after this entire process has been completed, others not even then, and still others before the completion or soon after the beginning of treatment.

The best is the first group. Patient and analyst are satisfied and no one talks any more about the treatment. *The most precious material for evaluation of the results, however, is lost.*

The worst is the second group. Here criticism of analysis is the loudest. *But one group of patients who cannot be cured by psychoanalysis in no way diminishes the value of psychoanalysis as a therapeutic method.* First of all, this type of patient is not cured by any other method, so far as I am informed. Secondly, not even in physical medicine are all patients cured. Besides, there are those cases for whom it would not be desirable to be deprived of their neurosis, patients for whom it would be more difficult to endure the misery of reality than it is to endure the misery of illness. Parenthetically, slight hysteria may protect a young girl from the dangers of promiscuity.

With the third group, the assessment of the value of psychoanalysis as a curative method is somewhat more complicated.

Some patients lose their symptoms after a short analysis and wish to break off the treatment. Since the analyst has hardly scratched the surface of their neurosis, he advises them not to stop. But, as they themselves feel cured and satisfied, they praise the analyst and nevertheless do stop. The best the analyst can do in such cases is to be prepared to take them back as soon as they suffer a relapse, or hope that nature will take care of the curative process initiated by him.

Other patients, again, likewise lose their symptoms prematurely, but after a longer treatment, characterized by reproduction of a considerable amount of repressed material. A patient came to me for treatment of excruciating pains which still persisted after he had gone through a gastro-enterostomy and resection of the stomach for the cure of his peptic ulcers. When he was almost entirely free of pains after about half a year of treatment, he showed an intention of stopping the analysis. I discouraged him, of course, since I understood only a fraction of the abundant

material, and consequently he understood even less. It was obvious
that this material required a thorough working through, which
could not possibly have been accomplished within such a short
period.

Another patient, a fetishist, sexually impotent, to a great extent
lost his interest in the fetish after a year and a half of treatment,
fell in love with a girl, and even became sexually potent with her.
He was enthusiastic about the results of his treatment and intended
to marry the girl at once. Although I do not like to arrogate to
myself the role of fate, nevertheless I discouraged the patient from
marrying for the same reason for which I did not let the other
patient stop his analysis: the material was not sufficiently worked
through. In addition, I feared that marriage would interfere with
the analysis and, in my opinion, an undisturbed continuation of
the analysis was more important for the patient than immediate
marriage.

*So we find ourselves, at times, confronted with a paradoxical
situation in which the patient and his family are satisfied with the
therapeutic results, and the analyst is not.*

Analysis of course does not merely free the patient from his symptoms. It does more for him: within certain limits, it changes his
character. There hardly exists a symptom neurosis without a character neurosis. They form a complemental series at the one end of
which the symptom prevails, at the other end of which the character in itself seems to be a kind of symptom. The disappearance
of a symptom cannot be considered permanent so long as the
corresponding character trait or attitude of the ego persists.
It also happens, of course, that the symptom disappears only
after the corresponding attitude of the ego or of its behavior
has been analyzed. Anyway, while the disappearance of the symptom is often dramatic and very impressive, the character change is
mostly latent and for a long time unnoticed by the patient as well
as by his environment. Only much later and in special circumstances may it become obvious how much the patient's behavior
has changed. Therefore, the disappearance of the symptom is more
appreciated than the change of the ego. However, the change of
character does not always please the environment. For instance, the
husband who was a submissive, meek, and passive person has be-

come active and independent. The wife, herself active and independent, may not like this change. *The question whether loss of symptom or change of character is more important is immaterial, for it is the change of ego reactions which makes the cure of a symptom dependable, at least most of the time.*

The secondary gain of illness is often a serious obstacle to a complete cure. If the symptom lives with the ego in a kind of symbiosis and is not felt as a foreign body, it is very difficult to effect a real cure. The same is true of character disorders. As long as certain pathological character traits or ego attitudes are not felt as foreign, as something which is in disharmony with the other ego strivings—no matter how detrimental they may be for the whole personality—the character is not accessible for analysis. Such character deviations are protected by narcissism, by self-love which would not even admit a character weakness. For these reasons it is difficult to treat character neuroses. However, it is not the psychoanalytic method that can be held responsible for failures, but the peculiar structure of these neuroses.

Symptoms as well as neurotic character traits indicate a split in the ego. From symptoms, the patients suffer; from character distortions, they do not suffer consciously; and if they suffer misfortunes or disappointments, they usually ascribe them to external circumstances. They lack insight into the causative part played by their ego.

In the neurotic struggle between ego and id, where the ego fights for the supremacy of reality, a part of the total ego is finally overwhelmed by the id, then repressed and cut off from the unaffected parts of the ego. The repressed part undergoes certain changes, for instance regression, and appears then as a strange character trait which is neither understood by the intact ego nor accepted into its organization. Consequently, two or more ego attitudes coexist, each independent of the other. I have not in mind now the evident splits of the ego in schizophrenia, depersonalization, or fetishism. I have in mind rather those seemingly insignificant splits which may even pass unnoticed.

It is obvious that an ego from which a part has been cut off is weakened. Certainly, through analysis, through converting the unconscious part of the ego into a conscious one, the estranged part is integrated with the intact ego. *The gain for the patient is clear: the ego becomes more independent of the instincts and gains mastery over them; it becomes solidified, hence stronger. But how evaluate this success?* The integration of the ego is far less impressive than the disappearance of a symptom; besides, the rift in the ego is not always healed completely, often there remains a scar in place of the rift. *Yet, more often than not, the patients are happy when the ego is only partially solidified and do not even know how much could still be done. After all, whose ego is made of one piece hewn out of solid rock?*

In order to interrupt these dry, theoretical considerations, I should like to insert at least one clinical example of the meaning of an apparently insignificant distortion of the ego. The patient who suffered from ulcer pains was a physician. He once mentioned casually that he did not display his doctor's diploma in his office, nor a doctor's sign at his door, nor ever carry a doctor's bag. He used to carry a briefcase on his professional visits, something which in no way resembles a doctor's bag.

His father was a great scholar who had tried to convey his knowledge to the son. But the son was an inattentive pupil, forgetting his lessons from one day to the next. When he finished high school, he declared his intention to study medicine. His father objected, maintaining that he had neither talent nor inclination for study. In spite of this opposition, he went to college and registered as a premedical student. However, he took only a minimum of science courses and instead devoted most of his time to the study of the classics. In the course of these studies he wrote a theme which he showed to his much-admired professor before it was finished. The latter was very impressed with the paper and warned him not to rush its completion but to continue to work on it patiently during the forthcoming vacation; he told him, moreover, that he planned to publish the paper after its completion. The student never touched it again, turned all his energy to science, entered medical school and became a doctor, though consistently hiding the external evidence of his profession.

He played two parts: that of a doctor, which he consciously wanted to be, and that of a nondoctor, which he evidently also wished to be, though unconsciously. It is easy to guess that the latter represented a deferred obedience to his father who had not wanted him to be a doctor. Yet a deeper factor may have been responsible for this split in his ego. When studying with his father as a young boy, he would press his hand against his penis under the desk and think about all the occasions when he had seen his father's genitalia. Hiding the evidence of his profession, he certainly exhibited deferred obedience to his father, an obedience based on his homosexual attachment to him. This attachment was so strong that he transferred it into a sublimated, faithful and lasting friendship with the same professor whose praise had caused him to drop his studies of the classics and to turn completely to medicine. That is, of course, not the whole story; but it is sufficient, first, to catch a glimpse of the deeply rooted conflict and, secondly, to imagine the relief the patient felt when he became aware of the roots of his ambiguities in relation to his profession.

Integration of the ego means essentially synthesis or assimilation of the repressed material. All that which is repressed, instincts as well as parts of the ego, is under the domination of the primary process. Everything in the id is in a constant state of fluidity. In addition, the unconscious has no sense of time, no sensitivity for contradictions, and no ability to distinguish between psychic and external reality. The ego, a preconscious psychic agency, is dominated by the secondary process. The psychic energy of the ego is not fluid; it is bound. Freud says that the binding of psychic energy manifests itself in the tendency of the ego to synthesize the amorphous psychic material incoming from the id. The ego develops a sensitivity for contradictions, tries to eliminate them, to unify what belongs together and to segregate what does not belong together, to generalize, and so on. It also acquires the sense of time and reality. If we compare, then, the patient's state of mind before his analysis with his state of mind afterwards, we can see the following picture: before the analysis, he confused the past with the present. Afterwards he is able to distinguish between his ideas and wishes belonging to the past and those which can be materialized in the present. While, before, he was confused to a certain extent as to mental and external reality, he has now learned to adapt himself to reality, for instance to see that his wife is not his mother, that what he expected from his mother in the past he cannot expect from his wife in the present, and so forth.

Of course, not all these changes can clearly be seen together in *one* patient. In one case a particular change predominates; in another case, a different change. Only in an ideal case can all these changes be seen together. Ideals are indeed rare and can seldom be materialized in real life. Why expect more than the possible from analysis? Not only is mental activity enormously complicated, but so is the curative process. In fact, when we try to separate all the changes effected by treatment, we do so rather for didactic purposes. *For the healing process initiated by the analytic treatment seems to be nonselective, but taking its own course to embrace the total personality. It is true, though, that one case is better integrated, and the other not so well. Exactly why this happens, we cannot say most of the time.*

So I could go on indefinitely trying to find reliable, unequivocal criteria for the evaluation of the results of psychoanalytic treatment. I doubt whether I should be successful.

However, since all mental activity is regulated by an economic factor, illness is likewise regulated by this factor. If we consider mental disorders as to their effect, the following becomes evident: in schizophrenia the patient, by overcathecting preconscious ideas, struggles to regain reality; in other words, to reconstruct the lost object world. The clamorous symptoms, hallucinations, and delusions thus represent a spontaneous attempt at recovery, an attempt to re-establish psychic equilibrium, toward which the ill as well as the healthy are striving. A similar attempt is made in transference neuroses; in conversion hysteria, the psychic conflict is brought to an end with the establishment of the symptom; in phobias and compulsive neuroses, the conflict is appeased over and over again by attempts to stabilize the symptom. The patient then gains a certain degree of peace, as long as the countercathexis can bind enough energy in the symptom.

The concept of balance of powers within the psychic systems, of a psychic equilibrium, suggests, therefore, that the entire concept of psychic health or illness is indeed based on quantitative factors. When the interplay of certain amounts of psychic energies ends in an equilibrium, then the strivings of the id are in harmony with those of the ego and superego, and we see a picture of mental health. A disturbance of this equilibrium produces disharmonies within the personality, and we have the picture of mental illness.

However, the tendency to smooth out psychic conflicts and to bring about a balance of powers is so irresistible that even in illness such an equilibrium of energies is, in a sense, established, although this equilibrium is of a labile nature. *If we could measure the quantities of psychic energies, it would be easier to determine the extent of mental health or illness.* But we cannot measure them.

Therefore we can only return to one of the oldest formulations concerning the results of psychoanalytic treatment. It is a very simple formula: when the patient is able to work and to love, he can be considered practically cured. Of course, this is not a scientific formula. However, deeper knowledge and understanding of psychoanalysis may at some future time provide us with more exact formulations.

INTRODUCTION TO THE *MINUTES OF THE VIENNA PSYCHOANALYTIC SOCIETY*

WHEN FREUD LEFT Vienna in 1938, he entrusted the *original* manuscripts of the Minutes of the Vienna Psychoanalytic Society to Dr. Paul Federn, who since Freud's illness had been acting president of the Society of which Freud was president. Federn soon followed Freud into exile, taking the Minutes with him. Thus he saved the manuscripts from destruction by the Nazis and preserved them for future publication.

The possession of the Minutes imbued Federn with a great sense of responsibility, toward Freud and toward psychoanalysis. He often talked about them: one gained the impression that he felt it to be his duty to publish them as soon as possible. Ill health, lack of time and funds, however, prevented him from consummating his plans. He was able to publish only one protocol—in *Samiksa,* an Indian psychoanalytic journal. His desire to insure that the Minutes would be presented to the world led him to provide in his last will and testament for their publication after his death. To that end he appointed me to edit the Minutes and to arrange for their publication together with his son Ernst.

The Minutes begin with the year 1906 and continue until 1915. From 1906 to 1915, Otto Rank was the official, salaried secretary of the Society, entrusted with the task of recording its meetings. The Minutes for that period contain records of the scientific portions of the meetings, as well as attendance lists of all meetings. In 1915 Rank had to leave Vienna for military service in the First World

---

Reprinted from *Minutes of the Vienna Psychoanalytic Society*, Vol. I, Edited by Herman Nunberg and Ernst Federn. New York: International Universities Press, 1962, pp. xvii-xxxii.

War. There are some records of discussions at meetings held between 1915 and 1918; however, except for one protocol of a meeting in November, 1918, they are so fragmentary as to be virtually unintelligible. We also have Minutes of the meetings which were held from 1918 to the end of 1933; these, however, are of no substantial interest. They consist only of brief records of the business parts of the meetings, attendance lists of members and guests, and abbreviated titles of scientific papers presented. They do not record the scientific discussions that took place.

Although the quality of the discussions was very uneven—sometimes logical and orderly, at other times emotional and confused—Rank carried out his task with deep understanding and great skill. His records were not stenographic; rather than attempting a precise account of all that was said, Rank seems to have taken extensive notes of the discussions and to have edited them later. For the most part, they express with remarkable lucidity what was said in the discussions.

Nevertheless, some of the Minutes are not easy to understand; some papers are rendered in a form that is too abbreviated, while others are mentioned only by their titles. Some speakers discuss one part of an unrecorded paper, others comment on another part. Thus, the Minutes are, at times, difficult to read. After 1910 they became shorter; finally, the contractions and omissions became so numerous that the reader can only surmise a great deal of what was said in the discussions. To some extent we have tried to explicate these unclear sections in our annotations. But we have restricted the annotations to the minimum necessary for comprehension of the text, because we prefer to abstain from influencing the reader's judgment of these Minutes. The careful reader, in spite of the hurdles encountered, will be rewarded by a growing insight into, and understanding of, the problems which at the time occupied the mind of the analyst.

The meetings started in 1902 as Psychological Wednesday Evenings in Freud's own apartment; later they became known as the Wednesday Evening Meetings. The Wednesday was retained as a tradition, as it were, when later on, after the transformation of this loose circle into the Vienna Psychoanalytic Society, its members met regularly each Wednesday evening. There are no records of the Wednesday Evenings for the period from 1902 to 1906. In 1908, when the Vienna Psychoanalytic Society was formed, the meetings became a function of the Society. In 1910, the meetings were moved from Freud's private apartment to the Doktoren Collegium (the College of Physicians). Until 1908, *everyone who attended the meetings was required to participate in the discussions;* from then on, participation was voluntary (Freud, 1914c).

The men who gathered around Freud were interested in psychology in the broadest sense of the word. Dissatisfied with what contemporary psychology had to offer, they looked for new ideas, for new guiding principles, which would help them gain a better understanding of man. Freud's teachings seemed to promise such help.

It is commonly known that from the very beginning Freud's new ideas were not well received by the medical profession; he was severely criticized by his colleagues, hated, and ostracized. Even some of his old friends deserted him.[1] Thus he became a lonesome man. But he was a sociable man as well; he could be a great and faithful friend. (The memoirs of Ludwig Binswanger [1956] are a telling testimony to this.) He loved to have people around him with whom he could communicate and exchange ideas. The loneliness into which he was driven—like all men who are ahead of their times—oppressed him; he would often say that the analyst should not be isolated, but that, on the contrary, he should associate with others and exchange ideas and experiences with them. In a letter to his friend Wilhelm Fliess he wrote that Fliess was his "Publicum," his audience (Freud, 1950). He needed a sounding board. When he realized that Fliess ceased to follow his ideas, he suffered intensely; finally the friendship broke up.

How strong his need for friendship was, and for recognition, is expressed in an address to the B'nai B'rith, a Jewish humanitarian fraternity, on the occasion of his seventieth birthday (Freud, 1926a). He recalled how much the warm reception accorded him and the opportunity for new human contacts offered there had meant to him at a time when he had been deserted by his colleagues and friends on account of his discoveries.

---

[1] In later years, he would jokingly say that people used to treat him like a freshly painted wall: nobody dared to touch him. (From a communication by Ludwig Jekels.)

A few years after Freud's relationship with Fliess had ended it was the Wednesday Evening Group which became his sounding board. He attended the meetings regularly and until his illness hardly ever missed a session.

Who were the men who formed the Wednesday Evening Group, and why did they become psychoanalysts?

On the one hand there was a group of men in search of new ideas and of a leader, and on the other hand there was a lonely man who had made important new discoveries and wished to share them with others. So, upon the suggestion of Dr. Wilhelm Stekel who had been successfully treated by Freud, Freud agreed to hold weekly meetings with this group. The aim of these meetings was discussion of psychological problems. Thus, the Wednesday Evening Meetings came into being.

The group was heterogeneous; it consisted of physicians, educators, writers, and others. In short, its members represented a cross-section of the intellectuals at the beginning of the century. Different as they were in their backgrounds and personalities, they were held together by their common discontent with the conditions that prevailed in psychiatry, education, and other fields dealing with the human mind.

During this period a host of ideas was in the process of fermentation in many parts of Europe. It was the time when, in psychiatry, the Nancy School's ideas about hypnotism and the teachings of Charcot were spreading from France all over Europe; when Kraepelin in Germany was trying to bring order into psychiatry, when the Swiss Eugen Bleuler became the leading psychiatrist, and when Wundt exercised his world-wide influence upon contemporary psychology. It was also the time when Darwin's work influenced contemporary scientific thinking, but, as far as psychiatry and psychology are concerned, Freud was, to my knowledge, the only one who applied Darwin's theories.

During the same period the philosophies of Schopenhauer and Nietzsche were making their mark upon the minds of intellectuals in Germany; Dostoevski's novels were widely read; Strindberg had written his *Confessions of a Fool;* Wedekind's *Spring's Awakening* had just appeared; and many other events of importance to the intellectual life of Europe were taking place.

Just as the world in which the Wednesday Evening men lived was torn by conflicts, so were they themselves. We have learned from our analyses that in order to heal inner conflicts it is necessary first to bare their sources and thus to understand them. We have also learned that we often project our own conflicts onto the external world. It seems safe to assume that the urge of these men to understand and to heal their fellowmen reflected to a great extent their own need for help. And, indeed, at the meetings of the Society they discussed not only the problems of others, but also their own difficulties; they revealed their inner conflicts, confessed their masturbation, their fantasies and reminiscences concerning their parents, friends, wives and children. It is true that they seem to have been neurotics, but no more so than many others who are not considered ill. I remember the jokes that circulated among us, young psychiatrists, to the effect that psychiatrists are schizophrenics, and that their choice of this profession represents an attempt at self-healing. Actually, some of the first psychoanalysts had undergone psychoanalysis for therapeutic reasons; others undertook a self-analysis if they did not believe themselves sick enough to ask for another's help. Since the publication of Freud's letters to Fliess (Freud, 1950), it is no longer a secret that he himself had a neurosis which he overcame by self-analysis, a Herculean feat if we consider the circumstances in which this analysis was performed.

Once, when fitness for performing psychoanalytic treatment was under discussion, Freud remarked that, curiously enough, neurotics proved to be good practical psychologists. Parenthetically, it may be noted that a man who is *genuinely* interested in psychology projects his unconscious or preconscious preoccupation with his own psyche onto the psychology of others. However, the blind spots caused by his own conflicts interfere with the ability of such a man fully to understand another. In order to eliminate such weak spots in the analyst's understanding of his patient, Freud—as these Minutes show—suggested at an early time that analysts be analyzed. This clearly demonstrates Freud's realization, soon after he began his work, that not only can the doctor exert an influence over his patient, but that the patient can influence the doctor as well. When the patient's conflicts coincide with those of the doctor, the latter may not see them; he may misunderstand them or identify with the patient. This phenomenon, which belongs to the sphere of what later was called countertransference, was an early topic of discussion in the Society.[2]

Thus, the Wednesday Evening men, in order to carry out their urge to help their fellowmen, above all had to understand themselves. By discussing intimate problems with one another, they hoped to help their patients as well as themselves. This hope, stemming from their belief in analysis, united them in their devotion to Freud; in identifying with him as their leader, they became the first pioneers of analysis.

At the outset they formed an almost harmonious group. Each member showed intense interest in the topic under discussion, whether it was a clinical case, a poet or artist and his work, a teacher, a pupil, or a criminal. Papers were read, books and magazine articles were reviewed, and a variety of problems discussed: biology, animal psychology, psychiatry, sociology, mythology, religion, art and literature, education and criminology, even the association and psychogalvanic experiments. It is worth mentioning that the members borrowed protocols of the meetings, studied and then returned them; this too is faithfully recorded by the secretary.

The reader should keep in mind that the discussions of the first few years were largely based on Freud's early work and that the discussants had not yet acquired wide analytic experience. Consequently we find much guesswork, many premature statements, etc. Moreover, one must not forget that a major part of the discussions was spontaneous, unprepared reaction to papers heard the same evening. Thus not all comments were consistent and logical.

In the discussions the participants stimulated each other and even Freud. For example, Adler very early stressed the importance of aggression in psychic life. Freud accepted this idea and paid more attention to it from then on; however, he integrated the aggressive instinct with his theory of instincts only much later, in the paper

[2] At the Congress in Budapest in 1918, I moved that the future psychoanalyst be required to undergo an analysis himself. The motion was rejected because Rank and Tausk energetically opposed it. It was only in 1926 at the Congress in Bad Homburg that this rule was adopted.

"Instincts and Their Vicissitudes" (1915). His theory of instincts took its final shape in *Beyond the Pleasure Principle* (1920).

It was a process of give-and-take which took place in these discussions. Naturally, Freud gave more than the others could take. There was, of course, a tremendous gap between their understanding of psychoanalysis and his. While they were merely beginners, he had already laid the foundations of his monumental edifice. They came to a rich table, indeed, but not all of them could digest what was offered. Yet, while they still knew very little of psychoanalysis, they were eager to learn. And they learned quickly; they listened with rapt attention whenever Freud talked, they tried to absorb every word he uttered, and they made common cause with him. No doubt, this devotion to Freud and his ideas required great courage at that time, for the psychoanalyst exposed himself to severe criticism and ridicule which frequently drove him into isolation. Some members were reluctant to publish psychoanalytic articles; others published under a pseudonym.

In spite of all the difficulties, those early followers of Freud did not hesitate to consider themselves his pupils and, for a while, worked with him in harmony. But this harmony did not last very long. As in other group formations, here too, ambivalence began to exercise a negative influence. Perhaps this explains the fact that some of these men, in spite of their attraction to depth psychology and their devotion to Freud, still had resistances precisely to what consciously they were attempting to learn; a situation, incidentally, which applies even today to some individual analysts and groups.

Indeed, some members of the Society could not face the Unconscious as revealed by psychoanalysis. As Freud once, after a paper given by Paul Schilder, remarked, they could not breathe in the sticky atmosphere of the dark underground, of the "sewers," as it were, but longed to bask in the bright sunshine on the surface. Of course, all of us would prefer to breathe fresh air, were it possible for the psychoanalyst to indulge in surface psychology. As was to be expected, those who preferred surface psychology soon abandoned psychoanalysis altogether. Within the Society, on the other hand, factions were formed, and rivalries developed, accompanied by quarrels about the priority of ideas and a competitive attitude which manifested itself even toward Freud. There were those who attempted to introduce into the discussions extraneous ideas which clashed with the basic concepts of psychoanalysis. The reasons for the introduction of such elements were many; foremost among them, however, were resistances to psychoanalysis, supported by personal predilections of a philosophical nature and by ambitions. These members tried to impose their own ideas upon the group and, in so doing, impeded the progress of the work of the Society. Finally they had to resign.

Elimination of some members did not weaken the Society. On the contrary, the membership was steadily growing, and the discussions became more substantial and better organized; it was easier to follow the development of certain ideas and to see how they were slowly taking definite shape. Obviously, the resignation of the dissident members made the group more coherent. In this atmosphere of greater harmony some personalities were steadily growing in stature.

As mentioned before, the range of topics dealt with at the meetings was very wide. The discussions, at times, became passionate, confused, and difficult to manage. But Freud never lost control of the group as a whole; he proved a masterful leader. With incomparable superiority he knew how to deal with these intelligent but emotional people. He was always able to bring order into the chaos and to calm the excited spirits. Often, with one observation, one word, he succeeded in showing the essential point of a problem, and in making it crystal clear. While giving everyone full freedom to express his opinions, he did not permit the discussions to run wild. He guided them with admirable skill, always remaining objective. He praised where praise was deserved, he disapproved where criticism was necessary. So he criticized Rank severely for the way in which he presented his material, but praised him for its content; he praised Adler for his contributions to ego psychology, but criticized him by pointing out that Adler's psychology was a psychology of the conscious rather than of the unconscious. There were, it is true, instances in which Freud was a very sharp critic, but on the whole he was mild and forebearing, patient and lenient. He tried to mediate in the conflicts of ideas and personalities. He was extremely tolerant of the convictions and ideas of others. However, his patience and tolerance had certain limits. As long as it was not absolutely clear to him that the divergent ideas threatened his *basic* doctrines, he did not interfere and did not oppose them. Only when it became evident to him that the edifice of *his* analysis was threatened, he was inexorable.

The best example of his patience and tolerance is the case of Alfred Adler. As a member of the group, Adler started, slowly but systematically, to promote his own ideas which, in the end, proved to contradict the basic concepts of Freud. Yet, for a long time, Freud treated Adler with marked distinction: he even appointed Adler president of the Society, a position which he held until the final breach.

On the one hand, Adler overstressed the biological basis of neurosis in maintaining that this illness is the result of an attempt to overcompensate psychically for the inferiority of one organ or another. On the other hand, he overemphasized the significance of the social, that is to say, of the external factor for the causation of neurosis. Being a Social Democrat, he seems to have attempted to reconcile the Marxist doctrine of class struggle with his own ideas about the psychic conflict. He asserts that the *psychic,* the *inner* conflict is an analogy to the *social, external* conflict between the dispossessed and the ruling class. According to him, the inferior, the weak, is the feminine factor, whereas the superior, the strong, is the masculine factor. A neurosis occurs, so he says, when an individual protests against the inferiority of an organ by psychic overcompensation for the malfunction of this organ. The leitmotif in every neurosis is the idea: "I want to be a man"; this is what Adler terms the masculine protest. Thus, on the one hand, he sexualizes the process of repression by substituting for the psychic conflict the concept of the masculine protest, which implies, of course, that the whole conflict is a struggle between the *homosexual* part of the personality and the *heterosexual* part. On the other hand, he desexualizes the sexual instinct, because he sees in the masculine protest not the intent to help man satisfy the yearning for sexual fulfillment but his yearning for power.

The Adlerian doctrine developed further, with many ramifications, but I cannot give a detailed account of it here. These few words of condensed description, however, should suffice to show that it was incompatible with Freudian psychology. Freud's pupils expected him to take a stand on these questions. Yet, for a long time, Freud remained silent while the majority of the group denounced Adler's innovations. Finally, Adler and his followers resigned. In a later period, when Freud's pupils called his attention to the deviations of Jung and Rank, Freud behaved in a similar way; indeed, it was extremely difficult for him to drop one whom he had once chosen as his friend. The letters to Fliess give us an idea of what the break with Fliess meant to him. The Minutes show how long it was before Freud permitted a rupture to come about between Adler and himself, even though Adler was not nearly so close to him as Fliess had been.

Jung's deviating ideas were not too much discussed at the meetings since he did not belong to the Vienna group and came to Vienna only very rarely. Therefore there is little in the Minutes that would give an indication of Freud's personal reaction to Jung's defection. However, the fact itself that he had chosen Jung his successor, had made him president of the International Psychoanalytic Association, and editor of the *Jahrbuch* would permit us to conclude what he must have felt when Jung deserted him, even if we did not have other sources from which we know how he suffered. Freud had distinctly favored Jung and his Swiss group, and had thus caused jealousy and hurt feelings in the Vienna group. But it is quite incorrect to attribute—as Jones (1953-1957) does in his Freud biography—this resentment to the inferiority feelings of the Jew who suspects anti-Semitism everywhere.

The separation from Rank, which occurred long after 1915, was perhaps the most difficult one for Freud, who had been extremely fond of Rank and thought very highly of his capabilities. He had made him editor of *Imago* and the *Internationale Zeitschrift für Psychoanalyse,* and, from the correspondence which Jessie Taft (1958) published in her biography of Rank, we learn that Freud had seen in him his successor who would further develop his ideas.

In all these cases, Freud broke off the relations, in spite of his personal attachments, when he became convinced that the basic tenets of psychoanalysis were at stake. It seems that Freud felt it to be his duty to protect psychoanalysis, as a father would his child, and to spread the truth as he saw it.

I have just used the phrase "as he saw it"—that is to say, as he saw what was happening in the human mind. For many years I had the opportunity to watch Freud during discussions in the meetings of the Society. When a speaker's remarks aroused his particular interest or when he was trying to make his own point especially clear, he would lift his head and look intensely, with extreme concentration, at a point in space, as if he were seeing something there.[3] This tendency to *see* what he was thinking is reflected in his writings. They contain many pictorial elements, even when dealing with highly theoretical concepts. If his doctrines were considered fantastic speculations by some, we may say that he first looked and then believed, and did not first believe and then see. Only a man with such a vision could discover and see the laws governing the intricate labyrinth of the human mind. I think he greatly underrated his talents when he said in a letter to Fliess that he had a "miserable space-perception" (Freud, 1950).

His adherents could not see all that he saw; they did not have his vision. They could not follow him completely. At the time that these Minutes begin, in 1906, Freud had already written many important articles and most of his basic books, such as the *Studies on Hysteria* (together with Breuer) (1895), *The Interpretation of Dreams* (1900), followed a little later by *The Psychopathology of Everyday Life* (1901), the *Three Contributions to the Theory of Sexuality* (1905c), and *Jokes and Their Relation to the Unconscious* (1905b). Not all of the discussants, however, were thoroughly familiar with these works. This may account for many misunderstandings. On the other hand, some of the misunderstandings were —as has already been indicated—due to resistances such as we all have against our repressed unconscious. Indeed, psychoanalytic insight could only be assimilated through constant psychic struggle, in the same way as we witness it in our daily work with patients.

As the study of the Minutes discloses, the members of the group saw far more in psychoanalysis than a psychopathology and a method of treating sick people. They knew that man is a social being as well as a biological entity. They recognized that the relations of man with his environment are expressed not only in his behavior but also in works of art and literature, in religion, and in

---

[3] This expression is beautifully caught in the etching by Pollack, in which Freud sits behind his desk surrounded by his collection of antique art objects.

social institutions. Therefore, they found it necessary to concern themselves not only with the sick human being but also with literature, religion, philosophy, anthropology, sociology, and so forth. There were, in fact, many debates about the interaction of biological, social, and historical factors in the development of the individual as well as of mankind.

In those early years it was difficult to obtain suitable case material for psychoanalytic study. But this material was easily available from nonclinical sources. This may explain the striking fact that at the outset, and even later, problems of art, literature, mythology, religion, education, were discussed more than were problems of psychiatry.

Among the numerous discussions there were, of course, also those about psychoanalytic theory. However, the discussants were more concerned, at that time, with the *meaning* of the unconscious than with its theoretical significance. Although Freud, at times, indulged in theoretical speculations, which were, of course, always tested on clinical material, he did not encourage his pupils to do the same. For instance, when I once got into a discussion with Tausk about the nature of attention, Freud interrupted us with the remark that these problems were too *"difficiles."* If we read today his "Project" (1895) in *The Origins of Psychoanalysis,* where he deals with the same problem, we can well understand his warning to be cautious.

And yet, Freud was criticized at different times and by various critics for indulging in excessive speculation without regard for clinical experience, as he was for overemphasizing sexuality, for paying no attention to the aggressive drives, for ignoring that man has an ego and that it is influenced by sociological factors, in short, for recognizing only biological factors as working on the human mind, and neglecting ideological ones, and so forth.

These Minutes present quite a different picture. Although it is true that in the span of time they cover, analysis *seems* to have been based solely on the libido theory, the attentive reader will find this belief erroneous. For even at that time, not only the sex or life instincts but also the aggressive or death instincts were under discussion. Moreover, Freud repeatedly stressed the contrast between libidinal and ego instincts and emphasized the fact that repression is a function of the ego, as are sublimation and the sense of guilt. As Freud indicated on many occasions, he did not like to be forced to formulate new concepts before they had matured in his mind. The concepts in question were of such a fundamental nature that he had to see them clearly in his own mind before he would convey them *in extenso* to others.

The discussions in the Society disclose, perhaps more clearly than his books and essays, how Freud's mind worked. What we see first is meticulous scientific observation, as is appropriate for a man who for years peered through a microscope in search of facts; observation combined with a soaring fantasy which is restrained by criticism, a need for causality, for systematization and integration. He was not a wishful thinker; he carefully scrutinized the complicated material spread before him by his pupils until he could see the reality behind the façade. He could not compromise once he had seen the truth.

Naturally, in the course of the years, while constantly working on his discoveries, Freud developed and modified his concepts. Because of this he was charged with inconsistency and confusion. These modifications were, however, the legitimate result of growing experience and ever-deepening insight into the workings of the human mind. One can easily discover in these records when it was that Freud made remarks indicating new problems. With very few exceptions, no one grasped their whole significance at the time. These problems gradually became crystallized in the works that he published between 1911 and 1923. To mention only a few of these works: "On Narcissism" (1914b), the papers on metapsychology (1911-1917), *Beyond the Pleasure Principle* (1920), *Group Psychology and the Analysis of the Ego* (1921), *The Ego and the Id* (1923a). Discussion of these works took place in the meetings of the Society; but after 1915 there are no records of these discussions.

The Minutes show that the Society underwent repeated changes. From an obscure initial group there developed the well-known and influential Viennese Society and the International Psychoanalytic Association. In the course of these developments, some members resigned, but most remained faithful until the dissolution of the Society in 1938 when Hitler occupied Austria. Of the original Wednesday Evening members, however, only Federn, Hitschmann, and Sadger remained to the very end. They developed steadily and each in his own way contributed his share to the growth of psychoanalysis. Since the death of Federn in 1952 and of Hitschmann in 1957, none of the original pioneers is left.

We do not deem it appropriate to enlarge upon the personalities of the Society. The Minutes speak for themselves; we believe that the reader will develop his own opinion about them. Similar considerations guided us in our task of editing the Minutes. We had the choice of selecting from the material what seemed to us most important, or of publishing all of the material as it is preserved, regardless of the importance or insignificance of some remarks.

It is for the following reasons that we decided to publish *all of the material*.[4] First, we wished to let the reader see for himself how these men influenced each other and how they accepted or rejected what was offered them; and that at times, they were dominated by emotions, prejudices, and influences alien to psychoanalysis. We wanted to spread before the reader those struggles taking place in the Vienna Society which helped its members to overcome their resistances and paved the way to their maturation as psychoanalysts. Secondly, we believe that it is impossible to give a fair account of the relationship between Freud and his pupils without presenting the material in its entirety. Against the background of his disciples, his figure stands out as the embodiment of an unattainable ideal. He leads them through the labyrinth of psychoanalytic theory and technique. They indeed attempt to follow him and identify with him. Yet, this identification was possible only to a certain extent. For he was so far ahead of them that at times it was difficult to follow him.

These Minutes also have a historical significance; they throw light on the way in which psychoanalysis developed and permit us to catch a glimpse of how and when Freud began to emerge from his isolation. They show us how he regained contact with the external world. Thus, we hope that the publication of the protocols will be a contribution to the knowledge of how psychoanalysis came

---

[4] As mentioned before, Federn (1947) published one protocol in the *Samiksa*, under the title: "Professor Freud: The Beginning of a Case History." In this publication Federn was selective, quoting only some discussants and omitting the remarks of others. His presentation of the protocol is thus incomplete.

of age, spread, and developed. However, the Minutes are of value for an additional and maybe more important reason: even today, primarily from Freud's remarks, one can learn much from them about the theory and technique of psychoanalysis.

In closing, we cannot think of a better way to illustrate what the meetings meant to the participants than to quote two of them; the first is Lou Andreas-Salomé, Nietzsche's and Rilke's friend, who was a writer and philosopher and became in her mature years a devoted follower of Freud. She was a guest at the meetings of the Vienna Society in the academic year 1912-1913. After the last session she attended, she made an entry in her Diary, from which I quote:

"I almost raised my hand and asked for permission to speak because I wanted to say the following: Gentlemen: I never wished to participate in the discussions; I let you do the discussing for me; the thanking, however, the thanking I want to do myself. To thank psychoanalysis, especially for demanding more than solitary work at the desk and thus having brought me here, to a kind of fraternity. Indeed, it is no vague mixture of science and sectarianism which makes psychoanalysis such a living force, but it is the fact that analysis has made of the supreme principle of all scientific endeavor, namely, of honesty, its own vital principle. This it applies continuously and over and again, even within the most individual reality; thus it subjects life to insight—just as, on the other hand, psychoanalysis has bent to life the narrow, withered knowledge of academic psychology, thus laying the foundations of its pre-eminent scientific achievement. This is the very reason why, within this circle and beyond, splits arise and disputes—and it is more difficult to settle these than any others, without endangering the continuity of results and methods.... Yet, at the same time, it is beautiful to see men facing one another in honest battle. So much more is it my, the woman's part to thank. To thank all these evenings, even the dull ones, for the sake of the One who chaired them and gave them of his time" (Andreas-Salomé, 1912-1913).

The second participant is Max Graf, an esteemed musicologist and professor at the Vienna Academy of Music, who was a permanent member of the Society. In the foreword to his *Richard Wagner im "Fliegenden Holländer": Ein Beitrag zur Psychologie künst-*

lerischen Schaffens [*Richard Wagner in the "Flying Dutchman":
A Contribution to the Psychology of Artistic Creativity*], he said the
following:

"With this little book, I would like to keep alive the spirit of
those discussions of psychological problems within a small society
which, during a number of years, met each week in Professor
Freud's warm and friendly home. This group of friends undertook
the task of testing, in a great many contexts, Freudian ideas and
concepts. In this circle, I read a paper about Richard Wagner's
The Flying Dutchman. The present work grew out of this lecture.
The ideas which I develop here are the result of an uninterrupted
exchange of thoughts with Professor Freud, and of many suggestions gleaned from discussions in his house, suggestions which
slowly ripened over the years. The present article is, then, the
fruit of an exchange of thoughts and ideas extending over many
years; it would be impossible to separate those which I owe to the
guidance of Professor Freud, and those which should be attributed
to the criticism of several of my colleagues. Thus, I dedicate this
study to the memory of those stimulating and exciting hours spent
in mutual intellectual strivings with the circle of friends" (Graf,
1911).

CURIOSITY

LADIES AND GENTLEMEN:

For a long time I have wished to demonstrate, by using a case in treatment, how an analysis unfolds. However, when I set myself to work, I found that this is an almost impossible undertaking as the presentation of the full analysis of a case would require an excessive amount of time. Nevertheless, I should like you to take at least a brief look into the psychoanalytic workshop: I shall try to show, by means of a fragment of an analysis, how a theoretical understanding of certain problems gradually evolves. Even from such an abridged proceeding one can learn how complicated an analysis is, how intricate psychic processes are, and how cautious one should be in his theoretical conclusions.

The analysis of each case offers many problems; as I have to limit myself only to one, I have selected the problem of curiosity because it dominates the life of the patient I am going to present. We shall see that for the understanding of a single problem the patient's entire life must serve as a background. Even so, many questions will remain unanswered.

In the course of his investigations Freud learned, as he remarks, that psychic phenomena can best be studied in pathological exaggeration. For instance, as long as ego and superego are integrated, the individual is not aware of his conscience; only when there is a conflict and they are split does he become aware of the existence of his conscience.

For the observer, likewise, it is often difficult to conclude from the behavior of the so-called normal person that he has a conscience or superego, whereas he certainly can do so with much greater ease when he watches an individual in conflict, that is, in an abnormal

This work consists of an expanded version of the Freud Anniversary Lecture given at The New York Academy of Medicine on May 17, 1960 (Nunberg, 1961).

state. When phenomena are pathologically exaggerated they can be seen better than when they are in the normal state of integration with other phenomena. Thus we hope from the investigation of the patient's main symptom, curiosity, to be able to reach some conclusions about the normal development and function of this phenomenon. Briefly, the purpose of this paper is twofold: to give an idea of analytic procedure as well as to show the metamorphosis and the meaning of curiosity.

Before I begin, I should like to state that I cannot offer new basic insights into a problem which has been treated extensively in psychoanalytic literature. In addition to Freud's fundamental work in the *Three Essays on the Theory of Sexuality* (1905c), *Leonardo da Vinci and a Memory of His Childhood* (1910), and some other papers, there are quite a number of other psychoanalytic contributions to the same topic.

The extremely complex phenomenon of curiosity expresses itself in many ways, such as looking, listening, touching. Of course, in one instance one form of expression may prevail, in another a different one. Whenever I speak here of looking, touching, hearing, etc., I am referring to manifestations of curiosity. Through the gratification of curiosity one acquires a certain stock of knowledge, which may again lead to new problems and the formulation of new questions. Curiosity may therefore also be called an *urge for knowledge*.

Our patient suffered from the compulsion to ask questions and to look for answers. He had simple questions and answers as well as complicated ones. Some questions and answers were satisfactory to him and others were not. Both types of questions were accompanied by anxiety. When an answer was satisfactory, the anxiety disappeared; when it was unsatisfactory, the anxiety built up to panic. Among the variety of his questions were, for instance, the following: What is speaking? How does it take place? How does it start? Questions about the start, the beginning, overwhelmed him very often, in the most unexpected disguises. On one occasion he asked, "Do I say things which are original?" When I asked him to explain the meaning of the word "original," he answered promptly, "It means childbirth, how you are born." Upon my request for further clarification he said, "Do you not see, the word 'original' is 'origin' and that means 'beginning,' how the child is started; how it is born." Thus, without further analysis, it was evident that these questions contained in a disguised form the question of how man is born. Similarly, the question "how thoughts start" meant how a thought is born, and the questions about origin and formation of words had a similar meaning.

This type of question was accompanied by slight anxiety. Another type was coupled with somewhat greater anxiety which, however, could be checked by an answer that included the words, "to a certain degree." An example: "Do I love people?" Answer: "Everybody loves everybody to a certain degree." This answer was satisfactory to him; it is easy to see why: he evaded the issue by generalization and at the same time restricted the validity of the answer by adding the words, "to a certain degree." It was a kind of compromise in which one part of the sentence contradicted the other. In brief, the answer was ambivalent.

A third type of question looked as follows: "Are there times when you say things which have a regular top-surface-do-aspect?" Answer: "Everything a person does has a regular surface-do-aspect, unless he says something, to a degree." Neither the form of these questions nor that of the answers satisfied him, and the more he tried to change the formulations, the more complicated and nonsensical they became. Finally, he became confused, dizzy, nauseated, and the full attack of panic set in. It would last from a few days to four, five, or six months. During the attacks he had to stay home, secluded in his darkened bedroom, unable to go to work.

There is no doubt as to the diagnosis: this is an obsessional neurosis. We know then that we have to expect a regression of the libido to the anal-sadistic phase and a strict, overdemanding superego. I have published a short fragment of this case (Nunberg, 1955, pp. 343-346). I reported there that the patient became aware of his first attack when he was sixteen years old. On his way home from school he had to ask himself when, precisely, the period of Renaissance began and when it ended. Of course, he could not find a satisfactory answer. When he spoke again about this attack, the following recollection came to his mind. One morning—he was about ten years old—his sister came down to the kitchen carrying a bundle. Asked what it contained, she gave no answer but ran outside and threw it into the garbage can. He followed her, took the bundle out, unwrapped it, and found a bloody cloth. Enormously embarrassed, he threw it back and never mentioned this incident again. Obviously, with one part of his ego he knew quite well that the bundle contained a sanitary napkin, but with another part he denied this knowledge to himself.

The question when the period of the Renaissance begins and when it ends thus means: when does the menstrual period begin and when does it end? Since the word "Re-naissance" means "rebirth," this question again deals with birth, the origin of man. Certainly, all of the patient's questions have a sexual background. Sexual curiosity plays, indeed, an important role in the normal life of children and adults, as well as in certain types of perversion and neurosis. To follow up the vicissitudes of curiosity, however, we must learn more about our patient's life.

He had an interesting relationship with his sister, who was four years his senior. Perhaps his earliest childhood recollection referred to the fact that she had almost bitten off his toe when he was about a year old. He did not remember the fact as such, nor did he remember when he had heard about it for the first time, but he had the feeling that he had known of it all his life. During the analysis he asked his sister for more information about this incident. She confirmed his "recollection" and even asked him whether he still had the scar on his toe. Up to his sixth year the relationship between the two children was highly ambivalent. There was much fighting between them; when he complained, his mother would take his side and punish the sister.

He loved his mother passionately and was very attached to her. The father disapproved of this excessive attachment and endeavored to counterbalance it by teaching him how to wrestle, to box, swim, etc. When, in spite of his efforts, he saw no change in the boy, the father became impatient, chided the child for behaving like a girl, called him a sissy and threatened "to cut him from his mother's apron strings." The harder the father tried to separate him from his mother, the more he clung to her. In order to stimulate his masculinity, his father sent him to summer camp as soon as he was six years old. Immediately after his return home, the father took the whole family to Europe. The children were placed in two separate though neighboring schools and the parents left. After a year had elapsed, they took the children back home.

This experience seems to have been the turning point in the patient's life. Before the trip he loved his mother and was ambivalent to the sister. This changed while he was abroad. It appeared as if he had lost his love for the mother and had begun to love the sister. When he returned home, he felt like a stranger in the family, talked neither to mother nor father, but became increasingly close to the sister. Obviously, the love for the sister had been substituted for the love of his mother.

When he was about nine years old, or perhaps somewhat younger, anxiety dreams about a man with a gun and a *flashlight* trying to force himself into his room began to disturb his sleep. Awakened by anxiety, he would ask his sister in the adjoining room to let him come into her bed. When she consented, he slipped quietly into her room. Before settling in her bed, however, he had to perform a certain ritual: he had to lie down, his head at her feet and his back toward hers, while no part of his body was allowed to touch hers. When I asked him whether he had always succeeded in keeping a proper distance between himself and the sister, he remarked that he had no sexual thoughts about or desires for her (as if he understood what my question implied). Yet he developed a kind of negative reaction. That is, it became his habit to be very careful not to touch her; in fact, he avoided coming close to her. This avoidance of touching persisted into adulthood, became generalized, and extended even to his own children. He feared that by touching he might harm them.

The clandestine relation with his sister continued until his sixteenth year. When he was fifteen the family moved to an apartment where he shared the bedroom with his sister. They had twin beds like a married couple, but since the beds were separated by a bed table, there was less chance of touching than of seeing one another. He took great pains *not to see her nude* and *not to be seen nude by her,* which was perhaps more important to him. *On the other hand, he looked and peeped with great pleasure* when it did not concern her. For instance, when girl friends came to visit her and stayed overnight (on such occasions he would sleep in the living room), he peeped through the keyhole trying to get a glimpse of them while they were *dressing* or *undressing,* and he had sexual desires for and dreams about them.

The avoidance of both looking and touching thus was a reaction formation against the urges to do so. All of his defenses, however, including the repression proper, could not withstand the increased demands of the libido in puberty. Especially in the last year in which he shared the bedroom with his sister, he was disturbed by the ever-growing intensity of his sexual urges as well as by wet dreams, the contents of which he could not remember. Yet in spite of his sexual hypersensitivity, he did not masturbate until his sister was married and left the parental home. He was then sixteen years old. Whenever he would meet her afterwards, he was embarrassed and unable to talk to her, just as he had been unable to talk to his mother after his disappointment in her in Europe. Obviously he felt that she had deserted him, just as the mother had done.

Until her marriage the sister was sexually taboo to him. Afterwards, he would speculate about her sexual relations with her husband and ask himself many questions about her sexuality. But there was no satisfactory answer. So he would walk the streets and look at women, asking himself how their sex organs looked and whether they had sexual relations. He went to movies, to burlesque shows, strip-tease performances; he would peep into neighbors' windows, and the like.

It is obvious that he could control his sexual feelings as long as he shared the room with his sister, but as soon as he was left to himself, the repressed sexuality exploded and appeared first as a perversion in the shape of sexual curiosity. In other words, *instead of choosing another sexual object after the loss of the sister, he made a regression to sexual curiosity.*

When in this period he peeped into a neighbor's window and saw a nude man, he was so impressed by the size of his penis that in great distress he asked himself repeatedly, "How can a man do that to a woman?"—meaning how can a man be so cruel to a woman. In truth he wanted to know whether his father was as cruel to his mother.

He reacted to the session in which he related this experience with the following dream. He was in bed with his wife making love to her but had the feeling that his son was watching him. When he turned toward the child's bed, he saw him lying quietly there but he was not sure whether the boy was actually asleep or only pretending to be. His son's attitude seemed familiar to him; it reminded him that he himself had often pretended to sleep when sleeping was expected of him. Then he remembered his own crib in his parents' bedroom and the noises which would wake him up at night. One could sense the unformulated questions of the little child, questions which the mature man tried to answer in his neurosis (Nunberg, 1955, p. 346).

In this dream the patient projects himself into his son, at the same time identifying himself with his father. The son, who represents the patient, watches him as he himself had once watched his father. Watching means looking with the purpose of finding out something, often without a clear formulation of a question. A child cannot ask questions before he can talk. Yet he is able to express feelings and emotions such as joy, pain, surprise, astonishment, curiosity by the intonation of his voice, by a gesture, by the posture of his body. The child in the dream did not talk, he lifted his head and looked at the father. Watching the father, looking at that early age, may dramatize a question, as if the child were asking, "What are you doing?"

We know that all children are sexually curious, but also that they give up this curiosity in the course of development. Our patient, however, seems to have retained much of it and satisfied it in a more or less disguised form in many ways, masturbatory fantasies among them. As indicated before, he did not masturbate until his sister was married. Then he began to masturbate with the following fantasy. He put a woman, most frequently his father's secretary, on an operating table, tied her and made her helpless, then undressed her and looked at her until he became sexually very excited. In this fantasy, looking is a sadistic act. As a mature man he would ask himself, while in the act of copulating with his wife, whether he derived more pleasure from looking, touching, and squeezing her than from intercourse. This man, who treated his wife with utmost consideration, had to have her face lighted during copulation so that he could see whether she showed signs of pain. His curiosity thus was mixed with a great deal of sadism.

His scoptophilic, sadistic fantasy persisted for a long time without change. Before that, in prepuberty, he had another fantasy which was of rather a masochistic nature. In order to understand the relationship between the two, we have to go back to the period following his return from Europe.

We remember his father's disapproval of the boy's excessive attachment to the mother and of his femininity, and I have reported that he separated his son from her for a year. After the family had returned home, the boy made up his mind to become a real man. He took up a variety of sports, such as boxing, football, etc., and in the course of time became a first-rate athlete, a champion. Yet he failed to impress his father with the numerous trophies he brought home. He was not interested in girls, except for his sister, but formed many friendships with boys. His best friend, Timmy, was also an excellent athlete. Timmy was not a strong boy of athletic build; he was rather girlish, slim, weak-looking, but agile and alert. Their friendship was so great that they never played against one another in any competitive game, but always together on one team against others. They also played fantasy games together, one of which they called the *pirate game*. They were then between nine and eleven years old. The game was played in the following way: they would lie on their stomachs on separate beds; our patient would be the leader, calling out each step of the game in the manner of a radio announcer. He would say, for instance, "Now we climb up the pirate ship; now we draw our swords and fight the pirates." Suddenly they would notice that the pirates were women, not men as they had expected, whereupon they would stop fighting and surrender. It was a matter of honor to him not to fight women. The female pirates captured him, tied him to the ship's mast and made him helpless; then they undressed the upper part of his body down to the waist, looked at him, and asked where the treasure was hidden. He did not betray the secret and saw himself as a hero. When he refused to answer, the female leader gave the order to whip him. When he still remained silent, she ordered that his trousers be taken off. At this point he became very excited sexually and broke off the fantasy game.

This fantasy was the opposite of the postpubertal fantasy. In the latter he was active, sadistic, *looking* at the helpless nude woman; in the former he was passive, masochistic, undressed and *looked at by the woman.* In both fantasies the sexual excitement became overwhelming; in the later one by *searchingly looking* at a woman, in the earlier one by *being asked questions and looked at by a woman.*

The content of the pirate fantasy was composed of real and psychic elements.[1] The concept of the pirate ships and hidden treasures stems, of course, from stories and moving pictures. The costumes in which the pirate women were dressed stemmed from experiences in the attic of the parental home. From early childhood on the patient and his sister used to play there with costumes they had found in a chest. She would dress in such a costume and dance before him to his great delight. The pirate leader, dressed in this costume, thus represented (in one layer) the sister. We remember: when he would come to her bed at night, frightened by a dream, he denied himself the pleasure of touching or looking at her, because, he said, he was afraid he might harm her. In the pirate game he took on a passive role, as if he were saying, "Not I am curious about the pirate woman (my sister), not I want to touch her or to see her nude, but she wants to touch (to beat) me and to look at me." The whip of the pirate woman reminded him of the cat-o'-nine-tails hanging from the kitchen wall throughout his childhood. Whenever he was naughty, his mother would threaten to whip him, but never did. Finally, he wished she would do it.

As the whip is a well-known penis symbol, we may assume that the patient equipped the pirate woman, the sister and mother substitute, with a symbolic penis. If this interpretation is correct, we have here a classic example of the concept of the woman with a penis, found so often in both men and women. His friend Timmy, a male, reminded him of his sister in many ways, such as in his slight build and the rhythm of his movements. The fact that

[1] Fantasies are reactions of the ego to the urges of the id, on the one hand, and to the demands of reality, on the other; they are a compromise between the two. All small children have fantasies which may be considered unconscious at that age. In latency they become conscious in a distorted form; we may say that they are preconscious. All fantasies undergo changes in the course of development; they may be repressed and are then transformed into character traits; they may be dormant, that is inactive, and take no effect on the behavior of the individual. Under certain circumstances they may become active, that is, charged with energy, and then they influence the individual's creativity or lead to perversions or neuroses.

he refused to play against him in competitive games was even more convincing. He said he could not beat his best friend. When he fought with his sister and in the end hit her, his father would get very angry and warn him sternly not to do that again, stressing that one does not do that to a girl. In the pirate game he could not fight the pirates as soon as he discovered that they were women, and he had to be as considerate of Timmy as he was expected to be of his sister.[2]

The pirate fantasy during which each boy was masturbating for himself was in fact a mutual masturbation fantasy. If we add that the patient many times felt the urge to jump upon his friend and to rub his penis against Timmy's, we recognize that the wish for sexual gratification was displaced from the sister onto the friend. If it is true that Timmy represented her, then she was a bisexual creature in his eyes—a male and a female.

The house to which the family moved when the patient was fifteen years old was a great distance from the old residence. It made him very unhappy that he could no longer see his friend daily. Moreover, as Timmy's friendship cooled off gradually, he felt deserted, depressed, and lonesome. The frustration of the homosexual friendship may well have contributed more to his final breakdown than his sister's marriage. Frustrated homosexuality seems to have been a factor in his regression to infantile, aggressive sexual curiosity.

Now we have to ask ourselves how and when he acquired the idea that his sister had a penis—an idea which contradicted the perception of his sense organs. It was difficult to establish the exact time at which he first noticed the difference between his own and her sexual organs. It is certain, however, that he was very young when he first asked his mother questions about the difference, long before the trip to Europe. He did not believe her answers and found one for himself: the father had cut off the sister's penis. This was consistent with his ideas about sexual intercourse in which the woman is hurt and injured by the man. However, he very soon became dissatisfied with this solution, and became anxious and

---

[2] A certain type of homosexual retains in his object choice some of the features characteristic of his repressed first sexual object. The patient had first repressed the love of which his mother was the object by substituting the sister for her; then he exchanged the latter for Timmy.

restless. After much doubting and brooding, he came to the conclusion that the sister had a penis but that it was hidden high up in the abdomen, *for protection.*

It is interesting to note that the painful perception of the difference between himself and his sister stimulated his curiosity. The explanation which he gave himself first provoked restlessness and anxiety. This anxiety, which can only be interpreted as castration anxiety, in turn stimulated other questions, speculations and answers, which seemed to be aimed at providing reassurance and comfort. With the reassuring answer that the sister, a woman, has a penis, his anxiety disappeared for a while. Even though his answers were incorrect, the questions, speculations, and quasilogical deductions still are a sign of intellectual activity; indeed, not infrequently do painful experiences give the impetus to intellectual and artistic creativity.[3]

Let us now continue with the analysis of the pirate fantasy. Two events occurred immediately before its emergence. Under our patient's leadership, a group of boys in school ganged up on one of their schoolmates and tried to undress him; he was a frail, blond, girlish-looking boy. When our patient noticed how desperately he defended himself and how he suffered, he felt pity for him and guilt and ceased to participate in the assault. Shortly thereafter a group of strange boys accosted him and asked whether he had a sister. Upon his affirmative answer they demanded her address. Sensing that something was wrong, he gave them false information. After they had left, Timmy told him that they belonged to a gang

[3] I see in this phenomenon, which evolves at the very beginning of the latency period, a parallel to the intellectualization in puberty as observed by Anna Freud (1936). According to her, the intensified intellectual activity of the adolescent helps him in mastering the increased pressure of the libido in puberty. It seems that in our case—and in others which I have observed—castration fear on the one hand supports the inhibitions demanded by upbringing, and checks infantile curiosity with all its consequences, while on the other hand it stimulates the development of mental activity. This is another manifestation of the importance of the castration complex. As Freud has said, not only can it influence the mental development (as it does in our case), but also the character development and is the factor which is decisive in regard to an individual's health or illness. The castration complex is ubiquitous and seems to be inherited, like the oedipus complex. External events and traumata, like those castration threats on the part of the patient's mother, may, at the most, modify or enforce the castration complex, but they do not create it.

of boys who kidnapped girls, tied, undressed, and looked at them. Although he condemned the supposed activities of these boys, he felt a strange sexual excitement. It was soon after this that the pirate games with Timmy began.

In these games he carried out the exact opposite of what the gang of boys was supposed to do to the girls and what he himself had wanted to do with the girlish boy in school. These boys were sadistic and looked at nude girls; in the pirate game the girls were sadistic, undressed him and looked at him. The idea of active looking changed into passive feelings of being looked at. It was only years later that he permitted himself to do in his fantasy with the secretary what he had been afraid the boys were going to do to his sister and what he had wanted to do to the sister substitute. However, the appearance of the gang immediately after the assault on the girlish boy seems to have weakened his ego in his effort to repress his desire for the sister. Yet he did not succumb to the temptation, but reinforced the repression by reversing the desire to look and to touch into its opposite, that is, into being looked at and beaten in the pirate fantasy.

When he boarded the pirate ship in this game, he expected to find men there and was prepared to fight them, but instead found women dressed like men. Our patient had numerous anxiety dreams in which he was savagely fighting with a man. There is no doubt that the man represented his father. He was never afraid of his mother or of the pirate woman in the fantasy, but of the father. It is, therefore, likely that he substituted the mother for the father at the last moment, as if he were saying that the pirate woman was less dangerous than the pirate man. Thus the pirate fantasy was a bisexual fantasy: heterosexual in so far as it was conscious, homosexual as well as dangerous in so far as it was unconscious.

We indicated a moment ago that the secretary fantasy was a straight reversal of the pirate fantasy of his prepuberty years, in which he was passive and masochistic. Moreover, in the secretary fantasy the woman is entirely a woman, not a bisexual being. This fantasy represents, in a sense, a progress from passivity and homosexuality to activity and heterosexuality. He stressed many times that he felt the greatest sexual excitement when, in the secretary fantasy, he overpowered the woman and tore the blouse from her body, just as in the pirate fantasy he felt the greatest excitement when the woman threatened to remove his trousers. Obviously, looking, which was in his mind the same as investigating, became alternately a sadistic and a masochistic act.

The repressed wish to look, to investigate, to be active and aggressive appeared, as mentioned before, in the pirate fantasy as its counterpart, the fear of being looked at and examined. (The intensity of his fear of being looked at can be judged from the fact that after years of married life and fatherhood he was unable to undress in his wife's presence.) It may thus be assumed that the pirate fantasy on the whole was a defense against his aggression toward the sister, the aggression which became conscious as a sexual urge aimed at a sister (mother) substitute in the secretary fantasy.

The patient himself rationalized his fear of being looked at with a fear of being laughed at. The latter stemmed, in fact, from his sister's laughing at him and pointing her finger at his penis when she saw him naked as a little boy. He remembered an incident in his fifth year when she came into the bathroom while he was standing nude in the bathtub. He became frightened because the way she looked at him made him feel that she would take his penis away from him, that she might castrate him by looking. His fear of being seen nude expresses both fear of castration and fear of exposing his "inferior" penis.

When in the fantasy the pirate woman gave the order to beat him, he had the mental picture of his own back covered with red, bloody streaks. Evidently he split himself and saw or hallucinated his own back in projection in the external world. It reminded him of an experience he had had when he was four years old. A lady took him and her little son to a bathhouse on the beach. She asked the children to turn to the wall and not to look while she was undressing, but our patient turned around and looked at her. She caught him at it and said sternly, "No peeking!" However, he had had enough time to catch a glimpse of her back, which seemed to him covered with red, bloody streaks, as if after a whipping. Thus he identified in the pirate fantasy with a beaten, injured woman. In one layer the fantasy of being beaten by a woman means the fulfillment of his old wish to be whipped by his mother. But we have interpreted the pirate woman as a woman with a penis, that is, a man. If we take into account that a fantasy, like a dream, is always overdetermined, we may say that he is beaten not only by a woman but also by a man. If we further remember that in his imagination the father beat and injured the mother at night, we must assume that, in the deepest layer of his fantasy, the patient identified with his mother as beaten by his father. Being afraid to expose his genitals as well as being afraid to look at a woman's stems from the same source, the castration complex. In the first case he fears castration; in the second he is afraid to look at a human being who has no penis.

Yet there was a time when he was not afraid to be exposed and looked at. About half a year after the beginning of his analysis his sister told him something which she thought might be useful in his treatment. When he was two and a half years old a maid played with him sexually on the bathroom floor. He could not remember any event of that kind, but a picture came to his mind of himself lying on the bathroom floor and the maid or nurse kissing his penis. Subsequently, whenever he thought of his sister's story, he saw the nurse or maid kissing his penis; in the end he began to believe that the picture was not an imagination but the recollection of a real event.[4] Since it was difficult to ascertain what really happened, I consented to his asking his sister about the details. The sister, who was six and a half years old at the time when the event supposedly took place, confirmed his "hallucinated" recollection and added that their mother dismissed the maid immediately when she came home and learned what had happened. The mother gave a different version. She remembered that upon coming home one afternoon she found the *nursemaid* drunk on the floor before the bathroom and the boy holding his penis and crying because he could not urinate. She dismissed the maid on the spot and took the child to the doctor. He informed her that the boy's penis was infected and advised to keep it clean. The mother, who had a compulsive character, took the doctor's advice very seriously, washed the boy's penis often, and warned him constantly not to touch it and to keep it clean. Should he fail to obey, she threatened, his penis would get *infected* again and fall off. Under this pressure he washed his penis carefully indeed, probably mas-

---

[4] It happens frequently that what emerges first as a vision or hallucination in the course of an analysis proves to be a real recollection.

turbating at the same time. Later he became very neat and clean, washed his hands exceedingly often, perhaps once every hour, though never to such an extent that it would interfere with his daily activities in business and elsewhere. Only after the discussion of his anality, he revealed that in the beginning of his analysis he had always omitted to express the thought, "and not to be infected," when he was talking about "how a man can put his penis in the dirty, messy genitalium of a woman." His anality which, as will be seen later, played also a considerable part in his infantile birth and pregnancy theories, thus contributed to the formation of certain character traits such as his neatness and overcleanliness, and to the development of his disgust at the female genitalia (Freud, 1908a). In addition, it stimulated the formation of the castration complex in the form of fear of *infection* by the woman.

Let us now return to the bathroom scene. How is the difference between the versions of sister and mother to be understood? It is likely that the sister gave an account of what she saw and the mother one of her own experience. Assuming that the sister's report is correct, how is it possible that she remembered all the details unless she was present and participated in the boy's seduction, or even stimulated him herself, later projecting this onto the nursemaid? This seems quite probable if we take into account that she was very aggressive, a tomboy, that she had actually almost bitten off his toe when he was about a year old, and that, on the other hand, the patient hardly remembered nurse or maid but seemed to remember the kissing of his penis. The mother's version is easy to explain. She may well have come home another time and found the drunken maid and the crying boy outside the bathroom. In the patient's feeling, however, the bathroom scene and the scene in the doctor's office were so closely linked that they almost constituted a unity. Perhaps we can understand this if we consider that both had a common denominator: gratification in the state of passivity. In the doctor's office he was lying on his back on a couch or table while the doctor was doing something to him under a strong light and two women in white, the mother and the nurse, were at his sides *looking at him*. In the bathroom scene he was lying on his back while two women (nurse and/or[5] maid) were kissing his penis.

_____
[5] In the unconscious "or" often means "and."

He had no other association to the scene in the doctor's office except one which would always come to his mind whenever he thought of this scene, namely, a mental picture of himself playing some athletic competitive game, such as baseball, while thousands of people were watching and admiring him, and he was feeling a hero. He retained this fantasy unchanged into adulthood. He had it every night before falling asleep; it was like "a mother's good-night kiss," he remarked once. He produced this fantasy also when he would wake up at night and could not go back to sleep; it worked like a hypnotic.

The gratification of being looked at and admired is certainly a narcissistic one; the technique for achieving this goal, that is, showing oneself, is called exhibitionism. It is a counterpart to voyeurism or scoptophilia and, perhaps in a broader sense, to curiosity. Scoptophilia as well as the desire to touch, listen, taste, or smell, can be gratified by the stimulation of an erotogenic zone, such as the eye, the skin, the ear. Exhibitionism cannot be satisfied by stimulation of an erotogenic zone, since there is none for the exhibitionistic drive. It can be satisfied only by identification with the onlooker, that is, with an object of the external world. When the patient was gratified by the fantasy of a woman looking at him in the pirate game or by the fantasy of a crowd watching him playing some athletic game, he regressed to the time of the scene in the doctor's office, to the narcissistic gratification in exhibitionism, that is, to the early times when mother looked at him with admiring affection.

The scene in the doctor's office has still another connotation: he was struck by the fact that the doctor used a glaring light for examining his penis. Repeatedly he called my attention to this light, which he called a flashlight, as if he were trying to tell me that this was something very important. Actually, a flashlight played an important role during his childhood until puberty. As mentioned before, he had a repetitive dream in which he lay in bed in his room, his face turned to the wall, when suddenly he heard heavy steps of a man coming up the stairs and approaching his room. He turned around in his bed in order to see who was coming and was hit by a strong flashlight when the man opened the door and tried to find him. He awoke with anxiety and went to his sister's bed.

So the scene in the doctor's office seems to have branched out in several directions: (1) fear of genital infection through contact with a woman; (2) reaction formations against anal stimuli and wishes; (3) fear of castration by the father when found by him with a flashlight, i.e., when being watched by him; and (4) narcissistic gratification derived from the feeling of being watched by others. This last ramification is of great importance for it throws into relief that showing oneself nude not only gives narcissistic pleasure but, as an attempt to seduce the onlooker, may also become a danger. In other words, to be admired by mother gives pleasure, while to be admired by a man may be dangerous.

It may appear that all this has not much to do with the problem of curiosity; the following material will lead us slowly back to this problem. We return to our patient's trip to Europe.

On the boat he had many anxiety dreams of which he remembered only one: somebody throws him overboard into the ocean; he sees the ship moving away from him, farther and farther; he tries to swim, to hold on to something, perhaps a board, but there is no help, the waves are closing in and he feels desperate, alone, helpless. He woke up in panic.

Knowing the background of this dream, one had no great difficulty in understanding it, at least to a certain point. On the ship the boy had been told of the impending separation from his family, and he was full of worries and fears. Since a ship very often symbolizes a woman, we may interpret the boat in the dream as a symbol of his mother. Being thrown into the ocean means, then, being separated from her. The father was the only person who could perform this brutal act. We recall that the father considered him effeminate and too much attached to his mother and had threatened "to cut him off her apron strings"; therefore we must conclude that the dreamer was afraid to be separated from his mother by castration. If this interpretation is correct, we understand the panic which woke him up, a panic which frustrated the wish-fulfillment tendency of the dream. Translated into conscious language the dream says: I submit to my father's wish to separate from my mother, but if it implies castration I will not do so. Thus the attempt to please the father is frustrated by castration fear.

This dream is overdetermined, as are all dreams. The patient's mind was occupied with many thoughts on that trip, one of which pursued him with particular persistence. It concerned the Count

of Monte Cristo, the hero of Alexandre Dumas' novel.[6] He felt
compelled to visualize over and over again the episode in which
the hero was captured by his enemies, dragged into prison, sewn
into a sack, and thrown into a canal, a sewer. The Count cuts the
sack open from within, slips out of it and swims from the sewer
into open, clean water, thus escaping from the dreadful and disgusting prison.

The fascination which this episode had for our patient is easily
accounted for by one of his birth theories. Supplementing his old
belief that the father was beating and injuring the mother in
sexual intercourse, he imagined at a later stage of development
that the child is born when the doctor cuts the mother's abdomen
open with a knife. Certainly the doctor is a substitute for the father
and the knife a symbol of his penis. In the novel there is no doctor
who cuts the sack, but it is the prisoner himself who does it. Obviously, the child identified with the Count, who is his own
obstetrician; in other words, he gave birth to himself, he was
reborn. Besides the fact that all birth fantasies are both active and
passive, our patient himself stressed many times that thinking
about the baby in the mother's body, he always saw and felt himself as the baby. The cesspool in which the hero is swimming struck
again a familiar note. The boy's idea was that the unborn baby is
swimming in urine and feces inside the mother, as if he knew the
old proverb, *"Inter faeces et urinam nascimur."* He would speculate how a child could live there, see in the dark, breathe, eat, and
get out of there. One gains the impression that he had endeavored
to look inside the mother, to penetrate into her, as in later years
he tried to penetrate secrets by peeping. We find offshoots of this
problem in the questions he asked himself in later years, such as,
"Do I inhale or exhale when I am hitting the [golf]ball?" To
which he would answer, "You neither inhale nor exhale by the
mouth; you keep it shut; you suck in the air by your anus."

None of these thoughts, questions, and fantasies appear in the
manifest dream, but they are contained in the latent dream
thoughts; they are represented by the Count, who serves as an
intermediary link. (We know that omissions in the dream serve

[6] It was difficult to ascertain how a child of his age came to be acquainted
with this novel. One of his aunts who read innumerable stories to him throughout his childhood may have chosen that one, too.

the purpose of disguise.) All the latent dream thoughts attached to the Count lead us to understand that the dream expresses not only separation and castration wishes but also anal-sadistic birth ideas. What separates the baby more radically from the mother than birth, and what causes more anxiety? The fact that the manifest dream does not contain the slightest hint of anal or sadistic urges is sufficient to show how deeply repressed these anal urges were even at that time.

The multiple determinants of the manifest dream expressed themselves in still another detail which at first seemed insignificant. The dreamer was trying to catch a board "to hold on to" in the ocean. A piece of wood, a board, symbolizes the mother or her breast; hence we may assume that the dreamer was trying to attach himself to the mother's breast in order to undo the separation. And in reality, the woman's breasts played an enormous role in the patient's love life; they held an almost fetishlike fascination for him. Until the age of four or five he was a passionate thumb sucker. He remembered clearly that when he masturbated while sucking his finger, he had a mental picture of his mother's breasts with him in bed. In her effort to wean him from thumb sucking, she used to threaten that his finger would be sucked in and disappear in his stomach. When he compared the two thumbs, it seemed to him that his pleasure-finger was really getting smaller, and he became afraid of losing it. When she warned him against eating fruit pits, another fear was added: he became afraid that an apple tree, an orange tree, or another fruit tree might grow in his stomach. There is no doubt that the thumb symbolically played the role of breasts as well as that of penis, while the fruits growing in his stomach symbolized children.[7] He had so many pregnancy and birth fantasies that it is almost impossible to enumerate them. Even the swimming in the ocean of the manifest dream represents a pregnancy fantasy demonstrating the dangers of birth. For water in a dream has always a symbolic relation to the mother's womb, pregnancy and birth. Derivatives of these fantasies manifested themselves, as we have seen, in innocuous questions, like the one about originality, the origin of speech and thinking, the Renais-

[7] About the transition from breast to penis, see Freud's *Leonardo da Vinci* (1910); and about the symbolic meaning of the thumb, see Rank's (1913) analyses of Grimm's fairy tales.

sance period, etc. From early childhood until the time of his illness he was almost wholly absorbed with the problems of birth; and in his illness these problems constituted at least one component of each of his questions.

It is difficult to say when he first began to ask these questions. The analysis of his dream about the primal scene led us to the conclusion that he already had questions in very early childhood, even though he was not yet able to express them in words. He remembered that he asked mother and sister questions about birth even before he was four years old and that either he received the usual evasive answers or was met with laughter. Of course he rejected the answers; he formed his own theory, namely, that the doctor cuts the baby out of the mother's body. Evidently this theory was an extension of his earlier ideas about father injuring mother at night. So deeply ingrained was this theory that later in life whenever his wife was in labor he would become panicky and enormously afraid that mother and child would be killed.

Freud suggests that curiosity may be stimulated by a birth in the family, but no birth occurred in the patient's environment during his early childhood. Freud further suggests that death may have the same effect, for death is associated with life, thus with birth. In fact, the patient's grandmother died when he was three years old. A day before her death he was taken to her sickroom and became terribly frightened at the sight of her enormously distended abdomen. When he saw the next day that his mother was very unhappy and was told that the grandmother had died, he thought that her stomach had burst. In the analysis he made a connection between her death and the enemas which his mother used to give him in his childhood. She would urge him to hold the water in his "stomach," and he would try to obey her; but when the pains became very strong he became afraid that his stomach would burst. When his mother did not permit him to flush the toilet because she wished to check his evacuation, he would ask himself whether she was looking for a baby he had produced. There is no doubt that he established a connection between his grandmother's distended belly and his anal-birth fantasies. However, it was difficult to decide whether he had already made this connection at the age of three years, at the time of her death, or made it later, and perhaps in the analysis projected his birth fantasies into the distant past. Although it was not yet possible to ascertain exactly when the child began to think about childbirth, it seemed clear that these problems emerged spontaneously when he was less than three years old.

In view of the complexity of psychic processes and of the fact that they are interwoven, let us now turn our attention again to the relationship between orality and looking which was expressed, for example, in the entanglement of the bathroom scene and the doctor's-office scene. This relationship became very clear in a particular transference situation.

When the patient's attacks had disappeared and he felt cured, the analysis was discontinued for the time being. It is well known that improvement is often used as a resistance which stalls for long periods a profitable continuation of the analysis. In such cases I have found it better to dismiss the patient in the certainty that he will return after some time. In fact, after eight months a slight new attack brought the patient back to treatment.

I have pointed out elsewhere (1925) that recovery from illness means to the patient something different from what it means to the doctor, even though on the conscious level it seems to have the same meaning for both: to cure and to be cured. In the unconscious, however, it frequently implies to the patient the ability to enjoy the same gratification as in illness, but without inhibitions. This is, of course, a handicap for the treatment right at the beginning of the analysis. The sooner the analyst uncovers the specific meaning of the unconscious wish for recovery in each case, the easier the analysis will be. However, it is not always possible to detect the full extent of this meaning at the beginning of treatment, since the wish has different aspects on different levels. In the course of treatment the wish for recovery is absorbed and replaced by the transference.

Prior to the analysis with me the patient was in treatment with a psychotherapist. That treatment consisted of a sort of question-and-answer game. The patient asked questions and the doctor replied. When the patient saw after some time that he was making no progress he left this therapist. When he came to me he tried to play the same game. When he realized that I would not collaborate he gave me to understand that he did not believe in analysis. A while later, he expressed the conviction that he could not be cured at all, neither by his first doctor nor by me. Nevertheless, in spite of all his resistances he stayed in analysis and came regularly every day.

After his confession he began to associate and to provide enough material to enable me to make some interpretations. Soon, however, I saw that he did not accept them. Of course, I looked for signs of transference. He was very correct with me, friendly but without emotion; he was reserved, cool, as if he had erected a wall between us.

In this attitude toward me I saw a repetition of his attitude toward his mother after his return from Europe, when he began to ignore her and not to talk to her. He himself said that he felt at that time as if a wall were separating them. Just as the confession of his distrust in analysis did not change much, so it was that my explanation of his behavior toward me, by relating it to his attitude toward his mother, also produced little change. However, it brought out material from which I learned that he was literally unable to accept anything from his father, not even gifts for his children which at times would have been substantial. Under these circumstances it was as puzzling that he had forced his father to take him into his business as it was that he came regularly for his analysis while refusing to accept any interpretation. The father had not wanted him to join the business; he would have preferred that the son continue his studies. Nevertheless, the patient left college and persuaded the father that his business was the only suitable place of work for him. Once there, he opposed his father constantly and did not accept his guidance.[8]

[8] Freud remarks that the refusal to accept anything from one's father implies the wish to reject his influence, the wish not to be his son. In my monograph on bisexuality and circumcision (1947) I dealt with rejection of and submission to the father's wish. The rejection was explained by the fear of being castrated by the father and thus transformed into a woman, the submission to the father's will by acceptance of the feminine, *passive* role. If we yield to our inclination for generalization, we may say that emotional acceptance of the analyst's interpretation means to the patient acceptance of the feminine, passive role—a danger. The refusal to accept interpretations plays a great role in the treatment and is both result and major source of resistances. This is true of women as well as of men. Freud has said several times that an analysis may have been carried out quite correctly, and yet the patient may not change. It is then left to the patient whether he is going to accept the interpretations—that means whether he will submit to the analyst's influence. This point of view leads to a comparison between psychoanalytic therapy and hypnosis. See Freud, *Group Psychology and the Analysis of the Ego* (1921), and Nunberg, "Transference and Reality" (1951).

The patient wanted from me direct answers to his questions; we may thus assume that his questions during the attacks were unconsciously addressed to his father, from whom he had also wanted direct answers, that is, sexual enlightenment. Most boys wish their fathers to introduce them to the mysteries of sex, i.e., they wish their fathers would teach them how sexual intercourse is performed and how children are made, which amounts to the wish for participation in these mysteries. Our patient asked his mother sexual questions and felt her answers to be unsatisfactory; he asked his sister, and she laughed at him; he wanted to ask his father but was too afraid of him. Why was he more afraid to put these questions to father than to mother or sister? As we know, he reacted to his sexual questions with fantasies in which his father played a prominent and unfavorable role. Unconsciously, our patient had a strong homosexual attachment to him; the analysis of the attack that brought him back into treatment was almost entirely taken up by this topic.

The circumstances under which this attack occurred were the following. He was free of symptoms, felt happy as never before, was gaining weight, and was altogether satisfied with the results of his analysis. He was very grateful, thought often of me, and had the wish to visit and thank me, but never found time to do so. Then it happened that he wanted to go to a party with his wife. She telephoned a woman friend in order to make arrangements for going there together. He overheard the conversation, in the course of which the friend asked how they would come home, since the men were usually drunk at the end of such a party. His wife replied that he could drive them back, since he never became intoxicated, regardless of how much liquor he drank. The woman at the other end of the wire said that she would still watch him closely when he was drinking. He asked his wife to repeat what her friend had said and as soon as he fully understood, he became restless and a question forced itself upon his mind. He tried to suppress it but could not.

This was the question: "Are there times when you tell a story and are there times when you are telling things which are not stories?" Answer: "Everything that you say is a story to a degree." This was followed by other questions and answers, which ended in anxiety.

We have to ask ourselves first: why did overhearing the telephone conversation between his wife and her friend provoke an
attack; and second, what is the connection between this conversation and the questions about stories?

In reference to the telephone conversation he reminded me that
during his analysis he had often had the feeling that he was talking
to me over the phone; he was talking to me but could not see me.
This made him feel uneasy. Evidently he identified the woman at
the other end of the telephone line with me. He complained often
that he felt as if undressed, nude, when he had the impression that
I was looking at him. We remember: he was afraid of being looked
at and investigated. But what has the fear of being watched while
drinking to do with the questions about stories?

To him analysis meant telling stories, and stories meant fairy
tales—lies. Never, he said, had he lied in the analysis; however,
he said he had kept one thing from me, and that was the topic of
homosexuality and fellatio between men. This topic, and particularly oral relations with men, was so repulsive to him that he could
not even think about it. Therefore, he added, he had avoided talking about it to me. (That is not correct; in fact, he had discussed
this problem, but obviously repressed it again.)

Now we have perhaps found a reason for his failure to visit me
in spite of his wish to do so. We can even understand how this is
connected with his questions about stories, at least to some extent:
he was afraid to confess the truth about his oral homosexual
fantasies in relation to me, his analyst. He was, of course, unaware
of that when the attack set in, but instead was afraid of the woman
who would watch him drinking.

This woman in the role of a critical observer reminded him very
much of his mother. The latter would inspect his ears, mouth,
hands, even his excrements, and that at a time when he was no
longer a little child. She would keep her watchful eye on him even
at the dinner table. He used to drink much water, of which she
disapproved, urging him to drink milk instead. He liked milk but
could not take it without adding another flavor, such as coffee or
cocoa. Up to maturity he had imagined that there was always milk
in a woman's breasts, and that one had only to put one's mouth to
her nipples for milk to flow in abundance. As a child he compared
mother's nipples to the cow's teats and wondered why these were

so long and the nipples so small. He asked himself also why mother had breasts and father had not. After much speculation he came to the conclusion that breasts are a kind of penis displaced from below upward.

The following illustrates how deeply set such ideas were in his unconscious and how they influenced the adult's behavior. While in treatment he went to see his mother once and reported afterward that his improvement was so great that he felt free in her presence and was even able to look at her without embarrassment as she came out of her bedroom in a nightgown. However, he was surprised by what followed. At about that time she sold her two-story house and bought one which had only one floor. Discussing the change with her he remarked that he preferred the two-story home. Immediately thereafter he got an attack in which he had to ask himself *questions about stories*. It was impossible at the time to understand the full meaning of the attack. Only now, in the latest phase of his analysis, had it become possible. He said that stories meant to him not only fairy tales, lies, but also floors in a building. At that point an old cynical joke came to my mind: "What is a kiss? An inquiry on the second floor whether the first is free." He had been happy to have solved the problem of mother's sex (breasts equal penis moved upward) and now she had only *one* story, the lower floor.

There is still another meaning attached to "stories." Stories are lies, as he said. Mother lied much to him, particularly in matters of sexuality. He was a keen observer and noticed that her tongue was rough as if it had holes, while his own and his sister's were smooth and pink. Mother would tell the children that they would bite their tongues if they told a lie. It was true that he was afraid to lie, but if occasionally he lied nevertheless, he wondered whether he did not bite holes in his tongue. Speculating about the "holes" in mother's tongue, he came to the conclusion that they must have been caused by father's penis, which seemed to him sharp as a knife. If he lied, he had a hole in his tongue like mother. That would mean that he was a woman; but he had no holes in his tongue, therefore it was not true that he was a woman, just as it was not true that mother had "bought him at Macy's" and would send him back if he was naughty.

When he was a very young child, his mother had her teeth

pulled.[9] When he came into her bedroom in the morning and saw her false teeth in a glass beside her bed, he was puzzled. He pondered over it and finally found the explanation that father had knocked them out at night with his penis.

In an uninterrupted flow of associations he talked about his oral pregnancy and birth fantasies, as if he were connecting them with the parents' supposed oral activities at night. He added that when he learned later about homosexuality, he thought with horror that sexual intercourse between men might be performed orally. Out of the same horror, he said, he could not tell me that the woman whom he had observed through the window of the neighboring apartment was performing fellatio on the man. Immediately, however, he corrected himself, saying that he had not really seen the act, but that he had the impression that it was being performed, that in fact he imagined it afterward. The present attack had set in with the fear of the woman watching him while drinking. He imagined that in watching him she would be able to read his mind and discover that he had pleasure from drinking. *Actually, he was afraid that I would read his mind when I was watching him on the couch, that is, that I would detect his oral homosexual fantasies.*

As we remember, mother threatened him with (symbolic) castration when she caught him sucking his thumb. It was, however, extremely difficult for him to desist from it altogether; thumb sucking was his greatest pleasure. In order to prevent mother from watching him, he gave it up in daytime, but at night he covered his head with his blanket and indulged in thumb sucking and the accompanying fantasies. Most of his thinking and speculating took place under the blanket. He kept these thoughts a well-guarded secret and constantly feared betraying them. In the course of his analysis he became afraid that I would detect his secrets, that is, his desires, fantasies, thoughts, and speculations. As he felt that most of them were wrong, forbidden, they had to be hidden. His fear of being looked at, specifically included the fear of being caught at some wrongdoing. In order to protect himself from self-betrayal he developed a certain watchfulness which expressed itself

[9] This happened at the time when it was fashionable to pull teeth in order to remove the source of focal infection allegedly causing schizophrenia and other psychic disorders. His mother was indeed very neurotic.

in many traits, particularly in his cautious manner of talking, weighing every word carefully.

We are not surprised to learn that his questions about stories had still another connotation which fits perfectly in the mosaic of his thoughts. A storyteller meant to him a liar. He associated the word "lawyer" with the word "liar." From about his tenth to his nineteenth year he wanted to become a lawyer in order to defend criminals. In his fantasies, however, he did not see himself as a lawyer defending his client, but he saw himself in the courtroom, at one time as the prosecutor, another time as the defendant, thus *as the accuser and the accused*. As prosecutor he fired tormenting questions at the accused, i.e., at himself.

The problem of crime and punishment became ever more important to him; he spent much time speculating about it; he asked himself also whether he would hit his father back if he were hit by him, and whether he had the right to defend himself. At times he wished to have a gun for defending himself—from whom, he did not know.

Just as he felt crushed by the prosecutor's questioning in his courtroom fantasies, so he felt crushed and punished by the questions that he asked himself in his attacks. Many times he asked me why it was that he addressed himself in the second person, as, for instance, when he questioned himself, "Are there times when *you* tell stories . . ." There is no doubt—and he stressed this often—that he was punishing himself in these attacks. With this meaning of "stories" (lies) the circle seems almost closed. It is obvious that we have to do here with the relationship of the superego to the ego and the id.

The last attack began with fear of the woman who would by watching him discover that he derived pleasure from drinking. We have learned that he was actually afraid of my discovering his oral homosexual inclination. It was true, he remarked, that he considered this, as well as many of his other thoughts and wishes, highly immoral and was critical of it. But he could not understand why he was so afraid of me since nobody could possibly be more severely critical of him than he was himself.

His fear of being criticized was, of course, a manifestation of his conscience, of the fear of his superego, of which his analyst had become the representative in the outside world.

His first dream after the attack had a connection with this theme. There was a party where everything was confused, men were kissing women as well as men, everybody was kissing everybody else. Finally, he felt a *shadow* behind him, watching him. He awoke with anxiety. When he thought about this dream he was impressed by the "picture" of girls kissing girls and boys kissing boys as small children do who are not yet aware of the difference of sexes. Everybody loves everybody; they are free to love whomever they want. One of his obsessive questions at the beginning of the analysis was, as will be remembered, "Do I love people?" To which he answered, "Everybody loves everybody to a degree." At that time he was tormented by the question whether he loved men but did not have the courage to tell this to me. It was only now that he gave this supplementary information. Indeed, this time he came into analysis to talk freely about his homosexuality, which he considered a crime.

His fear of homosexuality was already so strong in his late high-school years that he was constantly on guard against an attack. He suspected teachers and schoolmates of the intention to seduce him; several times while walking in the street he had the feeling of being followed by a man and ran away in panic.[10] This fear that resembled a persecution mania was transitory and disappeared completely, while the fear of being looked at and investigated remained with him. The repetitive childhood dream of the man who searched for him with a flashlight is in a sense its precursor. He ran from the man to his sister as if looking for protection by her and, in a deeper layer, by the mother.[11] We shall refrain from going deeper into the topic of his homosexuality and return to the patient's curiosity, that is, to his questions.

When he was covered with his blanket, sucking his thumb and speculating about his mother's womb (he always used the word "stomach"), he was particularly disturbed by two problems: how are babies fed there and how do they get in? The question how

[10] It happens in the course of the treatment that patients recollect such paranoid ideas or episodes, and sometimes such ideas enter the transference situation, making the analysis temporarily very difficult. But if there are no other signs of paranoia, they disappear sooner or later.

[11] It is not a rare occurrence that a man looks to the woman for protection from his homosexuality.

they escape from there did not bother him at that time; he had found an answer to it in his anal-birth theory, which, by the way, he had abandoned before the trip to Europe.

The solution of the puzzle how the babies get into the woman's "stomach" was determined by his unconscious symbolic equation "thumb-breast-penis": the woman swallows the penis, and children grow out of it in her stomach. Another idea coexisted with this one: not only girls but boys also can have babies, and consequently, he fantasied, he had babies in his stomach. In fact, he identified with women, specifically with his mother. This identification played an important role in his attacks of panic.

When he entered mother's bedroom in the morning, he would find her in bed feeling ill and miserable, complaining of headaches, dizziness, and nausea. He held his father responsible for her misery, and the sight of her in such a pitiful state increased his hate for him and aroused his compassion for her. Compassion means suffering with another one, that is, identifying with him in so far as she or he is suffering. The identification with mother became particularly evident in two situations: in his attacks of seasickness on the trip to Europe, and, as mentioned before, in the attacks of panic which set in when his questions and answers failed to satisfy him.

His was such a severe case of seasickness that everybody— stewards and passengers alike—was amazed that a child as young as he was could suffer so much from this illness. He had headaches, was dizzy, nauseous, and he vomited. He covered himself overhead with a blanket and kept away from everyone except his mother, whom he permitted to comfort him.[12] The symptoms in his attacks of panic were similar, indeed almost identical: headache, dizziness,

---

[12] I do not wish to imply here that the cause of seasickness is exclusively a mental one. However, it should be mentioned that before the trip he suffered from car sickness; when he was riding in the car with his parents, father and mother used to sit in front while he was in the back seat. After a while he became nauseated and began to vomit, whereupon the mother moved to the back seat, took his head in her lap and stroked and comforted him. He became peaceful and happy and fell asleep in a state of bliss. One might say he formed almost a unity with his mother, a complete identification.

The identification with the mother was different from the one with the father; it took place in the ego rather than in the superego as the latter did. The first was more of a libidinal, the second more of an aggressive character.

nausea, vomiting, seclusion in his bedroom, shades drawn and lights out. Thus the seasickness and the attacks of panic reflected the condition in which he would find his mother when he entered her bedroom in the morning. It can hardly be doubted that he identified with her in the situation of suffering. As was pointed out, he imagined that his father had knocked out her teeth (castrated her), cut her, and forced her to swallow his penis. Thus he was dramatizing or acting out on himself what he imagined the father had done to his mother. Often in later life he complained that his attacks were tortures and punishments inflicted upon him.

But what has that to do with looking, investigating, questioning —in brief, with curiosity?

The first answer is that his attacks of panic set in when he could not find a satisfactory answer to one of his questions; that is, when his curiosity was frustrated. Secondly, it struck him that there was a difference in his reaction to the sight of each parent in nudity. He remembered clearly seeing his mother as she went about un-dressed in her bedroom, or as she sat in the bathtub. He did not feel ashamed or embarrassed. On the contrary, he liked to look at her, especially at her breasts.[13] But he could not remember having seen his father naked, although he must have on many occasions —in the bathroom, in locker and shower rooms, and in solaria where the father used to take him. Although all the men in these places, his father included, were naked, he himself put a towel around his hips. The adults tried to persuade him to remove the towel, they ridiculed him, but to no avail. On the one hand, he was afraid to look at his father's nudity; on the other, he was afraid to be looked at when naked. His fear of being looked at by men derives from fear of retaliation, that is, castration by the father for looking at him with aggressive intentions. In other words, he feared that his father would do to him what he himself wished to do to the father. (The biblical legend of Noah comes to mind who cursed his son when he became aware that the latter had looked at his nudity.) But where is the link with orality? The patient *maintained that when one sees something desirable, one wants to*

---

[13] Obviously this recollection refers to early childhood, not to latency or later years, for in these periods he would look surreptitiously at his mother while she was dressing or undressing, and as a mature man he became embarrassed when she dressed in his presence.

have, to eat it, just as he felt that his sister wanted to have his penis, to bite it off, when she *"looked at me with her greedy eyes."* But this is not sufficient to explain the relationship between the castration complex and orality.

Let me insert another detail here. When his mother urged him to drink milk, she would ask, "Do you not want to be as strong and tall as your father?" Certainly he always wanted to be as big and powerful as his father; but whenever he forced himself to drink milk, he was obsessed by thoughts about milking cows and squeezing their teats, and about playing with mother's breasts. In the transference situation he became aware that he had also wished to suck his father's penis (Nunberg, 1936). However, he hesitated for a long time to convey this idea to the analyst because it was unbearable to him. Moreover, in the unconscious a part stands for the whole; therefore swallowing the penis must have meant swallowing the whole father—an even more horrifying idea.

As you know, it is assumed that in prehistoric times the primeval father was killed by his sons and incorporated in an oral (cannibalistic) act, and that later, in further development, this physical act became a psychic one, which is called identification. Through this specific identification the superego develops, which is, in a sense, the psychic representation of the father in the ego and exercises a moral influence on the individual. If it functions properly, the individual in the course of development becomes gradually less dependent on the father's judgment than on the superego's.[14]

Alerted by this fragment of theory we can almost see how from the chaotic, unorganized mental life of the little child our patient's moral personality emerged. As a child he was afraid of his father in the external world; later on this fear decreased while the fear of and dependence on his superego increased. In the transference situation he was afraid that the analyst might know what he tried to hide, that he would know and see his homosexual and aggressive wishes toward the analyst. Thus he projected his superego onto the analyst. Since the latter was a substitute for the father—as is regularly the case in treatment—the patient re-established in

[14] See Freud, *Totem and Taboo* (1912-1913), *The Ego and the Id* (1923a), and other works.

this way the original situation where he was afraid of his father's omniscience. In his fear of being looked at by the father he projected onto him his own curiosity and aggression. Since the superego develops, as we have just recapitulated, by means of identification which is a derivative of oral incorporation and since it acts as a critical inner eye, we may assume that it stems not only from auditive impressions but also from visual ones. It is as if by consuming the father, the son acquired the omniscience the father of his childhood possessed. And what he wanted to know in childhood was what father was doing with mother. In other words, through identification with father he would acquire father's knowledge and be able to do with mother what father did.

Incidentally, we may perhaps have found a way to understand one aspect of the passage in Genesis which tells us that Adam *knew* Eve after he had eaten of the tree of knowledge. If we assume, as Theodor Reik (1957) does that the tree of knowledge represents a totem (father) god, the meaning of the myth would be that Adam, having swallowed the father (god) and identified with him, acquired his knowledge, i.e., sexual *knowledge*.[15] We know, indeed, from our analyses how fervently boys desire to be introduced to the mysteries of sex by their *fathers*. In other words, one can have sexual relations with mother when one acquires the necessary knowledge through identification with father.

Let us now return to our patient. As we have seen, the thought of drinking milk and becoming as strong as father set in motion the entire chain of associations connected with oral aggression against him. The aim of this oral aggressivity was, in a sense, fulfilled in the psychic incorporation of or identification with the father through which one becomes as tall, as strong, as omnipotent and omniscient as he is. The fusion of orality with scoptophilia may perhaps become more understandable if we think of the superego and its function, the conscience, as the result of incorporation. As you know, the word "conscience" stems from the

---

[15] I owe to Mr. Gerson Cohen of the New York Jewish Theological Seminary the following information. The Hebrew word *yada* means "to know," *lamad* means "to learn, to study." Only *yada* is used in the sexual sense; the basic meaning of both words is "experience." In the Ugaritic epic *Gilgamesh* the hero Enkidu becomes wise (i.e., has gained knowledge) and therefore like the gods, only after a sexual experience.

Latin *co-scire,* which means to know together with. The German word *Gewissen* has the same literal meaning. Theodor Reik reminds us that the word "remorse" is derived from the Latin *mordere,* which means "to bite"; its German counterpart is *Gewissensbisse*—which means "bites of conscience." Thus language gives us an almost pictorial presentation of the relationship between superego and ego, as if indicating: the superego "watches and bites" the ego.

After theoretical speculations it is advisable to direct one's attention again to reality. Our patient's sexual curiosity was beginning to subside before the trip to Europe. After his return home, however—he was then seven years old—his questions reemerged. Yet it was no longer so much in speculations, fantasies, and theories that he tried to find answers to them as in actions. As we know, he had not only the fantasy that he, a boy, could have a baby, but he identified himself also with the fantasied unborn baby. At that time he thought that a baby is born by micturation; however, he did not adhere long to this theory because it seemed impossible to him that a baby could pass through the small urethral orifice; thus he resorted to his old fantasy that a baby is cut out of the mother's womb and concluded in analogy that his child would have to be cut out of his penis. Then another difficulty presented itself to him: would not penis and child be injured by the surgeon's knife? In order to resolve this problem he resorted to an experiment. Having seen the cook taking peas out of the pod he took a knife and cut a pod open. When he found that he could not cut the pod without scratching the peas, he stopped the experiment. From that day on he could eat neither peas nor any other food that had to be removed from a shell, such as nuts, oysters, and the like. He had, of course, identified with pea and pod. Nevertheless, this experiment implies a certain progress; with it he took one step closer to reality. Up to that point he had only speculated and fantasied; now he projected his ideas and fantasies into the outside world and experimented there, like a scientist. His castration fear, however, caused him to desist from further experimentation. Had his castration complex been less powerful he might perhaps have become a scientific explorer.

He became no scientist but an excellent businessman. And although his infantile sexual curiosity did not bring him closer to

reality, it sharpened his thinking processes. It stimulated the emergence of manifold problems which he endeavored to solve by
complicated reasoning, by speculations, which in a sense, provided
a preparatory training for his future logical thinking. Naturally,
as long as his questions were dominated by the sexual instinct, his
answers were wrapped in "theories" and fantasies, far removed
from reality. Only when his curiosity gradually was cleared of the
sexual admixture did better reality testing and logical thinking
begin to evolve. His attempt to find an answer to his questions in
the pea-pod experiment was a manifestation of an intermediary
period in which he projected his fantasies into the external world
and looked there for an answer to his tormenting questions instead
of within himself. An example of the progressive development of
his reality testing and logical thinking is afforded by his behavior
after the return from Europe. We recall that he decided to take up
athletics in order to become manly and thereby to please his
father; before every contest he practiced very hard and calculated
every step of the game in advance, be it baseball, golf, or any other
sport, so that not a single move was left to chance. No wonder that
he became a champion and earned many trophies. He wanted to
become a man like father, and we know that identification with
the father facilitates adaptation to reality considerably. Goethe's
words come to mind:

> Vom Vater hab' ich die Statur,
> Des Lebens ernstes Führen,
> Vom Mütterchen die Frohnatur
> Und Lust zu fabulieren.

> [From Father I have looks and build
> And the serious conduct of living;
> My mother gave me gaiety
> And zest for spinning stories.]

The patient's attempts to solve sexual-aggressive problems evidently helped him in later life to solve problems in general, problems of a practical nature. He always carried a notebook in his
pocket in which he used to jot down all the questions he could not
solve immediately. When he entered his father's business he con-

tinued this habit, now in relation to the business. In an almost scientific manner he set up teams for investigating certain problems for which he had no explanation, and when his father retired, he reorganized the business, using the information gained in the course of these investigations. Gradually he succeeded in making his company one of the largest and most prosperous of its kind in the country. This man who never studied mechanical engineering was called upon for help by the factory manager, a trained engineer, when some machine was out of order and nobody was able to repair it. He would work there—sometimes for weeks—until he found the cause of failure, which his trained men had not been able to detect.

These few examples show how the infantile sexual curiosity lost the sexual component during the course of development and turned from fantasy to the solution of real problems. In other words, the infantile sexual curiosity was sublimated and paved the way for adaptation to reality.[16]

As stated at the beginning of this paper, all human beings are equipped with a certain amount of curiosity. It seems that its first manifestations appear in earliest childhood. Our patient's first dream tends to support the assumption that curiosity is already active in the primal scene when the infant wants to know what the parents are doing together. Of course, that wish cannot be conscious since the child has no ability nor facility to formulate a question. Since a primal scene may or may not have occurred, we have reason to believe that curiosity arises independently. It seems,

---

[16] The adaptation to reality is a very complex problem. Here is not the place to discuss it in detail; however, I would like to take this opportunity to correct a misunderstanding which is expressed in Dr. R. Loewenstein's paper on Masochism (1957, p. 211). He writes: "Hartmann refutes the theory advanced by Ferenczi and taken over by Nunberg according to which all adjustment to reality is based on masochism. He thinks the latter may be found in cases of psychoses (Nunberg) or may exist when reality is painful, but certainly not in adjustment to any kind of reality."

I do not understand how the authors arrived at this conclusion about my view on adaptation to reality. In my book, *Principles of Psychoanalysis* (1955; German edition, 1932, under the title, *Allgemeine Neurosenlehre*), to which the authors refer I stated that we have to distinguish between passive and active adaptation to reality and that passive adaptation is only an intermediary stage which is followed by active adaptation. Without active participation there is no effective adaptation to reality.

indeed, to set in shortly after birth. For the observer gets the impression that the suckling is searching for the erotogenic zones of his body. First it is the mouth which the baby tries to reach with his hands. As soon as he has found it, he puts his fingers in and sucks them with ecstatic pleasure. But he does not stop here in his explorations; he continues to search for other erotogenic zones. Unmistakable is the pleasure when he detects parts of his body, such as hands, toes, or earlobes. Finally he discovers the genital zone. It looks as if the child were born with a kind of instinct to investigate. Freud calls curiosity at times an instinct of investigation; at other times he says that such an instinct does not exist. Since curiosity manifests itself so early and with such urgency, it seems difficult to deny that it at least behaves like the derivative of an instinct. Anyway, it is clear that curiosity, in its earliest stages, is amalgamated with sexuality. In the course of development it loses its sexual component and, if we take into account the indefatigable compulsion to repeat inherent in curiosity, we cannot but agree with Freud that one of its functions is to help in mastering the external world, the reality. In the need for mastery we see a derivative of the aggressive instincts; indeed, infantile curiosity contains much aggression fused with the sexual instinct.

Infantile sexual curiosity is concerned mainly with three questions: where do children come from; what is the difference between a boy and a girl; and what are father and mother doing together? Usually answers to these questions are provided by the children themselves in the typical fantasies.

In our patient, however, the problems of conception and birth seem gradually to have pushed into the background all the other sexual questions. They persisted longer than the others and absorbed a great amount of psychic energy.

Although in normal development sexual curiosity can be mastered by the ego and inhibited to a high degree, in truth it cannot be suppressed completely. Everybody knows what role it plays in normal love life.

The question about the origin of man occupies not only the mind of the individual child but it has occupied mankind from primeval times onward. In most religions men projected the solution of this problem onto their gods, leaving to them the task of creating the first man. According to the biblical myth, God blew life into a piece of earth, thus creating Adam. In all mythologies earth is a symbol for the mother (Mother Earth). If we substitute "mother" for "earth" in the creation myth, we see that it has great similarity to one of our patient's fantasies about the birth of a child. Why birth had to be represented in a disguised and de-sexualized form in most of the creation myths, is a problem which does not belong in our context.

Originally, the patient asked what or who caused the child to be born; later on, why the machine in his factory stopped function-ing or why some products were selling better than others, etc. When he found the cause, he knew how to put the machine back into function or how to improve his business. A child tries to find out not only what the cause of an event is but also who creates the cause, rather who is the cause. Just as in childhood man feels compelled to fantasy about his origin, so he feels compelled in a more advanced stage of his development to think about the cause of some phenomena. From the phenomenological point of view causal thinking seems to be the manifestation of a need to connect two phenomena in such a manner that the second is determined by the first. This need, I called the *need for causality*.

I am not talking here about causality as a philosophical problem but about the *need* for causality, a psychological phenomenon. Everyone feels it as a wish to find, to establish the relationship between cause and effect. It is a deeply rooted need; it is known that the younger or the more primitive an individual is, the more easily he will find causal connections. To the primitive man or the little child, everything in the world around him seems animated and has its creator.

When the child sees a newborn baby he senses that the parents have something to do with his appearance, i.e., that a man and a woman do something with one another and the result is a new human being. All of this stimulates his curiosity. In a paper writ-ten a long time ago (1930) I derived the need for causality from this infantile sexual curiosity. It needed but one step further to recognize that the synthetic function of the ego stems from the same source. Its most comprehensive task is binding, unifying. This conception is based on Freud's instinct theory.[17] As you

---

[17] See Freud, *Beyond the Pleasure Principle* (1920).

know, he distinguishes two groups of instincts: the sexual or erotic and the aggressive or destructive instincts. The interaction of these two instinct groups reveals itself in the phenomenon which we call life. The sexual instincts or eros have the tendency to bring two individuals together and to join them in the act of love. When this libidinal instinct of the id enters the ego and is discharged in sexual union, a child is created. If it enters the ego and is not discharged in the sexual act, it loses its sexual character but retains the binding, unifying, creative quality of eros, though on a higher level. It permeates the ego and appears as its synthetic function. Because of its derivation from eros the synthetic function comprises also the creative faculty of the ego, just as the need for causality comprises the need to understand the phenomena of life and nature in general. If one understands a phenomenon one may perhaps be able to recreate it. That may be the meaning of Freud's statement that curiosity serves the purpose of mastering reality.

The original sexual curiosity of the child confronts him with a variety of problems that he tries to solve in his fantasies and "theories." In the attempt to solve similar problems mankind in its infancy resorted to the creation myths. In further development man searched for the elixir of life, for the stone of wisdom. Paracelsus and his followers expected to create the *homunculus* in the test tube; Darwin postulated his theory of evolution; and in our times man tries to penetrate the secrets of matter.

Curiosity and the need for causality are boundless. There are individuals whose urge to know is unlimited and whose ego seems to lose control over this urge and to become its prisoner. Individuals of this type may be utterly ruthless in their avidity for knowledge and totally unconcerned with the possible consequences of their search. They may not even be deterred by the prospect of comprehensive destruction, including their own, when they hope to come closer to their goal. One gets the impression that the pure instinct of destruction has been released in them. Indeed, Freud says that with sublimation there occurs not only desexualization but at the same time a defusion of the two groups of instincts which sets destructive instincts free. Since infantile sexual curiosity as such contains an aggressive element, we might say that the explorer, in a sense, returns to the level of the child who ruthlessly tries to satisfy his curiosity.

Curiosity may, on the one hand, be a blessing and stimulate intellectual performances of the highest value; on the other hand, it may lead to destruction if too much aggression is released. We may, perhaps, take comfort from the observation that nature often enhances the creative and constructive forces when excessive destructive power has been released.

REFERENCES

ABRAHAM, K. (1924), A Short Story of the Development of the Libido, Viewed in the Light of Mental Disorders. In *Selected Papers*. London: Hogarth Press, pp. 418-501.

ANDREAS-SALOMÉ, L. (1912-1913), *In der Schule bei Freud. Tagebuch eines Jahres, 1912/1913* [Studying with Freud. Diary of One Year, 1912/1913]. Zurich: Max Niehans Verlag, 1958.

APTEKMANN, E. (1911), Experimentelle Beiträge zur Psychologie des psychogalvanischen Phänomens [Experimental Contributions to the Psychology of the Psychogalvanic Phenomenon]. *Jhrb. psychoanal. & psychopathol. Forsch.*, 3:591-620.

BAILEY, F. & MILLER, A. M. (1909), *Textbook of Embryology*. New York: Wood & Co.

BINSWANGER, L. (1956), *Erinnerungen an Sigmund Freud*. Bern: Francke Verlag.

BLEULER, E. (1912), Das autistische Denken [Autistic Thinking]. *Jhrb. psychoanal. & psychopathol. Forsch.*, 4:1-39.

BRAUS, H. (1924), *Anatomie des Menschen* [Human Anatomy]. Berlin: Springer Verlag.

BRESLAU, *Hebrew-English Dictionary*. London: Unwin Bros.

BRUNSWICK, R. M. (1940), The Preoedipal Phase of the Libido Development. *Psychoanal. Quart.*, 9:293-319.

BRYK, F. (1941), *Circumcision of Man and Woman*. Neubrandenburg: Gustav Teller.

DEUTSCH, H. (1944), *The Psychology of Women*, Vol. I. New York: Grune & Stratton.

FEDERN, P. (1913), Beiträge zur Analyse des Sadismus und Masochismus. I. Die Quellen des männlichen Sadismus [Contribution to the Analysis of Sadism and Masochism. I. The Sources of Male Sadism]. *Int. Z. Psychoanal.*, 1:29-49.

FEDERN, P. (1914), Beiträge zur Analyse des Sadismus und Masochismus. II. Die libidinösen Quellen des Masochismus [Contribution to the Analysis of Sadism and Masochism. II. The Libidinous Sources of Masochism]. *Int. Z. Psychoanal.*, 2:105-130.

FEDERN, P. (1947), Professor Freud: The Beginning of a Case History. *Samiksa*, 1:305-311.

FELDMAN, A. A. (1944), Freud's *Moses and Monotheism* and the Three Stages of Israelitish Religion. *Psychoanal. Rev.*, 31:361-418.

FERENCZI, S. (1909), Introjektion und Übertragung [Introjection and Transference]. *Jhrb. psychoanal. & psychopathol. Forsch.*, 1:422-457.

FERENCZI, S. (1919), *Hysterie und Pathoneurosen* [Hysteria and Pathoneuroses]. Leipzig: Internationaler psychoanalytischer Verlag.

FERENCZI, S. (1924), *Thalassa: The Theory of Genitality*. Albany, N. Y.: The Psychoanalytic Quarterly, 1938.

FRAZER, J. G. (1925a), The Dying God. In *The Golden Bough*, Vol. II. London: Macmillan.

FRAZER, J. G. (1925b), The Magic Art. In *The Golden Bough*, Vol. II. London: Macmillan.

FRAZER, J. G. (1925c), Taboo and Peril of the Souls. In *The Golden Bough*, Vol. III. London: Macmillan.

FREUD, A. (1936), *The Ego and the Mechanisms of Defense*. New York: International Universities Press, 1946.

FREUD, S. (1900), *The Interpretation of Dreams*. London: George Allen & Unwin, 1913.

FREUD, S. (1901), *The Psychopathology of Everyday Life*. New York: Macmillan, 1914.

FREUD, S. (1905a), Fragment of an Analysis of a Case of Hysteria. *Collected Papers*, 3:13-146, 1925.

FREUD, S. (1905b), Jokes and Their Relation to the Unconscious. *Standard Edition*, 8:9-238, 1960.

FREUD, S. (1905c), Three Essays on the Theory of Sexuality. *Standard Edition*, 7:125-145, 1953.

FREUD, S. (1907), Obsessive Acts and Religious Practices. *Collected Papers*, 2:25-35, 1924.

FREUD, S. (1908a), Character and Anal Erotism. *Standard Edition*, 9:167-176, 1959.

FREUD, S. (1908b), On the Sexual Theories of Children. *Collected Papers*, 2:59-75, 1924.

FREUD, S. (1910), Leonardo da Vinci and a Memory of His Childhood. *Standard Edition*, 11:59-137, 1957.

FREUD, S. (1911a), Formulierungen über zwei Prinzipien des psychischen Geschehens [Formulations Regarding the Two Principles in Mental Functioning]. *Jhrb. psychoanal. & psychopathol. Forsch.*, 3:1-8.

FREUD, S. (1911b), Psychoanalytic Notes upon an Autobiographical Account of a Case of Paranoia. *Collected Papers*, 3:387-466, 1925.

FREUD, S. (1912), The Dynamics of Transference. *Collected Papers*, 2:312-322, 1924.

FREUD, S. (1912-1913), Totem and Taboo. *Standard Edition*, 13:1-162, 1955.

FREUD, S. (1914a), Further Recommendations in the Technique of Psycho-Analysis: Recollection, Repetition and Working Through. *Collected Papers*, 2:366-376, 1924.

FREUD, S. (1914b), On Narcissism. *Standard Edition*, 14:73-102, 1957.

FREUD, S. (1914c), On the History of the Psycho-Analytic Movement. *Standard Edition*, 14:3-66, 1957.

FREUD, S. (1915), Instincts and Their Vicissitudes. *Collected Papers*, 4:60-83, 1925.

FREUD, S. (1916-1917), *Introductory Lectures on Psycho-Analysis*. London: Hogarth Press, 1929.

FREUD, S. (1917a), A Child is Being Beaten. *Collected Papers*, 2:172-201, 1924.

FREUD, S. (1917b), On the Transformation of Instincts with Special Reference to Anal Erotism. *Collected Papers*, 2:164-171, 1924.

FREUD, S. (1919), The "Uncanny." *Collected Papers*, 4:368-407, 1925.

FREUD, S. (1920), Beyond the Pleasure Principle. *Standard Edition*, 18:7-64, 1955.

FREUD, S. (1921), *Group Psychology and the Analysis of the Ego. Standard Edition*, 18:67-143, 1955.

FREUD, S. (1923a), *The Ego and the Id*. London: Hogarth Press, 1948.

FREUD, S. (1923b), The Infantile Genital Organization of the Libido. A Supplement to the Theory of Sexuality. *Collected Papers*, 2:244-249, 1924.

FREUD, S. (1925), Some Psychological Consequences of the Anatomical Distinction between the Sexes. *Int. J. Psycho-Anal.*, 8:133-142, 1927.

FREUD, S. (1926a), Address to Members of the B'nai B'rith. *Standard Edition*, 20:271-274, 1959.

FREUD, S. (1926b), *The Problem of Anxiety (Inhibitions, Symptoms and Anxiety)*. New York: Psychoanalytic Quarterly Press & W. W. Norton, 1936.

FREUD, S. (1927), *The Future of an Illusion*. London: Hogarth Press, 1928.

FREUD, S. (1930), *Civilization and Its Discontents*. London: Hogarth Press.

FREUD, S. (1931a), Female Sexuality. *Int. J. Psycho-Anal.*, 13:281-297.

FREUD, S. (1931b), Libidinal Types. *Psychoanal. Quart.*, 1:3-6, 1932.

FREUD, S. (1933), *New Introductory Lectures on Psycho-Analysis*. London: Hogarth Press.

FREUD, S. (1936), A Disturbance of Memory on the Acropolis. *Collected Papers*, 5:302-312, 1950.

FREUD, S. (1937a), Analysis Terminable and Interminable. *Int. J. Psycho-Anal.*, 18:373-405.

FREUD, S. (1937b), Constructions in Analysis. *Int. J. Psycho-Anal.*, 19:377-387, 1938.

FREUD, S. (1939), *Moses and Monotheism*. London: Hogarth Press.

FREUD, S. (1940a), *An Outline of Psychoanalysis*. New York: W. W. Norton, 1949.

FREUD, S. (1940b), Medusa's Head. *Int. J. Psycho-Anal.*, 22:69-70, 1941.

FREUD, S. (1950), *The Origins of Psychoanalysis. Letters, Drafts and Notes to Wilhelm Fliess (1887-1902)*. New York: Basic Books, 1954.

FREUD, S. & Breuer, J. (1895), Studies on Hysteria. *Standard Edition*, 2:1-305, 1955.

FUERST, A. N., *A Hebrew Chaldee Lexicon to the Old Testament*.

GINSBERG, H. L. (1936), *The Ugarit Text*.

GRAF, M. (1911), Richard Wagner im *Fliegenden Holländer*: Ein Beitrag zur Psychologie künstlerischen Schaffens [Richard Wagner in *The Flying Dutchman*. A Contribution to the Psychology of Artistic Creation]. *Schriften zur angewandten Seelenkunde*, 9.

HOOKE, S. H. (1938), *The Origins of Early Semitic Ritual*. London: Publishers for the British Academy.

JEKELS, L. (1913), Einige Bemerkungen zur Trieblehre [Some Remarks on the Theory of Instinct]. *Int. Z. Psychoanal.*, 1:439-443.

JEKELS, L. (1917), The Riddle of Shakespeare's *Macbeth*. *Psychoanal. Rev.*, 30:361-385, 1943.

Jewish Encyclopaedia, Vol. IV. New York and London: Funk & Wagnalls.

JONES, E. (1953-1957), *The Life and Work of Sigmund Freud*, 3 Vols. New York: Basic Books.

JUNG, C. (1911), Wandlungen und Symbole der Libido [Changes and Symbols of the Libido]. *Jhrb. psychoanal. & psychopathol. Forsch.*, 3:120-227.

KATAN, M. (1952), Further Remarks about Schreber's Hallucinations. *Int. J. Psycho-Anal.*, 33: 429-432.

KLAUSNER, J. (1943), *From Jesus to Paul*. New York: Macmillan.

LENORMANT, F. (1880), *Les Origines de l'Histoire* [The Origins of History], Vol. I. Paris.

LEWIN, B. D. (1933), The Body as Phallus. *Psychoanal. Quart.*, 2:24-47.

LIPPS, T. (1907), *Vom Fühlen, Wollen und Denken*. Lipsk.

LOEWENSTEIN, R. M. (1957), A Contribution to the Psychoanalytic Theory of Masochism. *J. Amer. Psychoanal. Assn.*, 5:197-234.

MEYER, E. (1912), *Papyrus von Elephantine Hinrichs'sche Buchhandlung*. Leipzig.

NUNBERG, H. (1913), The Unfulfilled Wishes According to Freud's Teachings. *Neurologia Polska, 3*. *This Volume*, pp. 1-12.

NUNBERG, H. (1925), The Will to Recovery. In *Practice and Theory of Psychoanalysis*, Vol. I. New York: International Universities Press, 1948, pp. 75-88.

NUNBERG, H. (1926), The Sense of Guilt and the Need for Punishment. In *Practice and Theory of Psychoanalysis*, Vol. I. New York: International Universities Press, 1948, pp. 89-101.

NUNBERG, H. (1928), Problems of Therapy. In *Practice and Theory of Psychoanalysis*, Vol. I. New York: International Universities Press, 1948, pp. 105-119.

NUNBERG, H. (1930), The Synthetic Function of the Ego. In *Practice and Theory of Psychoanalysis*, Vol. I. New York: International Universities Press, 1948, pp. 120-136.

NUNBERG, H. (1932), *Allgemeine Neurosenlehre auf psychoanalytischer Grundlage* [General Theory of Neuroses, Based on Psychoanalysis]. Bern and Berlin: Hans Huber.

NUNBERG, H. (1936), Homosexuality, Magic and Aggression. In *Practice and Theory of Psychoanalysis*, Vol. I. New York: International Universities Press, 1948, pp. 150-164.

NUNBERG, H. (1937), Theory of the Therapeutic Results of Psychoanalysis. In *Practice and Theory of Psychoanalysis*, Vol. I. New York: International Universities Press, 1948, pp. 165-173.

NUNBERG, H. (1947), *Problems of Bisexuality as Reflected in Circumcision*. London: Hogarth Press, 1949. *This Volume*, pp. 13-93.

NUNBERG, H. (1948), *Practice and Theory of Psychoanalysis*, Vol. I. New York: International Universities Press.

NUNBERG, H. (1950), A Commentary on Freud's *An Outline of Psychoanalysis*. *Psychoanal. Quart.*, 19:227-250. *This Volume*, pp. 94-117.

NUNBERG, H. (1951), Transference and Reality. *Int. J. Psycho-Anal.*, 32:1-9. *This Volume*, pp. 118-133.

NUNBERG, H. (1952), Discussion of M. Katan's Paper on Schreber's Hallucination. *Int. J. Psycho-Anal.*, 33:454-456. *This Volume*, pp. 134-139.

NUNBERG, H. (1954), Evaluation of the Results of Psycho-Analytic Treatment. *Int. J. Psycho-Anal.*, 35:2-7. *This Volume*, pp. 140-151.

NUNBERG, H. (1955), *Principles of Psychoanalysis*, Vol. 1. New York: International Universities Press.

NUNBERG, H. (1961), *Curiosity*. New York: International Universities Press. *This Volume*, pp. 168-206.

NUNBERG, H. (1962), Introduction. In *Minutes of the Vienna Psychoanalytic Society*, Vol. I. Eds., Herman Nunberg and Ernst Federn. New York: International Universities Press, pp. xvii-xxxii. *This Volume*, pp. 152-167.

PFENNINGER, W. (1911), Untersuchungen über die Konstanz und den Wechsel der psychologischen Konstellation bei Normalen und Frühdementen

(Schizophrenen) [Investigations Concerning the Constancy and Variation of Psychological Constellations in Normal and Schizophrenic Subjects]. *Jhrb. psychoanal. & psychopathol. Forsch.*, 3:481-524.

PIKLER (1908), *Das Beharren und die Gegensätzlichkeit des Erlebens.* Stuttgart.

PLATO, *Symposium.* Translated by W. R. M. Lamb. Cambridge, Mass.: Harvard University Press.

RADO, S. (1940), A Critical Examination of the Concept of Bisexuality. *Psychosom. Med.*, 2:459-467.

RANK, O. (1909), *The Myth of the Birth of a Hero.* Washington, D. C.: Nerv. & Ment. Dis. Monogr. No. 18, 1914.

RANK, O. (1912), *Das Inzest-Motiv in Dichtung und Sage [The Incest Motif in Poetry and Saga].* Leipzig and Vienna: Franz Deuticke, 1926.

RANK, O. (1912-1914), *Psychoanalytische Beiträge zur Mythenforschung [Psychoanalytic Contributions to Research on Myths].* Leipzig, Vienna and Zurich: Internationaler psychoanalytischer Verlag, 1922.

RANK, O. (1913), Totemismus im Märchen; Rv. Grimm'schen Märchen [Totemism in Fairy Tales; Review of Grimm's Fairy Tales]. *Imago*, 2:594-596.

RANK, O. (1924), The Trauma of Birth and Its Importance for Psychoanalytic Therapy. *Psychoanal. Rev.*, 11:241-245.

REIK, T. (1914), Couvade and the Psychogenesis of the Fear of Retaliation. In *Ritual.* New York: International Universities Press, 1958, pp. 27-89.

REIK, T. (1915-1916), The Puberty Rites of Savages. In *Ritual.* New York: International Universities Press, 1958, pp. 91-166.

REIK, T. (1917), Das Kainszeichen [The Mark of Cain]. *Imago*, 5:31-42.

REIK, T. (1919), The Shofar (The Ram's Horn). In *Ritual.* New York: International Universities Press, 1958, pp. 221-361.

REIK, T. (1923), *Der eigene und der fremde Gott [One's Own and the Alien God].* Leipzig, Vienna and Zurich: Internationaler psychoanalytischer Verlag.

REIK, T. (1925), *Der Geständniszwang und Strafbedürfnis [Compulsion to Confess and Need for Punishment].* Leipzig, Vienna and Zurich: Internationaler psychoanalytischer Verlag.

REIK, T. (1957), *Myth and Guilt.* New York: George Braziller.

REINACH, S. (1928), *Cultes, Mythes et Religions*, Vol. II. Paris: Librairie Ernest Leroux.

RÓHEIM, G. (1942), Transition Rites. *Psychoanal. Quart.*, 11:336-374.

SILBERER, H. (1909), Bericht über eine Methode, gewisse symbolische Halluzinations-Erscheinungen hervorzurufen und zu beobachten [Report on a Method of Eliciting and Observing Certain Symbolic Hallucination Phenomena]. *Jhrb. psychoanal. & psychopathol. Forsch.*, 1:513-525.

STERBA, R. F. (1936), Zur Theorie der Übertragung [Critique of the Theory of Transference]. *Imago*, 22:456-470.

TAFT, J. (1958), *Otto Rank.* New York: Julian Press.

VAN OPHUIJSEN, J. H. W. (1920), On the Origin of the Feeling of Persecution. *Int. J. Psychoanal.*, 1:235-239.

WINTHUIS, J. (1928), *Das Zweigeschlechterleben bei den Zentralaustraliern und anderen Völkern [The Two-Sex System Among the Central Australians and Other Races].* Leipzig.

WOOLF, M. (1945), Prohibitions Against the Simultaneous Consumption of Milk and Flesh in Orthodox Jewish Law. *Int. J. Psycho-Anal.*, 26:169-177.

WOOLF, M., *Eating Prohibitions in Orthodox Jewish Law.*

NAME INDEX

Abraham, K., I: 90, 95, 97, 101n., 214n.; II: 5, 56, 207
Adler, A., I: 105; II: 157, 159, 160
Alexander, F., I: 105, 147, 149n., 166, 217n.
Andreas-Salome, Lou, II: 166, 207
Aptekman, E., II: 8n., 207

Bailey, F., II: 45n., 207
Bertschinger, I: 42, 47, 50, 55, 212n.
Binswanger, L., II: 154, 207
Bleuler, E., I: 3, 21, 209n., 211n.; II: 4n., 7n., 8, 8n., 10, 116, 155, 207
Braus, H., II: 45, 207
Breslau, II: 79n., 207
Breuer, J., I: 73, 214n.
Bryk, F., II: 82, 207

Cohen, G., II: 6, 199n.
Charcot, J., II: 155

Darwin, C., II: 155
Deutsch, H., II: 56, 207
Dostoevski, F., II: 155
Dumas, A., II: 185

Federn, P., II: 34n., 48, 56, 124, 152, 164, 165, 165n., 207
Feldman, A. A., II: 71, 74, 87, 88, 207
Ferenczi, S., I: 41, 58, 77, 150, 164n., 215n.; II: 20n., 34, 130, 202n., 207
Fliess, R., II: 154, 155, 156, 161, 162
Frazer, J. G., II: 66, 75n., 92, 208
Freud, A., II: 178n.
Freud, S., I: 20, 21, 22, 54, 60, 62, 63, 67, 73, 84, 87, 89, 94, 97, 99, 100, 101n., 105, 114, 119, 120, 122, 123, 127, 130, 135, 137, 138, 144, 145, 148, 149n., 150, 151, 157, 160, 164n., 165, 168, 169, 173, 185, 186, 187, 188, 189-190, 191, 195, 197, 198, 206, 207, 208, 211n., 212n., 213n., 214n., 215n., 216n., 218n.;

II: 5, 8, 8n., 10, 13, 14n., 23n., 25, 28, 29n., 31n., 34, 37-39, 39n., 44, 45, 46, 47, 48, 56, 56n., 60, 62, 64n., 68, 73, 74, 76n., 83, 84, 85, 88-92, 94, 119n., 124, 127, 129, 130, 131, 132, 135, 137, 138, 152, 154-169, 178n., 182, 186n., 187, 189, 189n., 198n., 203, 204, 204n., 205, 208-209
Friedman, P., II: 35n.
Fuerst, A. N., II: 35, 36, 209

Ginsberg, H. L., II: 86
Goethe, II: 201
Graf, M., II: 166, 209

Hartmann, H., I: 214n.; II: 119n., 202n.
Hitschmann, E., II: 164, 165
Hooke, S. H., II: 87, 209

Jefferson, T., II: 93
Jekels, L., I: 149n., 209n.; II: 48, 56, 154n., 209
Jones, E., II: 161, 209
Jung, C., I: 105; II: 5, 10, 161, 209

Kaplan, L., I: 212-213n.
Katan, M., II: 134, 209
Klausner, J., II: 85, 89, 209
Kraepelin, E., II: 155

Landauer, I: 42, 212n.
Lenormant, F., II: 26, 210
Lewin, B. D., I: 20, 210
Lipps, T., II: 2, 210
Loewenstein, R. M., II: 119n, 202n., 210

Mack Brunswick, R., II: 39, 47, 52
Maeder, A. E., II: 5
Meyer, E., II: 88, 210
Miller, A. M., II: 45, 207

Nietzsche, F. W., II: 155, 166
Nunberg, H., I: 149n., 217n.; II: 24, 28, 33, 53, 62, 68, 157n., 162, 163, 170, 174, 188, 189n., 198, 202n., 204, 210

I refers to Volume I; II refers to Volume II.

SUBJECT INDEX

Activity and passivity, II: 48ff., 56ff.
  and sexual drive, II: 63
Affect, I: 21-23
Aggression, I: 148, 159-164; II: 157
  and fusion of instincts, I: 145
  and homosexuality, I: 150f., 155, 160f.
  and identification, I: 195
  and need for punishment, I: 144
  turned against self, I: 141-144
Alloplastic and autoplastic phenomena, I: 40, 58
Ambivalence
  and guilt feelings, I: 43f., 93-95, 145f., 148; II: 158
Anal fantasy, II: 38f., 40
Anal-sadistic trends, II: 50-51f.
Analytic treatment, see Psychoanalytic therapy
Anxiety, I: 23; II: 114
Attention, I: 21-22

Bisexuality, II: 111
  and circumcision, II: 13-93
  and concept of God, II: 88
  and masturbation, II: 21ff.
  and reproduction fantasy, II: 36
  Freud's concept of, II: 45f.
  in biblical text, II: 26f.
  in male and female, II: 57

Castration complex, II: 14n., 64, 99-100, 111f., 178n.
Catatonia, see Catatonic attack
Catatonic attack, I: 4-23
  and ego disintegration, I: 22
  and hypochondria, I: 6, 14f., 18f.
  and libidinal cathexis, 27
  body innervations and sensations in, I: 14f.
  censorship in, I: 22
  delusions in, I: 7-13, 15, 16f., 20f., 26
  object libido in, I: 18f., 20, 21, 22
  objects in, I: 14, 17, 18, 20

pleasure-pain principle in, I: 17f.
  reality loss in, I: 24
  role of words in, I: 21, 26
Cathexis
  and hypercathexis, II: 104
  difference of in catatonia and hysteria, I: 23
Causality
  and curiosity, II: 204
  and instinctual drives, I: 123f.
  and rationalization, I: 122f.
  and schizophrenia, I: 20
  origins of, I: 123f.
Circumcision
  and bisexuality, I: 13-93
  and castration complex, II: 13, 63
  and femininity, II: 28, 54f.
  and homosexuality, II: 16, 90
  and masochism, II: 37f.
  and projected femininity, II: 28
  and regression, II: 40f.
  and sexual fantasy, II: 42ff.
  as trauma, II: 14, 30-34
  in biblical text, II: 84, 84n.
  reaction to and basic conflict, II: 90
Condensation, II: 106
Conflict, II: 160
  in psychic illness, I: 106
  libidinal, in schizophrenia, I: 24-59
  of ambivalence in schizophrenia, I: 29f.
  of transference in schizophrenia, I: 25, 211n.
Conscious, II: 95
Consciousness
  and mental illness, I: 133ff.
  in neurosis, II: 144
  in schizophrenia, II: 143f.
  normal and schizophrenic, I: 19, 21
  role of ego in, I: 134f.
Countertransference, II: 157
Curiosity, II: 168-206

Death instinct, II: 97
Defense mechanisms
  and ego weakness, I: 190f.
  in schizophrenia, I: 20, 209n.

I refers to Volume I; II refers to Volume II.

215

Compiled by W. Godfrey Cobliner, Ph.D.